LAST CALL

LAST CALL

AWAKEN TO CONSCIOUSNESS

JAMES GEORGE

Station Hill
of Barrytown

Published by Station Hill of Barrytown, the publishing project of the Institute for Publishing Arts, Inc., 120 Station Hill Road, Barrytown, NY 12507, New York, a not-for-profit, tax-exempt organization [501(c)(3)].

Online catalogue: www.stationhill.org
e-mail: publishers@stationhill.org

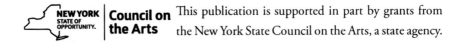 This publication is supported in part by grants from the New York State Council on the Arts, a state agency.

Cover and interior design by Susan Quasha
Cover Image: Susan Quasha

Library of Congress Cataloging-in-Publication Data

Names: George, James, 1918- author.
Title: Last call : awaken to consciousness / James George.
Description: Barrytown, NY : Station Hill of Barrytown, 2016.
Identifiers: LCCN 2015038863 | ISBN 9781581771565
Subjects: LCSH: Spirituality. | Consciousness. | Gurdjieff, Georges
   Ivanovitch, 1872-1949.
Classification: LCC BF1999 .G3883 2016 | DDC 204—dc23
LC record available at http://lccn.loc.gov/2015038863

To Barbara, my wonderful wife, who has helped me and so many others to see ourselves and the world in new ways. In addition, her award-winning skills have been an invaluable help in the editing of this book. And to our grandchildren, who will face the problems that our generation is leaving them, but with the benefit of having much more help and experience generally available than we had.

CONTENTS

LIST OF ILLUSTRATIONS

ACKNOWLEDGMENTS

If my friend John Robert Colombo had not generously volunteered his expert assistance in an effort to encourage me to gather together from my writings and interviews what I thought was still worth publishing, this book would not have appeared. I am grateful to him for helping me to overcome my passivity.

I am also grateful to my friend Lee Smolin, physicist and founding member of the Perimeter Institute, for encouraging me to publish.

Were it not for the kindness and skill of Luke Storms and Alex Bolduc, who scanned and organized the material I had selected from my files, this book could not have taken its present form and might never have appeared. Similarly, I am especially indebted to Robert McWhinney for organizing the materials of Chapter 2.

I am grateful to the editors of Parabola (Jeff Zaleski), Sufi (Alireza Nurbakhsh), A.U. Pope's *Survey of Persian Art* (Jay Gluck), *Born in Tibet* by Chögyam Trungpa (Walter Fordham), Hinduism Today, International Perspectives, All & Everything Conference Proceedings, and Bout de Papier for allowing me to republish my most meaningful articles, interviews, and book reviews, which they had published first.

I am also indebted to my interviewers, Walter Fordham, Sannyasin Senthilnathaswami, Richard Whittaker, and David Ulrich, for their skill and sensitivity in drawing me beyond what I thought I knew.

I wish to acknowledge the assistance of Ian McDonald of the Library of Parliament and Sophie Grenier of Foreign Affairs, Trade & Development Canada, in retrieving from International Perspectives a copy of the article republished in Chapter 17.

The publication of this last book is thanks to my old friends George and Susan Quasha, and my newer friend Sam Truitt of Station Hill Press in Barrytown, N.Y. Station Hill is the publisher of my two previous books. I am very grateful to them.

From my genetic history, I could not have expected to live so long. It has been hard work, and I must make grateful bows in several directions to my principal helpers. To my daughter, Dr. Dolphi Wertenbaker, supreme diagnostician and yoga teacher; to my family doctor, Dr. Karen Ko; to my Tibetan doctor, Shakya Dorje; to Elis Leung, Traditional Chinese Medicine; and to Dr. Eduardo Cardona, Fellow of the Royal Society of Medicine and Aryuvedic master. However, I do not regard long life as some kind of personal or collective achievement, for I have no doubt that it, like every moment of presence, is a gift from above.

This book is my final tribute to the teaching that has given me something to live for, the Work of Gurdjieff, as transmitted through Jeanne de Salzmann and Dr. Michel de Salzmann, and maintained through the community of the Gurdjieff Foundations internationally. So I conclude my acknowledgements with gratitude to my dear comrades in our groups in Toronto, Ottawa, Philadelphia, and Boulder who have contributed so much to my present understanding.

I STILL AM

I am!

When I read or hear those words, I can see again the apse of a small ruined chapel, the Baptistery of St. John, in Poitiers, about two hours by car southwest of Paris. The *Guide Michelin* says it is a 4th-century chapel and "the earliest Christian structure in France." Looking up at the tiled wall of the apse, as I did more than fifty years ago, I see the commanding presence of a radiant Christ, his right hand held out towards me, offering his teaching; and below two words in Latin: "EGO SUM." What, I wondered then, as I still ponder now, is the meaning of Christ's "I AM?"

Within a month of this visit, we began, at the Institut Gurdjieff in Paris, to hear from Mme. de Salzmann about "I AM" exercises that her mentor, G. I. Gurdjieff, had frequently given to his groups in Paris in the decade before he died in 1949. Gurdjieff had summarized these exercises very directly: "Inner, not identify. Outer, play role." In Russia before the 1917 Revolution, when asked to name what he was teaching, he had said that it could be called "esoteric Christianity." Thirty years later, when asked how old the "I AM" exercise was, he replied that it came from a time "before Europe was." And I remember the enigmatic affirmation of Christ: "Before Abraham was, I am." Whatever its antiquity, I AM has been the central practice and support of my inner world for the last fifty years. It still is. And I still am.

Today, the 24th of October, 2014, is officially "Global Oneness Day," and, as I sat quietly by myself this morning, I could feel an inner affirmation of this instinctive need that we all have—consciously or unconsciously—for a deep relationship with the Unknown One, with the Reality that I actually am, and that all of us are, when we are. For when I truly am present, even for a moment, I feel myself a particle of Life, that Life which animates you and me, humanity, organic life, the Earth, our solar system, and on up to the Source (whatever we call it) far beyond our knowing. When I remember that I am, not just mentally but with all my feeling/sensation/thought, it sounds a note, a call, that resonates with the higher harmonics of Life, rising octave by octave as far as I can go into the silence of accepting that I cannot know all that is.

Before I could write anything about this brief direct experience of the one-ness of Life on all levels, I am aware that I have already begun to be distract-ed by my automatic associations chattering on, as they always do, with the memories of my nearly one hundred years and the demands of the day ahead: bills to be paid, things to do—each of us has a list. As long as my attention is preoccupied with all those distractions from living the present moment, how could I possibly have any lasting awareness of being, of consciousness, of life? And without that, what am I? Nothing.

So I am not—and yet I am: teetering between these poles of being and not being. Remembering at this moment that I am and I can—while at the next I will forget that something within me always is, present and aware, without judgments or reactions. Relaxing with each breath, and praying for another moment, such as I have been given in the past, when the particle finds itself flooded with light in sudden communion with the One Whole.

And now, as you read these words in which I have tried to express a little of what, in my years of search in the East and in the West, I have found to be true about myself and the existential human condition, I expect that you may not remember your own similar experiences. They are easy to forget. We all have sceptical minds, encouraging us to do so. But we all also have a deep subconscious need calling us to just this sort of communion with this Life that essentially we all are. For only in that more awake state of awareness can I have a real relationship with my neighbour who is essentially the same as I am, when I am. When I am not, I have no neighbour; I am asleep and alone. Only when I am can I see and love my neighbour.

And only when I am, in the relativity of the flow of time, can I be relatively free of the associations enslaving my attention most of the time. As Gurdjieff says in *Views from the Real World*, in the chapter entitled "Is there a Way of Prolonging Life?" every normal person wants to live forever. The key to living longer is to understand that time is measured by associations, so being freer of associations lengthens my time in this body.

These are examples from the sacred secrets of all the great teachings. In more normal times, they are best preserved and transmitted individually and orally, for "sacred is secret." But today we are, for the first time in recorded history, living in a time when our technology enables us to destroy all life on this beautiful planet in "a bang or a whimper," as T.S. Eliot put it: in a massive nuclear exchange or a human-induced climate change that makes life as we know it unliveable. Today even the Dalai Lama risks assassination by some of his own people for daring to give their most secret Kalachakra teachings to totally unprepared people who are not even Buddhist. In Toronto he told a thousand such people that what he was calling "emptiness" they might understand better as "consciousness"—another way of saying, as Gurdjieff did, that we must free our attention from its inveterate tendency to identify with the next association that comes to mind. The Dalai Lama feels compelled to risk giving esoteric teachings publicly because of the dire crises we are all facing. Can we learn from his example? As we begin to understand the urgency of the crises we face, can that shock open us to a sudden acceptance of the remedies that have always been offered by our greatest and oldest teachings, our common sacred heritage on which we have been turning our backs in the West for the past two or three centuries?

Certainly it is time to change course before it is too late. "I AM" is the most effective way I know of changing levels, of waking up, of being able to transcend our self-centered ways that now threaten to destroy our civilization. I have verified this claim over many years and from my observation of some of the remarkable people that I have been fortunate to know. But you will have to verify this for yourself, if you begin to feel in yourself the struggle between your two natures—the automatic functional nature that runs the show almost all the time, and this conscious essential life or presence that is trying to be born and grow into a real soul—so that that you could become what you too were meant to be—a real man or a real woman—serving what cosmic purpose real human beings are designed to serve.

Many of my colleagues in the fight for effective action to be taken to stem the effects of man-made climate change are now being tempted to give up because we have been so widely ignored and fear it may now in fact be too late to avert a catastrophe. I share their distress, but I am not ready to give up. Indeed, in the past year, I have become more—not less—hopeful. I would like to take this opportunity to explain why, to whoever has ears to hear me.

In the first place, as many others have documented, the growth of the Internet, the amazing spread of cell phones and now smart phones to most of humanity, and the consequent exponential growth of all kinds of Non-Governmental Organizations (or NGOs) has made possible the instant spread of new ideas and inner spiritual and even esoteric practices. Moreover new technologies could well buy us more time to wean ourselves from our addictions to fossil fuels and nuclear energy even though sustainable sources of power are already affordable.

On June 9, 2015, the G-7 leaders of the world's major economies declared their intention to stop producing energy from fossil fuels by the end of the century. At about the same time, the Indian government has allowed word to get out of a previously secret research program that has made it possible to make machines that extract from the air (or, as they would say, from *prana*) two-and-a-half times more energy than goes in to them. One of India's largest electrical companies now has them in production on various scales, starting with a 20 kilowatt model for a house in a village without electricity. As this new technology spreads and becomes more efficient, it may be possible to cease using fossil fuels for energy very much sooner than the end of the century. From my own experience of having seen much more efficient zero-point energy generators in the United States, as I have recounted in *The Little Green Book on Awakening,* I know that this is a real possibility for saving the planet from the worst climate change scenarios. Since India is not beholden to any oil lobby and has had the courage and skill to develop this new technology, we can all breathe more hopefully now.

At the same time, there has been an astonishing release of esoteric information from all the great teachings, and even from ancient enclaves—such as the early Egyptians, the Gnostics, the Tibetans—and currently the Yazidis, whom ISIL seems determined to exterminate. In addition, there is now more caring for other human beings, for all creatures, and for the planet, which naturally follows from studying—and taking to heart—these great teachings. Yes, we do need to become better human beings, less self-involved and self-serving, more awake and in tune with the organic life of which we are a part. And I see once again that nothing less than an evolution of consciousness is called for. We were all designed to serve Nature, and we are failing, lacking even the wish for self-development in the sense of being or consciousness. New technologies can indeed help, but without a shift of consciousness they will never be enough. So where have I found help in awakening to such a shift in this increasingly secular world of ours?

All this fresh material, now publicly available, is feeding the appetite for more of it, and the rapid spread of a radical cultural re-evaluation of such ancient knowledge. Others have made similar observations.

For example, my friend Dr. Ravi Ravindra, when he was interviewed about the global crisis in 2011, articulated a point of view that I deeply share. I wish I could have said it so well. This is what he said:

> We may not be able to find a way past the current global crises, but a way may be found through us if we are willing and able to be instruments of subtler levels of energy which permeate the entire universe.
>
> If we contemplate the universe and the extremely intricate laws which govern the appearance and disappearance of galaxies as well as the emergence of the butterfly from a cocoon, it is difficult to persuade oneself that human beings are in control and are at the top of the spectrum of consciousness or intelligence. How can we not feel the sentiment expressed by Albert Einstein when he speaks of his "rapturous amazement at the harmony of natural law, which reveals an intelligence of such superiority that, compared with it, all the systematic thinking and acting of human beings is an utterly insignificant reflection?"
>
> It is the unanimous testimony of all the sages in the history of humanity that the entire universe is pervaded by subtle and conscious energies—variously labelled as the 'Holy Spirit', or the 'Buddha Mind', or 'Allah' or the 'Tao'. All spiritual traditions say that without the subtle and conscious energies of Brahman (or God or the Eternal) nothing can be done, but without human beings nothing will be done. We need to do our part as instruments of the all-pervasive

Intelligence. In our individual or collective hubris we forget the obvious—that we do not know all there is to know, and that neither the physical nor the spiritual universe is centered on any individual or on humanity or on the Earth. We need to search for our contribution to the continuing unfolding of the Mystery, not so much from ignorance but from innocence, open to unexpected voices and solutions.

Ahimsa—usually understood as non-violence or physical non-harming—is, in fact, closer to non-violation, non-imposition or non-manipulation. Ahimsa is the essential principle of all true ecology. Finding our place and playing our part, making room for and caring for other human beings, for all creatures, and for the planet naturally follows from this.

When I have to fill out a questionnaire and am asked what is my religion (with multiple choices), I am tempted to answer "all of the above." As it happened, I had four years with a Hindu Master, five with a Sufi Pir, and five with several Tibetan Rinpoches. But I am still a Christian, and now understand Christianity very differently thanks to having been for more than sixty years trying to understand and practice Gurdjieff's "Work," or "the Way of Consciousness," as it has been called recently. So I can appreciate Ramakrishna's conclusion, after consciously living several great teachings: they are all One. It has been my great good fortune to know remarkable teachers from many different traditions: Thomas Merton, Krishnamurti and Yogaswami, Dr. Javad Nurbakhsh, Trungpa Rinpoche, Dilgo Khyentse Rinpoche, Drugu Choegyal Rinpoche and Dudjom Rinpoche, even the Dalai Lama himself. And yet I have never felt a conflict between what I learned from them and what I have received from the Gurdjieff Work, as transmitted by Mme. de Salzmann, Dr. Michel de Salzmann and their successors. My contacts with other "ways" deepened my understanding of my own way, which in turn facilitated my rapid contacts with leaders of other ways.

When I first met them, both the Dalai Lama and Michel de Salzmann were in their twenties, and I watched over many years with increasing awe how quickly they grew, not only in understanding but, I felt, in their being. Their rigorous practices were not the same, but they were clearly transformative; and the quality of their emanations had changed dramatically. To a lesser extent, of course, I have felt similar changes in several of my Gurdjieffian friends, some of whom are still living. So I can say from personal experience that esoteric practices—and not only those that I have been trying to follow—can be remarkably effective. As we say in Gurdjieffian circles, "The Work works!" It is indeed a way of "conscience" in the French sense, which includes in one word both "conscience" and "consciousness."

Extrapolating much further, I wonder whether the image of Christ the King, the real Man, calling "I AM" from the apse of that early French Christian chapel, was, and I hope still is, speaking for an unbroken line of initiates stretching timelessly through history to keep humanity open to the possibility of a deathless Life for those who could persist in making the necessary efforts not to identify, and to live consciously. Did Jesus grow into the Christ who could say that he and the Father are One, and everything he (so to say) did was not his doing, but the action of the Father through him? Was it a similar law-conformable process that produced Muhammad, or the Buddha, or Krishna? Were they each trying to convey to humanity that their transcendence opens a door for us to follow in their footsteps?

Yes, I am way out of my depth. And yet I must point towards what I feel and know (not just mentally) is humanity's best hope for surviving our current crisis by achieving a rapid transformation in a significant number of humans now alive. Seen from this perspective, there are, I know, good grounds for hope that all is not yet lost on this planet. When we have tried our best, and see that by our own efforts we cannot transform ourselves, that without help from above we are nothing, then we may be able sincerely to ask Life, or Consciousness, the greatest forces in God's world, to help us. As Christ promised, "Seek and you will find; ask and you will be answered."

In other words, there is far more to Reality than what I can logically think or we can technologically invent. Gurdjieff entitled his last book *Life Is Real Only Then, When "I Am."* This is our first call, and also our last: the call to remember that I Am, the call to BE. Lord have mercy!

This body is not me; I am not caught in this body, I am life without boundaries, I have never been born and I have never died. Over there the wide ocean and the sky with many galaxies All manifests from the basis of consciousness. Since beginningless time I have always been free. Birth and death are only a door through which we go in and out. Birth and death are only a game of hide-and-seek. So smile to me and take my hand and wave good-bye. Tomorrow we shall meet again or even before. We shall always be meeting again at the true source, Always meeting again on the myriad paths of life.

THÍCH NHẤT HẠNH, *No Death, No Fear*

To die is to understand in a new way.

JEANNE DE SALZMANN

If you feel called to explore further this inner struggle towards what humanity is called to be, you might wish to read my two books already in print: *Asking for the Earth: Waking Up to the Spiritual/Ecological Crisis* (1995); and *The Little Green Book on Awakening* (2008). For this my final publication, I have selected from my various interviews, talks, book reviews and writings those pieces that I hope will shed some light on a rapidly darkening contemporary crisis that I see as fundamentally a spiritual crisis. As I see it, Nature is demanding that we transform ourselves or face elimination, since in our present mode humanity has become a threat to organic life on Earth.

I retired as an Ambassador in 1977 and most of my selections are from the period since I retired. As a final chapter, I have included some of my poems, realizing that prose of the head can never convey the emotional fire and light of the heart.

In some cases, I have added additional material in *italics,* as a preface to what I had said or written earlier.

My advice to readers uninterested in Gurdjieff and his Work is to skip chapters 1, 2, 18, and 19. The other twenty-three chapters are for you.

I have decided to put first an article I had submitted in 2004 to the *Gurd-jieff International Review*, but which was rejected. At that time I had shown it to Roger Lipsey in New York, who urged me not to publish my account of having interacted with a UFO on two occasions in 2002. In 2008, I did publish this UFO experience in greater detail in *The Little Green Book on Awakening*. The craft came within a quarter of a mile of us twice, so we could see its structure and cabin lights. But no human being could possibly see our hand movements from the craft at night, and this is why I called it a "tele-pathic video game," for the craft operator was clearly reading our thoughts, not reacting to our hand movements.

However, I said little in that book about my connection with the Gurdjieff Work. Now I feel I can no longer, in good conscience, conceal my conviction that Gurdjieff, in writing *Beelzebub's Tales to His Grandson*, was, at the same time, preparing humanity to interact with visitors from outer space who are, like Beelzebub, concerned about the state of affairs on planet Earth and are ready to do what they can to help us avert a catastrophe—if we are ready to abandon our self-serving ways and adapt ourselves to the harmony of Nature. Indeed, I feel considerable remorse of conscience for letting myself take the easier course of silence for so long. Surely I was not given this highly unusual experience to bury in my archives! So here it is, front and center, as part of my understanding of the Work that has been the foundation of who I am.

In the Massey Lectures of 2014, the former Canadian Governor General, Adrienne Clarkson, touchingly articulated what it means to "belong" in Can-ada, and the importance of a common vision as an act of imagination. This is from her final lecture:

> The Canadian literary critic Northrop Frye said, 'We partic-ipate in society by means of our imagination or the quality of our social vision. Our vision is what society is, what it could be, what it should be are all structures of metaphor because the metaphor is the unit of all imagination. Logi-cal thinking in this field seldom does more than rationalize these metaphorical visions.' What Frye is telling us is that we participate in each other's imagination even if we are not

consciously aware of doing so. We are a part of each other's
wishes, hopes, and, yes, dreams.

We are all, as she says, "part of one civilization." From my experience I have
come to see that this civilization—now so threatened—may not be just planetary. Since all Life is interconnected, it could be cosmic. Let me share with
you in this last book my enlarging vision.

JAMES GEORGE
Toronto, 2015

CHAPTER 1

GURDJIEFF'S SPACE TRAVELERS: ALLEGORY OR TRUTH?

In my lifetime, the scientific view of the Universe has been expanding dramatically. The figures given in this chapter, written in 2004, are already out of date. We now know that our galaxy alone, the Milky Way, contains 300 to 400 billion stars, with about 10 billion planets that are habitable. And there are between 100 and 200 billion galaxies! So it is no wonder that in 2014, NASA and the Library of Congress convened a global conference of scientists, theologians, philosophers, and historians to discuss how to prepare the world for contact with extraterrestrial life, since that was bound to happen soon, if it had not happened already. This is how Beelzebub puts it to his grandson, Hassein: "Now, my boy, I shall repeat once more, all your favorites, even the contemporary ones, are—like us and like all the other three-centered beings of our Megalocosmos—just such apparatuses for the Great Cosmic Trogoegocrat as were the original tetartocosmoses from whom arose the first ancestors of the beings now existing on the planet Earth, as well as those on all the other planets of our Universe."

When Gurdjieff was completing *Beelzebub's Tales* seventy years ago, space travel by human beings seemed a remote fantasy. It was almost inconceivable that the universe might have spawned forms of life elsewhere that were not only far more intelligent than us but so far advanced in their technology that they could observe us from space, after travelling from planets we knew must be many light years away from our remote corner of the cosmos. Since then, we have learned that there is not just one galaxy but billions, each with solar systems, probably each with planets. A few men have visited the moon, thousands of people have seen flying saucers and millions of dollars have been wasted on Commissions designed to prove that no such things exist. Like President Jimmy Carter, I have seen space ships and do not need further evidence. Before long we will have to be told the truth. Too many insiders have made too many disclosures already. But, like most others who have seen what is officially considered non-existent, I have not talked about it publicly until now. At eighty six, I am no longer so concerned to protect my so called credibility.

You may agree with me or not, but let me simply raise this question—if Beelzebub has not raised it with you already. Is our megalocosmos really populated by intelligent living beings with whom some form of interaction may be possible for humans? Are there benevolent, wise beings like Beelzebub who have been and still are observing our planet with increasing concern, as our technological prowess continues to exceed our rudimentary conscience, with results so painfully obvious to anyone with eyes to see? Was Gurdjieff, in writing *Beelzebub*, fictionalizing fact? It is a sign of our times that Steven Spielberg has fictionalized, in his film series *Taken*, many specific events that have occurred in the past fifty years. *Taken* was seen by over thirty million people last year. In any case, we can all agree that Gurdjieff was mythmaking for our benefit and instruction, but was he also preparing humanity for a future when we would be interacting on a daily basis with extra-terrestrial intelligent beings of a high order? Do we read *Beelzebub* as myth, or as mythologized truth?

Much depends, I suggest, on how we answer that question. If the answer, at least for a certain number of us, is perhaps it is true, then we may be ready for the shift in consciousness that is required, I now feel, if we are, individually and collectively, to mend our ways. If the answer is the usual one, "Myth, of course," the outlook for our species is not, I believe, appealing. For this response comes from the outmoded mind-set that is unaware of the havoc caused by our unconscious behaviour to our own kind and to our planet and therefore unaware that we could use some help from higher up the great chain of being.

When we consider that our species has killed in warfare a 100 million of us in the last century and is fouling our ecological nest at a rate likely to endanger all life on this Earth in this century, with or without the assistance of our nuclear arsenals, perhaps humanity's demise would not be a great cosmic catastrophe. But if we can wake up and change consciousness in time to radically reform our destructive ways, it would surely be better, for us and even for the cosmos that has spent a very long time getting us this far on the evolutionary road. The stakes have never been higher. It is my guess that, in writing *Beelzebub's Tales*, Gurdjieff was preparing future generations for this challenge by helping to enlarge our world view so that we could begin to assimilate the immense implications of the crisis that humanity would face in the 21st century. After reading *Beelzebub* for fifty years, it is just now dawning on me that we may be helped at this critical juncture by beings from extra-terrestrial civilizations that have the intelligence, compassion and technology to ease our passage through the "eye of the needle" on this endangered planet.

I now remember in a new way how many times Beelzebub expresses his concern, based on thousands of years of careful observations, about the deterioration of the consciousness of humans on this planet—"the almost entirely degenerated presences of these favourites of yours," as he puts it to his grandson, of those who have lost their wish for self-perfection. Perhaps we are becoming a cosmic problem and need help, if a larger catastrophe is to be avoided.

Let me make clear that I am pondering this great question with you, not putting any answer forward as a Gurdjieffian "article of faith." His tent is broad enough to harbour both those who favour "myth" and those who favour "truth." He makes no assertions, and you and I are left free to take it either way, or both ways—and later to change our minds. I have only recently changed my mind—or had it changed for me. With that caveat, let us look at the evidence in the text.

In his introductory chapter, "The Arousing of Thought," Gurdjieff warns us that he is not going to confine himself in this book "merely to this, in the objective sense, 'paltry Earth.' ... I shall of course also write of the Earth, but with such an impartial attitude that this comparatively small planet itself and also everything on it shall correspond to that place which in fact it occupies ... in our Great Universe."

In keeping with this cosmic perspective, the book begins with an explanation of why Beelzebub was flying through the Universe in "the ship *Karnak* of the 'transspace' communication," on his way to our solar system. And, almost incidentally, we learn that time as we calculate it on Earth, is not the same as it is "by objective time calculation." So, in these opening sentences, Gurdjieff prepares to overturn the foundations of our "normal" world. Space and time are not what we thought they were, in our provincial Earth-bound subjectivity. Space is not empty; intelligent embodied beings are travelling through it. And time is only relatively real—the "Ideally-Unique-Subjective Phenomenon," he calls it later. How beings perceive it depends, he says, "on the completeness of their own presence."

He does not expect us to understand what he is telling us all at once. He has already warned us that he intends "to destroy mercilessly," in our "mentation and feelings … the beliefs and views, by centuries rooted" in us, "about everything existing in the world." But mercifully he has also given us a way of swallowing what we do not yet understand by presenting it as merely his tale about a hero he has invented and called (provocatively) "Beelzebub." So we can play along with him in his game, not taking it all that seriously. For, if we did, we would have to stop reading. The challenge to our present world view would be too abrupt to continue. We need time to be able to surrender our egotistical vision and make room for a much larger one: a vision of the Sacred.

Indeed, I feel that I am only now beginning to see that Gurdjieff may have been cunningly preparing our minds to accept that "higher beings" from other star systems have actually been keeping planet Earth under observation for thousands of years, guiding us invisibly in the evolution of our consciousness and perhaps also in the development of our technology. And lest we mistakenly suppose that all this super attention is being focussed solely on our little Earth, he tells us that there are "four omnipresent platforms," or Egolionopties, from which the Four Quarters Maintainers keep a watchful eye on all that is happening everywhere in the Universe. From Beelzebub's perspective, it seems that our planet is, however, the cause of much anxiety on high and the focus of more than one Commission of higher beings sent by His Endlessness to take corrective action.

I might never have come to these conclusions if I had not had a remarkable experience two years ago [2006] at my log cabin on McGregor Lake, twenty miles north-east of Ottawa, in Quebec. Watching the stars appear one September evening, I was sitting with a close friend by the water. Suddenly she asked, "Is that the Pole Star over there?" "No," I replied, "the Pole Star is here, and what you are seeing is too bright and too twinkly to be a star; besides, it has begun to move. It must be a satellite." With that, the "star" sharply changed direction. Not a satellite. As we were wondering what it might be, we both intuitively began to wish, as strongly as we could, for the star to move, as we moved our hands, UP—and it did! DOWN—and it did! To the right … to the left … whichever way we focussed our attention and moved our hands, it immediately moved in that direction, not in a sweeping motion like an aircraft but in sharply defined angles that followed our movements instantly. It was like a telepathic video game that we were playing with whoever or whatever was controlling that space ship … and the game continued for at least half an hour before the visitor departed over the horizon.

The next evening after dark, there were our "friends," now only about a quarter of a mile away in the sky, ready to play with us again. It was difficult at night to see the exact shape of the craft, but it had a horizontal row of bright lights along a fat cigar-shaped body. It could pause in flight and remain stationary, then suddenly accelerate and change direction sharply. This time we were also shown how they could make their craft disappear—and reappear a few seconds later at another location. I remembered how Beelzebub, on the spaceship *Occasion*, had told his grandson: "We had, it is true, the possibility of making our ship … invisible … but we could not annihilate its presence," and so they had to move it from the Oxus River where boats could bump into it, to the Aral Sea where there was no such danger. Our space friends were taking the trouble to demonstrate to us that they had the same capability. Almost a year later, at McGregor Lake, they again played with me and went out of their way to show me that their ships can not only disappear over the horizon (as it did last year) but fly straight up into the zenith until lost in the stars. We move horizontally; they can move vertically.

Now, I begin to understand differently what Gurdjieff has been telling us for so many years. Yes, these incontrovertible experiences blew my mind. It has gone "back to abnormal" of course, but it has not been the same mind since then. And if I had never read about Beelzebub and spaceships, would I have even noticed that bright twinkling star, and wondered if it might respond to my intention? Probably I would—like most people—have never seen what was in front of my eyes. The cognitive dissonance in seeing what there was no basis in my experience for accepting would have wiped out any trace of the memory if Gurdjieff had not prepared me for a radical change of world view. The experience has therefore not been lost but has led me to ponder as never before on the nature of consciousness.

What is "consciousness?" If, with William Segal, we may suppose that what Gurdjieff calls the "Omnipresent Okidanokh" refers to the consciousness that fills all space, creates all life, and manifests as Love and Life in every form, then we can appreciate why he had to invent a special word for it, a word with which we would have none of our usual associations. He had told us that what he called the real consciousness was in what he called our "subconsciousness." Where does a free attention come from? What does "omnipresent" mean? What is that energetic seed in every manifested material form which can potentially relate to the Unmanifest, the Unknown? If there is embodied Intelligence in other parts of the Universe, in other beings, the next question is what makes it possible for very different embodiments to communicate? What is the linkage? What is the medium relating my consciousness with the consciousness of those in the spaceship who could demonstrably tune in and act on my intentions instantly without words?

If I may sound a more personal note, the fact that my son Graham and my grandson Carlo died a few months after my first encounter with a space craft over McGregor Lake has also changed how I am coming to see consciousness. Before they died, I was not sure whether anything can survive the death of the physical body. Now I am. My mind can have its doubts about the nature of life or consciousness, but something in me now knows that life cannot die. I know that "life" and "consciousness," whether embodied or not, are two names for the same timeless omnipresent mystery. It reminds me of Russell Targ's great quip that such shockingly unexpected experiences are "miracles masquerading as data." If our defence mechanisms do not prevent it, such experiences can awaken us to what we had never dreamed of in our philosophies: a totally new perception of the nature of reality, putting our entire world view in question, opening to a new awareness of what is and of what I am. The beauty of Gurdjieff's teaching is that he prepares us for such a shift of consciousness without ever encouraging our innate tendency to indulge in fantasy. *Beelzebub's Tales* is a very matter-of-fact myth with plenty of space for us to make our own discoveries and draw our own conclusions!

All these questions, it seems to me on reflection, point inescapably to a conclusion every Tradition and spiritual teaching has been proclaiming for thousands of years: that Consciousness (or Intelligence, or Love, or God, if you prefer) *is*, "always and everywhere." Is the dawning awareness of that mystery—the beginning of awakening, of presence, of enlightenment, in human beings—the awareness that in fact I AM that Consciousness with which my personal consciousness may, under certain conditions, be in some kind of resonant relation? Can we, at least at moments, be of one mind?

In the whole of what Gurdjieff calls "the Reasonable Whole," of which we are but particles, nothing is separate. Everything is interconnected. That is now what we understand from quantum physics, as well as from Beelzebub. It is one thing to accept this idea mentally, but quite another to know it. To be wordlessly aware of this Whole, at this moment, is presence. So many words pointing towards the indescribable.... But though the words fail us, every glimpse of Wholeness leaves in us an indelible imprint. Is it not so? Does this not give you hope? Does this experiential discovery not bring with it a totally new understanding of the world and everything in it—of the unity of Being?

Look again at Beelzebub's closing words in the chapter devoted to understanding war and how this terrible scourge of "periodic reciprocal destruction" may one day be eliminated: "It will only be with Time alone, thanks either to the guidance of a certain Being with very high Reason or to certain exceptional cosmic events." Does this mean that, since humans seem unable to stop wars, "others" may have to intervene? This may, he suggests, be justified for reasons beyond our little planet, since our "abnormalities unbecoming to three-brained beings" are maleficent, not only "for them themselves [but] for the whole of the Universe." When you let this verdict sink in, does it not seem inevitable that higher beings may have to help us at this delicate stage of our evolution?

Gurdjieff himself was surely no ordinary man. He once described himself as the "Herald of the Coming Good." At the beginning of *Beelzebub's Tales*, in his "Friendly Advice," he calls on us to "try and fathom the gist of my writings ... only then can my hope be actualized that according to your understanding you will obtain the specific benefit for yourself which I anticipate, and which I wish for you with all my being." What is this "benefit," this "good?" What would it take for a critical mass of human beings on this planet to transform their consciousness so that humans no longer live in the illusion that they are alone in the Universe, no longer kill millions of other humans in wars, no longer behave unconsciously and destructively towards their environment, no longer create a cosmic problem that even makes it difficult, he says, for beings on other planets to "perfect themselves in the sense of being?"

Gurdjieff proposes, specifically in the *Struggle of the Magicians*, that evil in the world comes from our unconscious actions, and the more conscious we become, "the less evil enters Thy creation." Beelzebub and his tribe are clearly more conscious than we are. They come from the planet Karatas, they come from Love. They are basically Good. Is it with implicit reference to them that, at the end of his life, he told Edwin Wolfe, among others: "Where I come from, many greater than me." Was he talking only about the Central Asian monastery he described in *Meetings with Remarkable Men*? Or Karatas? Certainly he had scant regard for the spiritual achievements of human consciousness in the West: "In the last three centuries, one and a half saints," was his cryptic and caustic assessment.

In the last few decades, I have been privileged, as a diplomat at the United Nations, NATO, in the Middle East and South Asia, to have seen world events unfold from the inside. I have seen how often people are manipulated by lies from the most authoritative sources. Until recently I believed the lies that UFOs were figments of the imagination of demented people. I have heard the lies about countries and cultures "we" did not like. Let us never be deceived in the future by "leaders" playing on our paranoia and pointing to the heavens as the source of the next wave of "terrorists" from whom they say they wish to protect us. If we take Gurdjieff at his word, we can see that those beings visiting us in their spaceships are acting from concern and making every effort to help—not harm—us. We would be on firmer ground to regard them as conscious agents of the Cosmic Good.

No one from another planet can do for us what we must inexorably do, here and now, for ourselves. The necessary change of consciousness on planet Earth still depends on us. But, if we take Beelzebub seriously, we may begin to see that there are indeed higher forces and higher beings, invisible to us. Their presence can be felt as if they were actually here now, ready and able to help ... if we can only do our part, if we can awaken enough to be aware. Then we will know in our hearts that the "others" are our friends. They also wish for the "Coming Good," in every dark corner of the evolving Universe. In that vastness, we are not alone.

CHAPTER 2

A CROSS FOR THE GRAVE OF MR. GURDJIEFF'S FATHER, IVAN GURDJIEFF (JOHAN GIORGIADES), 1834–1917

Since the early 1950s, when I first read a borrowed copy of the unpublished manuscript of *Meetings with Remarkable Men* and spent the night copying it by photography, I had been intrigued by Mr. Gurdjieff's injunction, at the end of the chapter on his father, that, having been unable to find and mark his father's grave himself, he wrote:

> I ... bid any of my sons, whether by blood or in spirit, to seek out, when he has the possibility, this solitary grave, abandoned by force of circumstances ensuing chiefly from that human scourge called the herd instinct, and there to set up a stone with the inscription:

> I AM THOU,
>
> THOU ART I,
>
> HE IS OURS,
>
> WE BOTH ARE HIS.
>
> SO MAY ALL BE
>
> FOR OUR NEIGHBOR

In the spring of 1975, while we were serving in Iran, my wife Carol and I unexpectedly found ourselves able to realize a long-standing dream of visiting the areas of the Caucasus mentioned in *Meetings* and *In Search of the Miraculous*, and perhaps even getting to Alexandropol where Mr. Gurdjieff's father had died while trying to protect his property during the Turkish invasion in 1917. Mme. de Salzmann had been staying with us that spring. She had told us where she thought he might have been buried and advised us to take with us from Tehran a Russian Orthodox cross with the required inscription. Our circumstances were propitious: we were in a neighboring country; our colleague, the Soviet Ambassador, was friendly; and we had a Canadian friend, Dr. George Volkoff, Professor of Physics at the University of British Columbia, who spoke Russian and happened to be going to Georgia anyway to address an academic conference in Tbilisi. His daughter, Alex, was the Canadian Press correspondent in Tehran. So, with the help of the Soviet Ambassador, Carol, Alex and I made our reservations, got our visas and set off by train from Tehran to join George Volkoff in Tbilisi.

At Djulfa, on the Soviet border, the Iranian train crossed the Araxas River, and we all had to change to a Soviet train for the rest of the journey to Yerevan in Soviet Armenia. No sooner had we found our places than the Russian station master came into our compartment smiling broadly, held out a large hand towards mine and said in what English he could muster, "Welcome to the Soviet Union, Mr. Ambassador! My name is Gurdjieff!"

You cannot imagine our complete astonishment. The name "Gurdjieff" is little known, even in the Caucasus. Not knowing what to say, I smiled in mute amazement. As the station master continued to shake my hand, my mind was racing to the large suitcase above my head where I had hidden the cross, counting on diplomatic immunity' to avoid having my baggage searched by the Soviet customs official who was following the station master. Then, to my intense relief, after this amicable exchange of greetings, both the station master and the customs official went on down the train, leaving us to our thoughts.

In Yerevan we had reserved an Intourist car that we were permitted to drive ourselves, provided we followed the route prescribed for us and stayed at the places reserved in advance. In this way we reached Tbilisi and found George Volkoff. Together we were treated to a special viewing of an entire basement of Scythian gold objects in the Georgian National Museum despite the fact that the curators had not yet had time to catalogue most of the objects strewn about on tables and even on the floor. What we were privileged to see that day was certainly far more sensational than the famous Scythian collections of the Hermitage that we visited on a later occasion.

For ten days we toured the Caucasus Mountains of Armenia and Georgia where Mr. Gurdjieff had passed so many years earlier: Echmiadzin, Mount Elbrus, Essentuki, Pyatigorsk, Kislovodsk, Mineralni Vodi. Much of these old towns remained the same as they must have been when Gurdjieff was there. On a mountainside near Pyatigorsk, we went to a concert of folk music. This too had not changed. But behind all these new impressions I continued to carry my preoccupation with the cross that I had smuggled into the country. I was still no closer to Alexandropol (now Leninakan) and the Intourist people were adamant that I could not under any conditions go there—it was a closed military area, no foreigners allowed. By telephone, I appealed to my good friend Bob Ford, the Canadian Ambassador in Moscow, but he replied that he had also been refused permission to visit the area. It looked as if I might have to take the cross back to Iran with me.

Before setting out on the return journey from Tbilisi to Yerevan and Tehran, I confided to Volkoff my plans for the cross and my frustration at being refused access to Alexandropol. Did he know any trustworthy Russian who could take the cross where we could not? Almost at once he had the answer— an Armenian priest whom he had just met at the conference and who was still in town. We immediately went to see him and delicately broached my request. Would it be possible for him to take the cross to Alexandropol at our expense, find the old Russian church (not the new one we knew had been constructed in recent times) and try to locate the grave of Gurdjieff's father? After all, we pleaded, his wife was Armenian. We could sense the priest's hesitation. To carry this cross with its English inscription could be a dangerous mission for him and we were virtually unknown to him. Finally, after a long silence, he spoke: "I will do this for you, but I will not take the further risk of writing to you about it, because all our letters sent abroad are read by the KGB. So, if I succeed, I will simply send you a postcard photo of the cross in its resting place in the church graveyard. The postcard will not carry my name or my address."

We agreed to this generous offer and returned to Tehran. Months went by. Almost half a year later we received this photo.

Figure 1: *The cross placed on the grave of Gurdjieff's father, Ivan*

Years went by. The Soviet Union collapsed. Visits to Alexandropol became possible, even for foreigners. Other Work people from London and from Montréal—perhaps other places—entered the old Russian churchyard in Alexandropol. They found that the church has no record of the name of Mr. Gurdjieff's father and the churchyard no longer has, along the back fence, a Russian Orthodox cross with an English inscription. But the effort was made; and we have it on good authority that "no conscious effort is ever wasted." Indeed, it brought me closer than I have ever been to the inner source of our Work. It brought me, I believe, to the greatest experience of my life, which I have partially described in the chapter on Chandolin in my book *Asking for the Earth*. More I cannot say.

Paris—April 17, 1975

Dearest Jim,

What a marvellous journey you are undertaking. The grave of Mr. G's father is indeed in Alexandropol. Zuber was there but on the Turkish side, so he could not see the grave which is on the Russian side. Maybe the name is not Gurdjieff but Gurdjian, Yvan Gurdjian. If you ask the service of the town, they must know it.

In Alexandropol the old church, where Father Borsh was, still exists.

I have asked Valia, the nephew, but he could not give any indication of what to look for. And I myself do not see. If you go to the Turkish bath in Tiflis you will see the place where 2 or 3 times a week everybody spent half a day.

The work around us is more and more deep and serious. Unfortunately some people like Schuon have really decided to harm us as much as possible. Have you read the article in "Study of Comparative Religions?" And it will continue in the next two issues. The easy way with which they accept every lie to give a wrong idea of G is for me the failure of their *revue*—failure to tell the truth. If you have not received it, I will send it to you. For them, it means everything is good if you wish to harm.

My dearest Jim. With my deep affection to you and Carol.

I wish I could see you more.

Yours,
J. de Salzmann

Paris—June 12, 1975

Dearest Jim,

I was very interested by what you wrote about the Caucasus. I think it is right to say that spirituality may have been suppressed, but underneath it is still alive.

I am grateful to you to have contacted the Armenian priest to try to find the grave. I am not sure he will take upon himself to do that, but who knows— everything is in the hands of God. It is possible to verify, to see and feel the current of a higher energy directing, pushing, acting on human nature. One is usually blind to it, being too much occupied to solve trifling questions, but when one begins to be aware of it, it becomes the most important thing. The currents are alive, of course not all on the same level. Some people act as transmitters. Of course not all have the same power. But there is the real life.

I will be very happy to see you in September. I will be at Crans at that time and will certainly see Dolphi when she comes to Chandolin. For the moment I am translating the two books in French with a small team of people, the *3rd Series* and *Views from the Real World*. It will take me part of the summer. After that comes the film.

I can say that the work here is alive and deep in spite of all the difficulties.

I was very happy to see Lhalungpa in California when I was there.

With my love to you and Carol—dear friend. I miss you.

Yours,

J. de Salzmann

October 18, 1975

Dearest Madame de Salzmann,

We have just had wonderful and for me almost unexpected news from an American Armenian, Mrs. Jacqueline Melkonian, that the cross is in place in the old Russian church graveyard of Alexandropol (now Leninakan). Dr. Volkoff, to whom Tehran we had entrusted it in Yerevan, left it with Father Reuben, who put up the cross in a cement mount on what he thinks is the right place—though we have no details as to how he found it or even exactly where it is. I have a battered photo which shows the cross in place near the back fence of a cemetery. The photo was given to Mrs. Melkonian in Yrevan by a friend of Father Reuben, Father Sarkis Tashjian, so as to avoid mailing it from the U.S.S.R., and Mrs. Melkonian sent it to Dr. Volkoff in Vancouver when she got back to the States last month. The message with the photo was that "Everything was done as you asked and the photo can show you." We have no address for Mrs. Melkonian.

But it looks as if Mr. Gurdjieff's wish has been fulfilled at last. *His* doing. I felt that strongly the moment the station master at Djulfa (where we had entered the U.S.S.R. from Iran) held out his hand to welcome us to the Soviet Union, saying in English, "Welcome to the Soviet Union, Mr. Ambassador. My name is Gurdjieff." Voila!

With our love and devotion always,
Jim

On October 12, 1999, the following letter was sent by Chris Thomson in London to Jack Cain and Bob McWhinney in Toronto:

The attached image is a color photo, taken this summer, of the gravestone erected in Gumri (formerly Alexandropol) some time ago, on the site of what is believed by some locals to be the burial place of Ivan (Adash) Gurdjieff.

Apparently some mysterious Russian visitors turned up out of nowhere, one day, and asked where the grave might be. There was then still living a very old man who had looked after the cemetery for many years and reckoned to know. The visitors, having ordered and paid for the stone, disappeared, never to be heard of again.

Beneath 'Ivan Gurdjieff 1834–1917', in Russian, is written "(*Adash*)" in Armenian. Beneath that is the famous epitaph from *Meetings*, in Russian.

This photo [not published here] is copyright Edward Stott, 1999.

I hope you can view it and print it without trouble.

Chris

CHAPTER 3

KNOWLEDGE, BEING, AND TRANSFORMATION

The University of Toronto's Center for Religious Studies and the Center for South Asian Studies asked me to give a lecture. It took place at Massey College on November 21, 1985. This is at the heart of what I am still trying to convey today.

I am happy to celebrate with you this afternoon my return to my University after an absence of forty-five years, a third of it in the East. Those of you who know another language understand that this facility has given them a whole new set of windows on the world, enabling them to see in a sort of stereo perspective what they had, with only one language, seen mono. Going deeply into the adventure of another culture, especially one of the traditional cultures of the East, is like that, only with an amplification of understanding, so that when we come home, as Eliot says, "We can know the place for the first time." I am not so sure I know the place, but I do have new impressions which I would not have had without that experience—impressions that are questions because they put so much in question, including me. It is the sort of questioning, I feel, from which understanding can be born. At the same time, they are not questions that are respectful of the established academic ways of thinking; they are rather challenging. In fact, I am finding a new openness in University circles to searching questions. We all begin to acknowledge that our world view is dissolving and reforming before our eyes: that ours is a culture in transition, and that the erosion of the "scientific certainties" of my youth is not a sign of collapse but of the rebirth of a culture on truer—but very different—foundations. I believe the new culture will be a lot closer to the global main stream of human experience represented by the great spiritual traditions than to what remains of the Newtonian mechanistic Universe.

So, I would like to speak from my experience about different ways of looking at the world as a whole, including ourselves, our knowledge, our being, our possibilities for change and even transformation, in the light of just about every other culture that has ever existed, or which still exists, on this planet. I am going to try to do this in less than an hour, so that you can speak too, and we can go into these great questions together. They are important questions for our time. Indeed, I begin to suspect that the future of life on Earth may depend on the quality of the human response to the predicament in which we find ourselves now.

For such an all-embracing search, we are going to have to go beyond the broad pastures of both Religious Studies and Asian Studies, though including both. We will, if you like, be using a transdisciplinary approach but going beyond that too, if it is understood as a mental discipline only, though of course it must include the mind and satisfy the mind.

A few years ago, when we were living in Paris, I found myself at dinner beside a Professor of Sociology at the Sorbonne. Not wishing to pass the time with small talk, I asked him, "What, in your opinion, Professor, is missing in our culture?" His reply surprised and delighted me. "What is missing is *being*," he said.

What do I mean by *being*?

Nothing is more elusive to describe or define, because, as my French professor friend said, being is in rather short supply in our culture. Being is what I am, my "*am*-ness," my life, but more specifically my relative degree of consciousness, individuality, and will. It is what has been distilled of the finer energies concentrated in my essence. It is weightless, yet gives those who have it weight, authority. Remember Napoleon's exclamation when Goethe, whom he had never met, walked into the room: "Now, there is a man!" Maybe not everyone is equally sensitive to the presence or absence of being, but most people can have some sense of it—in others, if not in themselves. But there is no known measurement of it and no definition that I have heard is satisfactory, e.g. "existence, one who lives, one's fundamental nature." The dictionary does not help us much. I prefer Napoleon. He is less cerebral and more instinctive. So is being. Perhaps we could say, "Being is the germ, the possibility, of my becoming what I truly am."

Whatever it is, being is not absurd. Henry Corbin, the great French Islamic scholar, told me in Tehran that there was one thing he was ashamed of in his academic career—having translated Heidegger into French; because it was through Corbin's translation that Jean-Paul Sartre got interested in the question of being. And from that has flowed more ink than truth.

What I found in South Asia and West Asia, where I represented Canada for 14 years, was that I could not really be a representative of my country and culture without understanding theirs. This meant, I soon discovered, going much deeper into their culture than a patronizing interest in their art, music and dance. It meant penetrating to the essentially religious core of their culture, whether that core was Hindu, Buddhist, Taoist, Muslim or Zoroastrian. And since I am trying to be a Christian, it meant uncovering the core of that tradition too. The traditional way for this search to proceed, I gradually found out, was to pose a very simple and very serious question to oneself that we hardly ever ask in polite university circles, though it is becoming more current outside academia, the question "Who am I?" What is the meaning and aim of my life, of the life of humanity, of life itself? And to try to find answers that satisfy the heart and the body, as well as the mind. So you see what I mean about going beyond the usual limits and methods of our own culture. It was a much more demanding and far more fascinating task than I could ever have guessed it would be at the beginning of my journey.

To show just how far apart our Western scientific culture now is from what could be called traditional cultures which are still alive mainly in the East, I am going to borrow an example cited earlier this year before the Royal Society of Canada by a Professor of both Physics and Religion at Dalhousie University, Dr. Ravi Ravindra. He first quoted the 8th Psalm:

> When I consider Thy heavens, the work of Thy fingers,
> The moon and the stars, which Thou hast ordained;
> What is man, that Thou art mindful of him?

Then he suggested that the scientist is more likely to put it this way today:

> When I consider the heavens, the work of our equations,
> The black holes and white dwarfs which we have ordained;
> What is God, that we are mindful of him?

It is indeed a different world view.

Over the years in the East, together with my precious co-explorer, my wife Carol, we learned that for Yogis and Bikkhus, Princes of the Church and Sufi Sheikhs, Rabbis, Roshis, and Rinpoches, as well as for you and for me, verbal formulations may be very different but the human experience at its highest and deepest is not. I think Thomas Merton, whom we introduced to some of our Tibetan friends in India, would have agreed that the truest experiential answers to the question "Who am I?" regardless of culture or faith, may be close to being the same. In the Judeo-Christian tradition, when God is asked by Moses to name Himself/Herself, the answer is "I am that I am" or "I am who am." "Be still, and know that I AM is God." This is about as close as we can come to defining God as Absolute Being. The South Asian answer in the oldest Vedas is still today a powerful mantra of Hindu practice: "Tat Vam Asi"—"That thou art." Nor is the Buddha field or the Dharmakaya essentially different. "One store—many departments," Yogaswami, an old Tamil Swami in Sri Lanka, used to tell us with a twinkle. But he also made sure we understood the enormous gap between knowing the answer in one's head and experiencing the state of being in which it was not theoretical but real, actual, here and now. For such a relationship, no other time, no other place, will do it. Now. Here. Where else could the Kingdom of Heaven possibly be?

Coming back to the West, to our meeting together, I can almost hear some of you thinking, "But what has all this metaphysical garbage got to do with my scientific studies? Science is producing spectacular results in the real world and I am not about to abandon it to go in search of 'being' when any logical positivist will tell you that being is a meaningless term."

If some of you are thinking in this vein, let me say that of course no one is asking you to give up anything. Whether or not you see it, your difficulty and mine is that we have both been heavily conditioned by our long intellectual training. We live largely in our heads, as most of us do in this culture. "I think, therefore I am." At least since Descartes all of us in the West have been taught to value knowledge, to train the mind, to work and to live with it, as if both my body and my emotions were either an obstacle or irrelevant. As a result, from the point of view of most other cultures, we are sadly limited to a certain kind of thinking, a certain level of thought, and only reactive contact with the rest of us.

For the vast majority of the people who live and have lived, it would be closer to the truth to turn Descartes on his head. "I am, therefore, I think"—and move and love and hate; but behind what I do, I am. Being, not knowledge, is primary.

Let us look ahead another 45 years. I wish I could come back and talk with you then. If we have not blown most of life off this planet, or fatally damaged our space ship by exploiting it for our ego satisfactions, not our real needs, we will, I hope and even expect, have come to a better balance between our knowledge and our being than we have today. We will have come into a new cultural environment, a new way of looking at the world, a new heaven and a new Earth. In academia, you call it a new paradigm. It will come, as I see it—it is coming—as a result of two strong influences powerfully at work today.

One of these influences is the sense of frustration we begin to experience with our existing paradigm, already obsolete and propped up by so many ingenious crutches that it might be simpler to let it die and start fresh. It is absurd to have one world view for physics and a totally different kind of story for organic life, including us. If purpose or mind is admissible in physics, it cannot be arbitrarily excluded from biology. Both need to address the questions of meaning which I have been raising today: the why, and not just the how, questions. For science to go forward again, it needs a broader, more complete perspective. It cannot be whole while ignoring the question we have today been calling being, and by dismissing the discussion of being as meaning less for science. According to the repository of human wisdom and experience represented by the sacred traditions of the East, the cure is not to know more but to experience a change of being which alone will permit us to enlarge our understanding. For when being does not grow with knowledge, understanding diminishes, and we are quite lawfully stopped. I think a good deal of the negativity that is so widespread today comes from that deeply unconscious frustration of half knowing that we have sold our birth right for a mess of potage.

The second strong influence, as I see it—you may disagree—is the seminal effect of the unprecedented influx of Eastern ideas and spiritual practices on the West. They are hopefully awakening or (as some now say) "raising" consciousness, teaching us to sit still, to make love longer, and even expanding the art of motorcycle maintenance to take on a significance, a self remembering awareness, it never had in the West before. This new explosion of interest in exploring inner space comes at precisely the moment when we are unravelling some of the secrets of outer space and beginning to prepare for manned flights to at least one or two of the planets of our solar system in the first decades of the next century. These momentous voyages, both in outer space and inner space, are likely to have an even more dramatic impact on the human psyche than the great age of seafaring discoveries about 500 years ago which helped to energize the last Renaissance of Western culture. Having seen atomic energy unlocked and the first steps towards releasing some of the energies of the unconscious during my lifetime, perhaps some of you may live to see humanity at the threshold of a quantum leap in our evolution when we shall be in touch not only with the forces of our subconscious but with higher energies that could without sentimentality be called spiritual. In times past, only the rare heroes of the spiritual journey have lived in contact with these higher energies; but, if they could, it must be possible for more of the rest of us to be open to the grace of such a benediction, at least from time to time, especially if it is necessary, as some teachings tell us, at this stage of the Earth s evolution, for a larger fraction of humanity to channel this energy.

For this human potential to be realized, however, we are going to need a spiritualized science and a scientific spirituality. I am not, of course referring to such distortions of the idea as scientology. I am remembering Prime Minister Nehru's visit to Ceylon (as it then was) in 1962 when he gave a remarkable discourse, while the Chinese armies poured across his northern border, in which he said that the hope of the future was in the combination of science and spirituality. He clearly hoped that India could play a leading role in that synthesis—and perhaps it still will. I am seeing the demystification of inner space research, called spiritual practice, by the application, with respect, of the rigour of scientific method combined with the free ranging emotional knowing of intuition, shorn of all sentimentality and superstition. I am seeing a science willing to explore the energies that can only be experienced, not measured—a science, like Einstein's, that dares to intuit equations and prove them rationally much later. I am seeing a spirituality in which the primary method is the work on oneself involved in patiently training the attention to connect with all the energies that can relate to a human being, not just the mental energies of ordinary associative thinking. I am seeing a biology in which causation from above is neither ruled out, nor doctrinally assumed, but which can be openly and honestly investigated. I am already seeing now a physics in which the old clockwork Universe of mechanistic reductionism has given way to a probabilistic relativism. I am seeing this new openness applied to the idea of whole systems, so that the relatively whole systems which constitute our visible world are seen to draw their anti-entropic energy from their relationship to greater wholes, to life itself, without which the clockwork should have unwound long ago. In short, I am seeing that the same laws apply to inner and outer space; and beyond there is implied an unknowable Law—maker Being Intelligence who IS, so to speak, above the Laws. So, if science concerns itself with all that is, science cannot exclude spirit (or higher energies) from its purview, any more than theology can claim to overrule science in some separate jurisdiction. There is only one reality. Physics and metaphysics are complementary approaches. Science cannot claim to be concerned with the whole of reality, and yet say that the experience of Dante, Bach, Blake and St. Theresa—human inner experience—is "off limits." If "God and the laws of structure and operation are one and the same Reality," as Spinoza taught, then there cannot be one for the physicist, one for the biologist, one for the theologian and one for the mystic—all different and inconsistent. The cause of the difficulty for all of us is the same—lack of being, and therefore limited understanding and no sense of the whole.

This inner feeling that I know much more than I understand, that I am somehow off balance, not at ease, like an exile from Paradise, is, I believe, rather wide spread today, in and out of Universities. I see that I am not what I could be—should be—so I suffer. But how could I suffer from my lack of being if I did not already know, at a deeper level, that I could be transformed? I must have that seed in myself somewhere, buried perhaps, but alive. It is the relation of knowledge to being that can open us to higher energies. That contact is transforming.

The literature is full of beautiful words about peak experiences, illumination, satori, union with the Divine, Christ consciousness, and much more. But for anyone the immediate awakening, from which genuine experiences of the heights begin, is to see that I am not. When I see that, I am no longer asleep. I am not just in my head. I have started to change.

With the work of Prigogine and von Bertalanffy, science is already working with the idea of different scales or levels of complexity, and with sub-systems forming parts of larger whole systems. Breakthrough occurs when a person, for example, is able to shift gears and move to a new level of complexity. Breakdown could be described as the reverse process, moving down the hierarchical scale instead of up. In this interconnected, interdependent whole that is the "system of systems," is it not possible, then, to suppose a hierarchy of mind or of being, in which the view from the top is broader, more inclusive, than how we see it at our level? In the cosmological interchange of energies, is it not possible that, in a certain specific sense, the higher feeds on the lower and the lower is food for the higher? This would give a very concrete meaning to the idea that our world is penetrated and formed by energies from above as well as by the operation of mechanical laws from below. Atomic theory has already taught us that matter and energy are not immutably separate but can be transformed from one to the other. It is not possible to look at the world as one system and myself as separate; I am part of it all. Like Jacob's ladder, I am a structure in which energies are all the time being transformed, some into the seeds of the next generation and others into waste products, moving up and down like the angels on the ladder. We know something about the lower rungs of ourselves, but what do we know about the upper? I can only wish for a being that could understand that.

If these attributes of being—consciousness, individuality, and will—do not mean much to contemporary science, could we find a common language in the genetic code, in DNA, in the double helix form, which belong (in traditional terminology) to essence? As we begin to know more about what Buckminster Fuller called the "design information" of our Universe, we already see how the same laws and principles can apply to consciousness, as well as to elementary particles or to the formation of galaxies. We are beginning to see that there is a real interface between our sciences and the mythical, mystical and religious heritages, newly understood. Every day now, scientists and educated mystics confirm that they are looking at the same patterns, the same reality, which is the basis for a new mutual appreciation. The trouble is that the metaphors of science have not yet been translated into the metaphors of the traditions with sufficient precision, and vice versa. So there is still confusion, but also the promise of what may come from this interface area in the next few years, if only we can up the being—and therefore the seeing.

Since Hiroshima shocked whatever we have left of our conscience, we have been told by men and women of vision, starting with Einstein, that the atomic age changed everything except our way of thinking, and that if we could not learn to think in a new way we were likely headed for the evolutionary scrap heap. But who wants to think in a new way, to stretch the existing paradigm, and risk being considered odd or eccentric? It takes more courage than most of us have to pioneer new ways of thinking or being. I remember how hard it was to convince my friend, Dr. Lyall Watson, the biologist and author, to publish his now famous story of the "hundredth monkey." In Japan, where our Threshold Foundation was organizing opposition to whaling, Lyall had been in touch with some Japanese colleagues who had been observing macaque monkeys on the outer islands for a couple of years. One winter, natural food supplies for the monkeys had run low and the scientists had begun feeding them yams. The trouble was that the soft yams picked up a lot of dirt on the ground that got in the teeth of the monkeys. Until one day a young female monkey had an inspiration. She washed her yam in the river before eating it. This improvement she gradually taught to her mother and then the rest of the family. Over the next few months yam washing spread slowly until about a hundred monkeys out of thousands were adopting the new practice. Then suddenly the scientists noticed that all the monkeys had switched to washing their yams; and not only on island A but on all the islands, some many miles away, where the monkeys were under observation. Overnight all the monkeys were in the new culture, spontaneously, without there being any apparent way for the practice to spread to far away islands. This was the part Lyall did not want to publish. How could such an observation be explained? He would be ridiculed be his peers. Yet he was convinced the Japanese were not telling him a tall story—they were as puzzled as he and as hesitant to publish themselves. I told Lyall that he had an obligation to report what he believed to be the facts and let others worry about explaining them later. To his credit, he did. And others have developed theories of "critical mass" to encourage the rest of us to not be so afraid to start something new, because it only takes a small amount of yeast to leaven a large lump of dough. Nevertheless, the fear is still there. But we do begin to see new possibilities.

The most important new possibility I would like us to see this afternoon is that we can think in a new way, be in a new way, and understand what we never could understand before.

Maybe what we need is a new department or faculty in this and other great Universities to focus the growing interest in holistic transdisciplinary studies: in von Bertalanffy's "system of systems," or anything looking in that direction. We might call it a Chair or a School of Ontological Studies, in recognition of the central place of being in the whole. It may sound strange to you now, but no stranger than a Department of Psychology, when that was first proposed. At the same time you realize the danger, if such a Chair falls into the hands of "empire builders." They will claim everything as part of their whole.

But why not try it? Last month there was a seminar in Washington, DC, under Smithsonian sponsorship on the question, "Can consciousness survive the death of the body?" Last June the Royal Society of Canada sponsored a symposium on "Origin and Evolution of the Universe: Evidence for Design?" And last July, Amherst University held a conference on "GAIA: Is the Earth a living being?" None of these questions would have had a hearing in respectable circles even ten years ago. The stage is set for a full dress examination of being that I hope will go well beyond theoretical studies.

Still, if the University is not quite ready for a School of Ontological Studies, complete with the most advanced bio-feedback devices for experiment, what about those of us here who may be interested starting a small informal group to pool information from our various disciplines and gather a sense of what general framework would best satisfy our demand for unity, symmetry and coherence in what we can discern as the cosmic order of laws, not excluding our experience of ourselves?

For what it may be worth, it is my conclusion that we are only just beginning to get a taste of what might be possible for humans to be and to think and to do in the next generations. A good deal has been made recently, by Sheldrake and others, of experiments with succeeding generations of rats, that have been going on since the 1930's, in which it seems to be demonstrably easier for each new generation of rats to survive swimming through a water maze in which many of their ancestors drowned.

The theories to explain this phenomenon are to me less interesting than the facts, and suggest, at least to me, that there may be ways (still little known in our part of the world but more widely acknowledged in traditional cultures) which actually can lead us towards the kind of being effort that may put us up a rung on Jacob's ladder where the view—our capacity to see—is quite different than before.

What is it that a St. John of the Cross and an Einstein hold in common? If we study that question objectively, with all the data on Einstein's inner world now available from the Princeton library, there is a remarkable congruence. Thinking becomes non-verbal, the body must be totally relaxed, the attention must be wholly concentrated, the energy of feeling enters as intuition, a light envelopes the body as if from "above," and there is an exchange within a larger field of force. A clarity ensues that does not automatically either demand or answer but can hold both possibilities simultaneously in a new kind of time and space, without past memory association or future expectation of any kind. In such a state of being I am no longer separate from everything but connected in a new way. I am present. I am alive. I am.

These words may not be of much help in experiencing this state, but road maps are necessary to find a direction in which I want to go, though the map is not the territory. Perhaps it helps to know that in every sphere of activity, inner and outer, others have pioneered a way for me, and because of their work it is a little more possible for my generation of "rats."

I was asked recently if the Threshold Foundation would support the collection of as complete a compendium of secret Tibetan teachings as could now be assembled and putting them into a computer, offer a data base on all such practices. I could imagine an 800 number to dial for access! How to explain the uselessness of such an enterprise? How to convey that what you can attempt depends lawfully on where you are on the ladder of being, which is exactly why such teachings have been kept secret, to prevent them being wasted on those not yet ready for them, and perhaps causing harm instead of helping. Yet we are so strongly resistant to the very idea of different levels of being. It is perhaps our biggest hurdle in coming to anything real in our culture.

Another biologist friend who dared to think in a new way—and paid for it with the "establishment"—was Gregory Bateson. It was his crime, or his distinction (whichever way you look at it), to try to satisfy his own intellectual honesty that could not be content with a mechanically unfolding Universe evolving by accident, purposelessly. Where the philosopher might prefer to speak of being, he felt more comfortable with mind; but for me the intent was the same. This is what he wrote in support of his life-long conviction that the primary aim of the scientist was to develop the capacity to see the "pattern that connects":

> The individual mind is immanent but not only in the body. It is immanent also in pathways and messages outside the body: and there is a larger Mind of which the individual mind is only a sub-system. This larger mind is comparable to God and is perhaps what some people mean by God, but it is still immanent in the total interconnected social system and planetary ecology.

For me, it seems clear that we would not have any capacity to see connections on any scale, large or small, if we ourselves were not connected, and whether we call the "connector" mind or being does not matter. My experience is that "having an idea about" something is a pretty thin connector, compared to what I feel when I genuinely love someone. Then it comes from a different place in myself: a much more central place than my mind, which I call my being. But of course one aspect of my being is consciousness; so I can think about my love too. In fact, my whole organism can only love in a complete sense if all its subsystems—body, thinking and feeling—are involved. Only then, I am. Anything else is partial, incomplete.

If bringing together all my parts is so important, how can I accomplish this? The traditional answer means very little to one who has not tried it persistently for some time, but it is awareness of myself, on the way to an awareness of Self. I am aware of my body through sensation, of my mind through observation, and when I continue quietly in a relaxed state feeling arises spontaneously. But nothing can be reached without a sensitive and trained attention; and this is not easy to develop. More head work alone will not change my thinking nor add to my stature, as the Gospel tells us. It will take the whole of me. The possibility exists because the germ is already deep in my essence, unspoiled by all the educational and environmental conditioning I have received throughout my life, which has fed only my personality, not me, not my being. I can write books about being, like Heidegger, but if I stay in my head I wither and dry up for lack of contact with the real life that is in me. How can I ever understand without practice, without more contact with being?

As an example of the impoverishment of meaning in our culture overflowing with data, let us take the history of one word, "credo." It was your Emeritus Professor, Wilfred Smith, who first told me what the root meaning is, and it is almost the opposite of what it has come to mean in the intellectual climate of today. The Sanskrit root is *kr*, the same root that becomes *coeur* in French, plus the Latin *dare*, "to give." So it does not mean "I accept or affirm intellectually certain postulates or articles of faith." It means, "I give my heart." This level of commitment is what used to be meant—and I hope soon will be again—by "I believe."

It is not for nothing that René Guénon called this age "The Reign of Quantity" and that in India they call it the Kali Yuga, which can be freely translated as "the pits." We may have an unequalled technology, but if we destroy ourselves and the planet through manifestations of our violence and egoism, what have we understood? Perhaps this is our last chance as a species to break out of the prison of our sleep and begin to realize some of the potential we have been considering this afternoon. We are suddenly, in one or two generations, being given all the information we need to explore inner space as successfully as we have outer space. The maps are in our hands. Now we have to go there. I have only a little time before I die. So have you, even if it is more than I have. None of us have time to lose.

The ideas I have been presenting to you this afternoon as the basis of a possible marriage between science and spirituality have been distilled in the wonderful contacts I have been privileged to have with both Eastern and Western teachings during the course of my life. I am grateful for all these teachings, but the thread that has brought it all together for me I owe to someone I never met, who also came from the West, and who spent many years of his life in South Asia, Central Asia, and the Middle East, before returning to the West a few years before his own country, Russia, had its 1917 revolution. With some pupils he then made his way to Europe, finally settling in France. To spread his teaching he visited the United States several times before his death in Paris in 1949. Only now, 36 years later, do we begin to have an appreciation of the stature of this mountain of a man, Gurdjieff, who laid the groundwork for a new synthesis on which the next Renaissance in our culture could, I believe, be based. It has taken me many years of work—work on myself, with the help of several of the great living teachers in contemporary Buddhism, Hinduism, Sufism, and Christianity—for me to understand something of the place and purpose of human life, and how it could serve a much higher energy than it does, in general, today. And still I feel I am just at the beginning of my quest.

The great traditions are, in a sense, timeless. But each found expression in a particular culture, for a particular psychology, which is past. What Gurdjieff tried to bring was the same essential truth in a form suited to our understanding today. I am constantly amazed to see how contemporary he is, how the influence of his ideas is spreading in a kind of underground which is drawing water from his well, mostly without acknowledging it.

One of his aphorisms, which I have tried to follow, is: "Take the knowledge of the West and the understanding of the East, and then search." This has been the theme of my talk. On another occasion, Gurdjieff said, "The study of the world and the study of man support each other. In studying the Universe and its laws man studies himself, and in studying himself he studies the Universe."

To conclude I should like to share with you these notes of what he said to his pupils one evening during the occupation of Paris in 1943 when everyone present had had to risk arrest for breaking the curfew in order to be at his table. It will give you a taste of the sort of food Gurdjieff served to nourish our wish to work on ourselves, with conscience and intentional suffering, for what he sometimes called "imperishable being:"

> During all your free time, count: one, two, three, four, five,
> six, up to fifty. Afterwards: fifty, forty-nine, forty-eight,

forty-seven, forty-six, etc., until you are back where you started. All the time. And if you do it seven times, five or ten minutes, sit down, relax and say to yourself: "I am," "I wish to be," "I can be," "not to use it to do evil, but good," "I will help my neighbour when I shall be. I am." After that, count again. But consciously, not automatically. You do that all your free time. The first time it will seem absurd to you. But when you have done it for two or three weeks, you will thank me with all your heart.

CHAPTER 4

WHEN EAST MEETS WEST—
BUT NOT VICE-VERSA

This article was written in Tehran in January, 1973, and was published in SUFI # 51.

A few days after this memorable exchange, Dr. Corbin dropped in to say goodbye before returning to Paris. As he was getting ready to leave, I asked him with great respect whether there was anything in his life that he now regretted. He was silent and then said thoughtfully: "Yes, I regret having translated Martin Heidegger into French so that Jean-Paul Sartre could misunderstand him!"

Yes, I thought, Sartre took existentialism negatively because it was just in his head. In the full experience of "I AM," with body sensation and feeling participating, there is no negativity and it is never absurd.

At lunch today I was the witness at one of those rare moments of meeting—or at least attempted meeting—between East and West. Yet even as I sit down to record it a few hours later, I know that the task is beyond me, and that I am no more capable of reproducing the full savour of that conversation in all its subtlety and freshness than I am of entering into the inner state of either of the two principal characters in this (at least for me) historic dialogue. Nor would a tape recorder have helped. Too much was going on at the nonverbal level. So, accepting the subjectivity of my perceptions, let me try to recall exactly what took place.

Dr. Javad Nourbakhsh had invited Dr. Henry Corbin to Sunday lunch, together with Dr. S. H. Nasr, Chancellor of Aryamehr University, Sir Peter Ramsbotham, the British Ambassador, Dr. William Chiddick, the American Persian scholar, Mr. N. Pourjavady of the Department of Philosophy at Tehran University, with two other Iranians (whose names I do not recall) and myself, at the Sufi Khanegah of the Nirmatullah Order in South Tehran. Dr. Nasr brought Sir Peter, and I brought Dr. Corbin.

After an affectionate embrace Dr. Nourbakhsh put Professor Corbin and Sir Peter in western-style comfort in chairs, while the rest of us sat on the floor, either cross-legged or with our legs under us, Sufi style. Tea was brought and with it half a dozen new publications supervised by Dr. Nourbakhsh, who presented them to Dr. Corbin. What more natural opening gambit than to exchange notes on their respective publication programs? Yet already something else was going on.

With the quickness and lightness of a cobra striking and recoiling itself, Dr. Nourbakhsh slyly threw at Dr. Corbin the question, "What is a Sufi?" Better than any other western scholar, H.C. could have described the life and works of all the great Persian Sufis of the past 1,300 years; but in front of the living representative of that tradition he was at first speechless. It was as if he did not hear the question. The conversation continued about books and research programs, new translations, and so on.

We moved next door for a delicious Persian lunch, but after we returned to our original places for fruit and tea, J. N. resumed his attempt to transmit something of his own understanding to H.C. and the rest of us. Certainly no western scholar has better deserved such a lesson from a Sufi master, for H.C. has spent a long and very industrious life bringing to light and making available to the West in translations the best of classical Persian Sufi thought. Indeed his efforts have produced a new generation of philosophers within Iran as well as in Europe, trained in a proper appreciation of the classical Sufi masters of Iran who had been previously largely neglected, both in the East and in the West.

A "perfect man," J. N. was saying, is one who knows God. But how can God be known? Not in words, not by the mind nor by the intelligence—only by love.

H.C. felt challenged and defended himself as best he could. He interpreted what was taking place as an attack against the rational intelligence of man, which was the very foundation of his own work and life. Was J. N. putting love above reason, above gnosis, above truth? Surely God himself had had to create creatures (and man in particular) so as to know Himself by being known by them, which for Corbin meant being known by man's mind, his intelligence. Duality was necessary, even for God. And for man, as Ibn Arabi had said, the fact of twoness must precede the knowledge of oneness. Without subject and object, can there be transcendence?

This did not, of course, satisfy the Sufi. He told us the story of the seeker who came to a Master asking him which, of all the names of God, was the supreme name. The Master had replied "that which is left when you have emptied yourself of everything in you that you know as yourself."

In the exchange that followed between the Western intellectual and the Eastern lover, it seemed apparent to all present except Corbin that he was being gently and lovingly cut down to size. If only he could have seen and accepted it. Beside J. N., Corbin (the older by thirty years) was revealed as a child before a father who knows how to take any heat out of the argument at the right time by humorously conceding his "total agreement" whenever H.C. found himself in a tight corner—and tightened up.

Referring to Corbin's own writing on Ruzbehan in which the Persian poet and philosopher described ecstatically how he had seen God "in the most beautiful of forms," I asked both of them what form this could be, since I could not imagine God in any form at all. For Corbin it was clearly the form of human love and he quoted also from Ibn Arabi's work on how God can finally be known as One, by transcending lover, beloved, and love itself.

Dr. Nasr then expanded the reference to Ibn Arabi, recalling his almost tantric doctrine of human love of man and woman as the supreme example of the merging of opposites in an experience (however transitory) of unity. Here again, as Dr. Corbin had been saying, a metaphysician finds proof of the passage from duality to unity in human experience, however we may explain it ontologically in terms of God's creation of man and woman in the first place.

This evoked a spirited rejoinder from J. N. who dismissed as mere intellectuality any authority, any book, and any process that could be put into any words. To describe the supreme Reality in words was already a limitation and so not THAT. Forget about Ibn Arabi and all the rest. Reality was One first and last, One before and after, One now and always One. Even to talk about a trinity of lover, beloved and love was a veil over the direct experience. When H.C. tried to say that it was duality in unity and unity in multiplicity, he was put down. Any description more or less satisfactory to our categories of thought might be beautiful, but it was nothing so long as it was an idea, "my" idea. (What was everything to H.C. was nothing to J.N., and vice versa. That is the important point.)

"Then why do you write books and have books published?" asked Corbin, with an almost audible "*touché*" sense of scoring. "To pass the time," laughed Nourbakhsh. What else to say?

The whole exchange was like a modern replay of Razali's classical Persian debate between love and intellect. Having heard this dialogue today, I am doubly sure that whatever is now attributed to Razali was cooked up afterwards more by the intellect than by the inspiration of love itself. Thought—even the highest metaphysical knowledge—unless powered by another circuit of feeling than the ordinary current that may be nothing more vibrant than associative sentiment, cannot lead to the energy of understanding that spoke in flashes of intensity through the eyes of the "mad" Sufi.

At lunch we had already talked a little about what has to die. For both Christianity and Islam, importance is given to a forty-day period of fasting and purification, as for example when Christ was tempted in the wilderness or when the Prophet of Islam was preparing to be a vehicle for the message of God. Dr. Nasr added that in Arabic and Persian numerology the letter *Mim* (which stands for death) has a number value of forty. (The same letter is echoed in European languages in the words *mort* and *mordre* or *mordant*.)

Can a camel pass through the eye of a needle? Can a man rich in ideas discard the lot in order to see God? For that not to be just another idea, he might have to be pretty close to what the world—whether East or West—would call a fool.

Perhaps only God's fool can really be in love, madly in love. The rest of us talk about it or write about it or think about it. But that is different.

Sadly, but with real human feeling, J. N. finally said goodbye to H.C. "with much respect." As I drove Dr. Corbin home, his justifying mind continued the argument, saying how the Sufi way was unbalanced, denying life, affirming the oneness of the most High to the neglect of the Earth on which we stand. Mystics might have beautiful visions, Corbin told me, but only the gnostic metaphysician brought heaven and Earth together in man, through knowledge.

While this understanding is fine on its level, I have no doubt that at a deeper level Corbin too was touched in a way his brilliant mind may never know—as we say, consciously—but touched nevertheless. "Die before you die," says the Sufi. But we from the West, dominated by a totally conditioned head brain, cannot even stop talking and get out from under it for a minute to feel wordlessly what that means. Who must die? Who am I? Who? Is there then nothing left? Nothing ... but that is All.

A few days later I saw Dr. Nourbakhsh again. When I mentioned Dr. Corbin, J. N. smiled and shook his head, as if acknowledging he had been unable to get through. "All his life," said J. N., "people have been saying to him 'Monsieur le Professeur, vous avez raison.'" "Yes," I agreed, "that's his difficulty." (And mine too, I saw afterwards, as J. N. had no doubt intended I should.)

We spoke of someone else, who had tried to see J. N. but couldn't. "He's a good man," I interceded. "All men are good," said J. N., "but I am not looking for good men; I am looking for fools."

Can two different levels—like parallel lines—meet at infinity? Not by taking thought. Only by God's love.

CHAPTER 5

YOGASWAMI: "WHO AM I?"

Thirty years after Yogaswami's death in 1964, I was asked by his pupils to write about my contacts with him during the last four years of his life. The following account tells of my visits to his hut in Columbuthurai. It was first published in Hinduism Today in 1994 and again on the 50th anniversary in 2014, when Parabola Magazine *republished it. A much longer version may be found on the Internet at https://www.youtube.com/watch?v=J1EE-8GPbFz0. The interview by Yogaswami's monks from Kauai's Hindu Monastery was recorded in 2011 in Toronto.*

> I was profoundly influenced by Swami. Though the state desired was thoughtless and wordless, he taught through a few favorite aphorisms in pithy expressions, to be plumbed later in silence. Three of these aphorisms I shall report here: "Just be!" or "Summa iru" when he said it in Tamil. "There is not even one thing wrong." "It is all perfect from the beginning." He applied these statements to the individual and to the cosmos. Order was a truth deeper than disorder. We don't have to develop or do anything, because, essentially, in our being, we are perfectly in order here and now—when we are here and now

The Tamils of Sri Lanka called him the Sage of Jaffna. His thousands of devotees, including many Singhalese Buddhists and Christians, called him a saint. Some of those closest to him referred to him as the Old Lion, or Bodhidharma reborn, for he could be very fierce and unpredictable, chasing away unwelcome supplicants with a stick. I just called him Swami. He was my introduction to Hinduism in its pure Vedanta form, and my teacher for the nearly four years I served as the Canadian High Commissioner in what was still called Ceylon in the early Sixties when I was there.

For the previous ten years I had been apprenticed in the Gurdjieff Work, and it was through a former student of P.D. Ouspensky, James Ramsbotham (Lord Soulbury), and his brother Peter, that, one hot afternoon, not long after our arrival in Ceylon, I found myself outside a modest thatched hut in Jaffna, on the northern shore of Ceylon, to keep my first appointment with Yogaswami.

I knocked quietly on the door, and a voice from within roared, "Is that the Canadian High Commissioner?" I opened the door to find him seated cross-legged on the floor—an erect, commanding presence clad in a white robe, with a generous topping of white hair and long white beard. "Well, Swami," I began, "that is just what I do, not what I am." "Then come and sit with me," he laughed uproariously.

I felt bonded with him from that moment. He helped me to go deeper towards the discovery of who I am, and to identify less with the role I played. Indeed, like his great Tamil contemporary, Ramana Maharshi of Arunachal-am, in South India, Yogaswami used "Who am I?" as a mantra as well as an existential question. He often chided me for running around the country, attending one official function after another, and neglecting the practice of sitting in meditation. When I got back to Ceylon from home leave in Canada, after visiting, on the way around the planet, France, Canada, Japan, Indonesia and Cambodia, he sat me down firmly beside him and told me that I was spending my life-energy uselessly, looking always outward for what could only be found within.

"You are all the time running about, doing something, instead of sitting still and just being. Why don't you sit at home and confront yourself as you are, asking yourself, not me, 'Who am I? Who am I? Who am I? Who am I? Who am I? Who am I?'" His voice rose in pitch, volume and intensity with each repetition of the question until he was screaming at me with all his force.

Then suddenly he was silent, very powerfully silent, filling the room with his unspoken teaching that went far beyond words, banishing my turning thoughts with his simple presence. In that moment I knew without any question that I AM; and that that is enough; no "who" needed. I just am. It is a lesson I keep having to relearn, re-experience, for the "doing" and the "thinking" takes me over again and again as soon as I forget.

Another time my wife and I brought our three children to see Yogaswami. Turning to the children, he asked each of them, "How old are you?" Our daughter said, "Nine," and the boys, "Eleven" and "Thirteen." To each in turn Yogaswami replied solemnly, "I am the same age as you." When the children protested that he couldn't be three different ages at once, and that he must be much older than their grandfather, Yogaswami just laughed, and winked at us, to see if we understood.

At the time we took it as his joke with the children, but slowly we came to see that he meant something profound, which it was for us to decipher. Now I think this was his way of saying indirectly that although the body may be of very different ages on its way from birth to death, something just as real as the body, and for which the body is only a vehicle, always was and always will be. In that sense, we are in essence all "the same age."

After I had met Yogaswami many times, I learned to prepare my questions carefully. One day, when I had done so, I approached his hut, took off my shoes, went in and sat down on a straw mat on the Earth floor, while he watched me with the attention that never seemed to fail him. "Swami," I began, "I think ..." "Already wrong!" he thundered. And my mind again went into the non-conceptual state that he was such a master at invoking, clearing the way for being.

Looking at the world as it is now, thirty years after his death, I wonder if he would utter the same aphorisms with the same conviction today. I expect he would, challenging us to go still deeper to understand what he meant. Reality cannot be imperfect or wrong; only we can be both wrong and imperfect, when we are not real, when we are not now!

As an Epilogue to this account of my own experiences with Yogaswami, I am adding this previously unpublished account of an initiatory exchange between him and his German pupil, Swami Gauribala in Jaffna, in 1951.

Gauribala had, for months, been trying to get Yogaswami to talk about the much-used Tamil mantra, *summa iru.* This can be roughly translated as "just be still!" But all that Yogaswami would say was "I don't know! *Summa iru* is foolishness."

Then one day Yogaswami suddenly asked Gauribala "Who are you?"

Gauribala: I don't know.

Yogaswami: That's just empty talk; you know very well who you are. Everybody knows who he is. Every creature knows that it is what it is. I am I.

Gauribala, quoting Shakespeare's *Twelfth Night,* "That that is, is."

Yogaswami: Yes! That that is, is. We is. We all is-ness!

Gauribala then tries to explain his views about *summa iru.*

Yogaswami: Ah, foolishness! Don't try to understand. Just say to yourself "that that is, is." So *summa iru* is.

I have this mind-stopping account by Gauribala in his own handwriting. He was a German poet named Peter Schoenfeld before World War 2, who, because of his Jewish ancestry, fled to India in 1939 and was incarcerated there during the war. He escaped to Tibet with Heinrich Harrer and others, but (because he spoke no Tibetan) was returned to British custody while Harrer was allowed to go on to Llasa. After the war, he came to Ceylon (Sri Lanka) and became a pupil of Yogaswami in Jaffna for the rest of his life.

CHAPTER 6

WALTER FORDHAM'S INTERVIEW FOR THE CHRONICLES OF CHÖGYAM TRUNGPA

Although perhaps best known as a distinguished Canadian diplomat and an effective environmental and political activist, James George is first and foremost a spiritual seeker. He has been a devoted student of the Gurdjieff Work for more than fifty years and was a close disciple of the late Madame de Salzmann, one of Gurdjieff's primary students. With her encouragement, he and his wife, Carol, explored the spiritual traditions that formed the foundation for Gurdjieff's early training. While stationed in India, Sri Lanka, and the Middle East, the Georges met with a number of remarkable men, including Krishnamurti, Thomas Merton, Yogaswami of Sri Lanka, Dr. Javad Nurbakhsh (Sufi master from Tehran), Dudjom Rinpoche, and Dilgo Khyentse Rinpoche. This underlying interest in spirituality is the thread that runs through all of James George's activities and accomplishments.

During the autumn months of 1968, James and Carol George hosted Trungpa Rinpoche in their home, the Canadian Embassy in Delhi. Of that period of time, Rinpoche wrote: "Returning from Bhutan through India [1968], I was delighted to meet again with His Holiness Karmapa and also His Holiness the Dalai Lama. I also made the acquaintance at this time of Mr. James George, the Canadian High Commissioner to India, and his wonderful family. Mr. George is a wise and benevolent man, an ideal statesman, who holds great respect and faith for the teachings of Buddhism." (Chögyam Trungpa, from the Epilogue to *Born In Tibet*).

As I think can be heard from the tone of this interview, James George is a very warm and accessible person, and a true friend to the Shambhala community. At the 2003 Kalapa Assembly, which he attended as the guest of honour, he spoke about the importance of applying our spiritual practice to the problems facing the larger world. I met with Mr. George in his Toronto apartment in June 2003 and asked him to talk about the life and legacy of Vidyadhara the Venerable Chögyam Trungpa Rinpoche. Here is what he had to say.

WALTER FORDHAM, October 2003

James George: Well Walter, I don't know that I can do justice to this occasion but I'm very honored to try, and even as we speak now, remembering Trungpa with much respect and much affection and asking his forgiveness for all the things I've forgotten that he told me and that you'd like to know. But some things have certainly remained very vivid, and I suppose partly because I got to writing about Shambhala. His interest in Shambhala certainly sparked my interest in it. But let me go back a bit and begin at the beginning.

My wife, Carol, and I went to India in September 1967, and I think it was the next summer she was in London to drive a Land Rover back to India with our kids. I joined them part of the way on the return trip to India. In that visit to London, I think she met Trungpa for the first time—that would probably be August of 1968, or July. So it was natural that, having invited him to look us up in Delhi when he got back to India, he did, and in fact lived with us for most of that autumn, I think, from October through December 1968. The culmination of that visit was a beautiful pilgrimage we made as a family with Trungpa, and I think Tendzin Parsons was also on that pilgrimage. Using our Land Rover, we went camping through all the Buddhist holy places in northern India, southern Nepal, Lumbini, Benares, Bodhgaya, and so on. It was a great time to be with him, and he of course made it very vivid, since I think it was in some cases, the first time he was able to visit these places.

It was, I think, during that visit in the fall of 1968 that Trungpa began to speak a little about Shambhala and Gesar of Ling, and I, as I've written, asked him to describe what he was able to tell me about Shambhala. He pulled out his mirror—a metal disk mirror that he wore on a cord around his neck—and started to look into it with deep concentration and describe Shambhala, just as if he was looking out the window. It was very vivid, and it got me researching Shambhala in a more serious way with a view to perhaps publishing something. Eventually I produced an article called *Searching for Shambhala*, which was published in *Search: Journey on the Inner Path*, edited by Jean Sulzberger. I had sent it to Trungpa in 1976 to see if I was allowed to publish this material, and he gave his permission. In this article, I was exploring whether Shambhala was an allegory or a real place or both. And since that's already published and on record, I don't need to speak more about that perhaps.

Trungpa, at that time, was not certain what he should be doing on this mission. I think it was a few months later in the early part of 1969 that he decided to team up with Akong Rinpoche at Samye Ling in Scotland [ed. note: Samye Ling was founded in 1967], and when he came to say goodbye to us before setting forth for Scotland and Samye Ling, I said to him, "You know, perhaps it's out of place to say this to you, but I see Samye Ling and Scotland as much too small for what you're going to be bringing to the West. You're going to have to wind up in America somewhere, because that's the big country." Even at that time, the lamas were telling us that the dharma is now in the West and when we would ask them what they meant, they would say "America." So I said to Trungpa, "Maybe your role is to bring the dharma to America and this would be a tremendous awakening, devoutly to be wished." And in due course, I guess that's what happened, although I never imagined at that time the scale of the awakening that he would create in such an extraordinarily short time.

The people he attracted, the intensity of the search, the shift in consciousness in so many of his pupils, I think, helped to shift the entire North American cultural scene in a significant way, and that shift is continuing. This is one of the green sprouts coming up through the wasteland that our culture of the thirties and forties and fifties had pretty well created to the detriment of the entire planet, which is suffering ecological distress and crisis. He saw very clearly that the energy that animates us in our sitting practice and on our cushions has to be brought out into life. He saw that this energy is the yeast that can facilitate a change that is absolutely necessary at the cellular level in individual people, and from there into the whole culture. He saw that bringing meditation into our daily lives would make it possible, in due course, to avoid a culture of destruction and war, and violence and fear, and generate a culture of consciousness, nonviolence, and fearlessness.

In that sense, I think he always intended the Shambhala Training as a kind of outreach into the world and at the same time an inner preparation for the Dzogchen teachings, the Mahamudra teachings about being present in the moment no matter what—just aware—not thinking, feeling perhaps, but not reacting and maintaining this awareness in the face of whatever happens out there in life, ordinary life. So there were no boundaries for him between the secular and the profane. There were no distinctions, finally, between samsara and nirvana.

When I visited Trungpa in Boulder at his home in 1983, he was seeing, as I was, that we were in a rather threatened strategic situation. At that time, the United States was positioning its Pershing nuclear missiles on the border of East Germany. If fired, these missiles would reach Moscow in about 12 minutes, and the danger of mistaken retaliation by misinterpreting radar signals seemed to be very great. I had been writing and campaigning about this dangerous situation in the peace movement, and I shared my views with Trungpa at that time. I think this supported his decision to move the center of his operations to Halifax, out of the United States, and out of Colorado—where the strategic command was located at Colorado Springs—and find a safer haven for his people and for his work. Of course he accomplished that move to Halifax only a year before he died. But the decision has stuck. You haven't moved back in any substantial degree, and I think Halifax and Nova Scotia have benefited from having this influx of practitioners who are committed to doing something more than sit in solitary or collective meditation. You have taken the practice into your lives and into the creation of a more enlightened society in so many practical ways.

There's something else I could share from an historical perspective. When I visited Trungpa in Colorado in 1983, he already had the court thing going and the formality around his person. I noticed that many of the protocols that he introduced had been lifted directly from his experience in Delhi living with us and observing how an ambassador functions and the formalities that surround him in a country like India, which loves formality. I think much of Trungpa's court formality was inspired by his experience of diplomatic life with us.

When I was on that visit, he asked me to stay. And I said, really I'm supposed to be back in Crestone tonight. So I took my leave and got into my car, and my car wouldn't start. It had been working perfectly when I arrived, but now it would not start. He kept me there for several hours that way before he released the car to start, which it did in due course. But it was interesting that he produced that. So that's another anecdote for you.

But these anecdotes only point to the real thing, which is the preparation of humanity for a level of consciousness that lives with awareness in the moment, and not just in the moment. We can learn to sustain that awareness by bringing it into our life, our conversation, our writing, our being, because it doesn't come from us personally. It comes from a much higher source that is waiting to get into humanity, if only we would wake up and get with it. So, for each one of us, this search for Shambhala is a practice of coming to this moment in a different modality of awareness. I think Trungpa Rinpoche's influence through so many lives, not only in North America, but in Europe and other countries, has been immense and little appreciated, because it has moved quietly and modestly and, for the most part, below the radar of the media.

I'm reminded of what Bernie Glassman has been doing in New York. The Greyston Foundation, which he started, provides housing for people, and operates a bakery that is a huge business now. Greyston has created a way for Zen to enter into relations with others who are practicing, whether they carry a Buddhist name or a Christian name or a Jewish name or a Gurdjieffian name. It doesn't matter because we're all seeing that, in origin, the human experience has gradually come to understand what could generate Bodhicitta and nonviolent awareness. All of our activities—whether we're trying to improve the conditions of the poor, or teach meditation to prisoners in the penitentiaries, or give bread to those who need it, homes to those that don't have them—are just the outer support for an inner practice of freedom from conditions. Without that practice, no awareness can develop. Without that practice we lose the connection to a greater consciousness, with which we have been blessed.

I think we all share the hope that human consciousness can evolve. We're probably not going to evolve much more physically, that's been done. But we don't want to be stuck with the consciousness that was appropriate for hunting and gathering and the violence that was even necessary to prevent ourselves being devoured by predators. We've now become the predators on the planet and are destroying our resources and each other—one-hundred-million dead from war in the last century alone. It's really shocking as a measure of human consciousness as it presently is. So that transformation must take place or we're down the tube and so is the planet. Therefore an evolution of consciousness is what I think fundamentally—aside from whatever lineage we represent—we're all trying to work for and search for, in ourselves, and collectively in our little groups.

When Trungpa came to America, he was not presenting the Buddhism of Tibet, exactly. When the dharma crossed the mountains with Padmasambhava, it had to change, and did. And with Trungpa, it had to cross the seas and change, and that change is still in progress. Of course anybody who is trying to change a tradition is up against enormous fundamentalist resistance, both from those who understand and want to protect something in the original that could be distorted, and from those who are just attached to a form and want to preserve it without really understanding the living spirit that gives it life. So he had to withstand pressures from all these different angles, and at the same time make something that someone like Allen Ginsberg could appreciate. I worked with Allen in New York for several years, and he owed an immense debt to Trungpa. Allen would never have been able to connect with the dharma if he had just been taught in the Tibetan style. So transplanting buddhadharma into a western context was a very tricky thing to attempt and to carry out, and Trungpa Rinpoche did it in a very short time.

We were friends of a remarkable English lady, Freda Bedi, later known as Sister Palmo, who should be recorded as a patron of Trungpa. She started the young lamas program with her own money; I was one of the trustees of her foundation for a while. She sent Akong, Trungpa, Sogyal, so many of the promising tulkus, to Oxford or Cambridge and gave them a university education, so that—knowing both languages in a sophisticated way—they could teach fluently in English and translate Tibetan texts into English. She understood that such translations would be so much better than the work done by Evans-Wentz, which were hopeless translations compared to what Larry Mermelstein and your group of translators in Halifax have been doing, as well as Chagdud's people, and others. It has been a remarkable job, comparable to the translation from Sanskrit into Tibetan, with long lasting effects and benefit, I'm sure.

Walter Fordham: Could you say anything about how Trungpa Rinpoche's life might be viewed by future generations?

JG: I don't know how his life will be assessed in the end. It's too soon. He's already recognized as a pioneer in bringing a fresh Buddhism from Tibet to North America and Europe. But he also needs to be seen as a spiritual pioneer in his own right. Look at the influence of someone like Longchenpa. He did it through his books and through his pupils, just as Trungpa did, and that influence is still touching lives today. There's a wonderful translation of the *Precious Treasury of the Basic Space of Phenomena* by Longchenpa that just came out from the Padma Publishing line of Chagdud Rinpoche, which I thought was splendid, sort of the heart of Dzogchen. I feel Trungpa was getting us ready to appreciate such teachings and be able to live them a bit, and to prepare others for the same transmissions.

He's been criticized for his lifestyle, but I don't feel that way. He was very frank with me about it. He said one time in India, "You know, my lineage of Trungpas have always had trouble with their emotions."

I'd like to read a poem that I think is appropriate, if you'll give me that book that's on the shelf beside you. This is René Daumal's poem translated from the French, written at the end of his short life when he had already become, I think, one of the outstanding pupils of Gurdjieff. René Daumal is quite well known in France as an avant-garde poet of the twenties and thirties. He died in 1944 at the age of 36. This poem was his last summing up.

> I am dead because I lack desire
> I lack desire because I think I have it
> I think I have it because I do not try to give.
> In trying to give, I see that I have nothing
> Seeing I have nothing, I then try to give of myself
> Trying to give of myself, I see that I am nothing
> Seeing that I am nothing, I desire to become
> And in desiring to become, I begin to live.

WF: That's marvellous. Thank you.

JG: Well I think that's paralleled in Trungpa's teaching. In *Cutting Through Spiritual Materialism*, he is teaching us how to awaken enough and how to surrender enough. I think one of his greatest teachings was at the end of that book: "…these moments of surrender where we just give up."

When Carol and I were back on leave from India in 1971, we visited Trungpa at Karme Chöling in Vermont. The three of us walked up to the great meadow together, and he was enjoying the spaciousness of it—saying what a wonderful energy it had, which we felt too. The next time we were there was in 1987 for his cremation, watching all those rainbows out of a clear sky, hearing all the lamas chanting, feeling so many thousands of people practicing together. You know, such an event is not a small thing. It leaves a mark on the culture, and it ripples out in ways we cannot understand.

WF: In your book, *Asking for the Earth*, I learned that Madame de Salzmann met Trungpa Rinpoche in India.

JG: Yes. I had two wonderful visits from Madame de Salzmann in India, but she met Trungpa in Paris. She met other lamas: Dudjom Rinpoche, Kangur Rinpoche, and I think Kalu Rinpoche and Chatral Rinpoche, while she was in India. They called her the Queen of the Dakinis, with great respect. They got on very well, and I have a picture I'll show you of Madame de Salzmann with Dudjom Rinpoche. I can't tell you much about Trungpa's meeting with Madame de Salzmann in Paris because I wasn't there at the time, but I had arranged it. Namkhai Norbu Rinpoche met her in Paris as well. [Ed. note: After the interview, Mr. George shared this excerpt from a letter he received from Mme. de Salzmann, dated 27 May 1969: "I was horrified to hear about the accident of Lama Trungpa. I like him very much—He is clean and true."]

WF: Is it possible that Madame de Salzmann wrote about her meeting with Trungpa Rinpoche in her journals?

JG: I don't think so. If she did, I don't know about it, and I think they might have told me. She was very interested in her contact with the Tibetans. She began to introduce sitting meditation practice in the late fifties and early sixties following her contacts with Zen masters. Madame de Salzmann visited Japan and met several of the leading Zen masters of the day before she met their equivalent, the Rinpoches, in the Tibetan tradition. She was very inter-ested in both streams of teachings, and I believe her interest has influenced how we, in the Gurdjieff Work, approach sittings.

When D.T. Suzuki came to our New York groups and saw our movements, our sacred dances, he said: "I wish we had this in Zen. We have a meditation walk, but it's not the same thing. It's not so demanding." He was very at-tracted to what Gurdjieff had done with the movements. I think that they are probably Gurdjieff's unique contribution: the attention created by a whole class moving as one. When the dancers can give up their own personality movements, and really listen to the music and really feel the connection with the other movers, and what animates all of them, they move together like a flock of birds turning absolutely together. You can analyze a movie of a flock of birds frame-by-frame, as they swirl in one direction or another, but you cannot find a leader. They just do it together. When one is in a state to dance together in that way, it's quite a different consciousness. Having had a taste of it while dancing, then there's the possibility that we might be able to reach that state again on a cushion, or in conversation, or whatever we're doing.

Trungpa was very interested in what Gurdjieff had tried to do because, in a way, he was trying to do the same thing. They both were confronted with the task of taking an understanding that was born out of eastern spirituality and (in Gurdjieff's case) the roots of eastern Christianity, and translating that into language that was accessible to contemporary culture.

Gurdjieff spent three-and-a-half years in Tibet. He wrote in *Meetings with Remarkable Men*, his autobiographical work, that he was taken to a central Asian monastery in Kashmir or Tibet called a monastery of the Sarmoung brotherhood. Now, Surmang, the seat of Trungpa's lineage, is just a transpos-ition of vowels, which I think, may conceal where Gurdjieff received much of his teaching. His essential teaching, his oral teaching (as distinct from what he wrote in his books) was all about what you would call Dzogchen, and I would call awareness or presence in this moment.

WF: Do you think that Gurdjieff made it all the way to Surmang?

JG: Yes, I do. I don't think he would have used that code word for his most sacred place of teaching, if he hadn't been there. I do think that's where he was. But there is no record of that, and he was very careful to cover up any traces of where he had been so that people wouldn't just go dashing off to find something that wasn't there anymore.

WF: In Trungpa Rinpoche's will, he said something to the effect that he didn't want anyone to systematize his teachings the way that Ouspensky had systematized Gurdjieff's teachings. He felt that Ouspensky had systematized Gurdjieff overzealously.

JG: Perhaps he did. We owe Ouspensky a lot for the clarity of his report, but we've been trying to get out from under that sort of systematizing ever since, and I think we are getting out of it. The fact that we can talk about Dzogchen commonalities and so on, is proof of that. Ouspensky recognized at the end of his life that he probably made a mistake in breaking with Gurdjieff over twenty years earlier. So all that time, Ouspensky was in England writing about what he called *The System*. After Ouspensky died in 1947, Madame Ouspensky called Gurdjieff back to New York to deal with all the Ouspensky people whom he had told to have nothing to do with Gurdjieff. And Gurdjieff told them, not in these words but in effect, "Start all over again. You've got it all in your heads, and you're not practicing in a right way. Don't let the spirit harden into some form; because, although it creates all forms, it is not the form. Only from the living juice of the spirit is anything alive coming through." This is just the sort of approach Trungpa might have made: shake things up. When forms become lifeless, they turn into idolatry. Idolatry is worshipping that which is less than the Unknown. To be entirely open, to surrender to the Unknowingness of the Unknown, is an extraordinary challenge, and it needs fearless warriors to respond.

WF: Do you recall if he corresponded with you at all during the years he was in North America?

JG: Really not, no. No significant letters, in any case. And yet whenever we could meet, we'd phone him, and meet him, and it was as if we'd never left each other.

WF: Well I know he always spoke so fondly of you. This has been a wonderful account. Thank you so very much for your insight and for your continued friendship and support for our community and for Trungpa Rinpoche's teachings.

CHAPTER 7

SEARCHING FOR SHAMBHALA

This was written in Tehran on January 13, 1976, A shorter version of this essay was published as a chapter in Jean Sulzberger's book, Search: Journey on the Inner Path.

Since the time of the Renaissance, Western culture has been on the way out, in the sense of being centrifugal. Its thrust has been outward in conquest, commerce, and conversion: until today its outreach has brought man to the moon. But man's awareness of the cosmos continues to expand. Ten billion light years do not bring us to the end of the universe but only to the limits of our present probes.

Curiously enough, the fantastic successes of outer space exploration seem to have unveiled more mysteries than they have solved. As we look outward today at the world of quarks and black holes and anti-matter, we are beginning to acknowledge (with more modesty than was fashionable a few generations ago) that we have barely begun to understand our cosmic surroundings and our place in the universe.

This awareness—new for modern man—of the limits of our science, of our understanding and of our consciousness, has encouraged what I consider a very healthy reawakening of interest in that other quest which so fascinated our ancestors—the exploration of man's inner space. The search for man's inner axis and for the center of his own being had its expression in many of the metaphysical myths that have come down to us from each of the major traditions in periods of man's history that were relatively more inward looking and centripetal. Now that the pendulum of attention is beginning to swing back from the outer towards the inner, from science to experience, it is time to take a fresh look at what some of these myths and traditions had to say about the idea of a center at those times in human history when it was taken for granted that everything important had to be centered and oriented—not only the temple, but the kingdom, palace, village, down to the most modest of nomadic dwellings, and including, of course, one's self. That we have lost so completely this attitude to building and to life is perhaps one of the surest indicators that our Western civilization has become quite literally "eccentric."

Wherever we look in ancient times and places, it was very different. Legends and allegories about the center of the world abound. In every culture there were cosmic mountains representing the axis of the world, capped by a sacred peak from which there were (typically) four rivers flowing off in the cardinal directions, watering four gardens and a whole mandala which was seen by that particular civilization as its ideal or archetype. There are many examples: for the Hindus, Mount Meru (Sumeru)—or Kailash; for the Zoroastrian Iranians, Hara Barzaiti, and for their Islamic descendants, Mount Qaf; Mount Zinnalo for the Laotian Buddhists; Himinbjorg for the Norsemen and for the ancient Greeks, Delphi, which they thought of as the *omphalos* or navel of the world.

In more strictly religious terms, other world "centers" have been rocks or meteorites such as the Muslim Ka'ba in Mecca. For the Jews, according to the Kabbala, the secret heart of the world was the Holy of Holies in the tabernacle of the Temple of the Most High set on Zion's Hill in the center of Jerusalem. For the Christians it was Golgotha which, as Mircea Eliade puts it, "was situated at the center of the world, since it was the summit of the cosmic mountain and at the same time the place where Adam had been created and buried. Thus the blood of the Saviour falls upon Adam's skull, buried precisely at the foot of the Cross, and redeems him."

Even Columbus believed that the world had a huge mountain at its center, binding heaven and Earth. Sailing off South America on his third voyage and noting the quantity of fresh water flowing into the ocean (from the Orinoco), he speculated that it might be from one of the rivers of Paradise pouring off the base of the world mountain.

These sacred mountains have their esoteric counterparts in another kind of tradition, often linked with the first—that of the hidden community of those who have realized man's potential for higher states of being and who have perhaps from time to time exerted an influence on the course of human history. This is the tradition of Shambhala, the sacred city in the mountains of central Asia which, according to Tibetan Bon and Buddhist, and to some Indian Hindu sources, represents the spiritual center of the world.

As with the cosmic mountain, there are many other examples which could be cited from other traditions but all point to the same hypothesis—that there is somewhere a community of men and women who have succeeded in finding and transmitting the knowledge of how to achieve the kind of psychic breakthrough to a higher consciousness that even the scientific world is beginning to acknowledge as possible for man. At this time and on this planet, has there been and is there perhaps still a brotherhood or a community or a monastery, or some kind of esoteric center, belonging to one of the great traditions of mankind—or in having surpassed the limitations of such particular labels—which has, in a concrete way, found what so many people who are not more than half asleep begin to look for today?

To say that such a center has existed does not mean that it still exists. Nor does it follow, even if it exists, that it could be located by satellite photography or tracked down by systematic ground expeditions. But so long as there is the remote possibility that such a place is real somewhere in our world, here and now, there will be those who will look for it. We can take Shambhala as the prototype of the object of this search.

Where and what is it?

I shall never forget an evening in our house in New Delhi in 1968 when we had the now well-known Tibetan teacher, Trungpa Rinpoche, staying with us. We had been asking him about the Tibetan tradition of Shambhala. To our astonishment he replied very quietly that, although he had never been there, he believed in its existence and could see it in his mirror whenever he went into deep meditation. That evening in our study he produced a small circular metal mirror of the Chinese type and after looking into it intently for some time began to describe what he saw. Within a circular range of high snow-peaked mountains there was a green valley with a beautiful city where extraordinary people lived, cut off from the outside world by their own volition. In the middle of the city there was a little palace or temple on the top of a hill composed of terraces. Around this hill there was a square walled enclosure, and around this again other enclosures where people lived and where there were temples and gardens, chortens and other sacred monuments. It sounded "out of this world." But there was Trungpa in our study describing what he saw as if he were looking out of the window.

Four years later, in 1972, when we were visiting Bhutan, we were invited to the house of one of the senior officials and nobles of Paro, Mr. Paljor Dorji, where my memory of Trungpa Rinpoche's description was refreshed by seeing a painting which Mr. Dorji told us was several centuries old, on a wood panel in his living room. It was a painting of Shambhala. A few months earlier we had been given a Tibetan map of Shambhala by Mr. Tenzing Namdak, the Tibetan Bon scholar and priest who had collaborated with D.N. Snellgrove in writing *The Nine Ways of Bon*, which enables a reader to receive an impression of what Shambhala meant to a Bon artist in Tibet five or six centuries ago and to a Bhutanese or Tibetan Buddhist about 200 years ago. Though the Bon version is much more stylized, both versions agree on essentials. It should be noted that the Bon version specifically places Shambhala on a cosmic mountain, whose nine stories represent for that tradition the nine ways of Bon. Moreover, the text which Tanzing Namdak translated for us from the Zhangzhung language (pre-Buddhist Tibetan from the vicinity of Mount Kailash) indicates by name the tribes and peoples living north, south, east and west of Shambhala. From this evidence we can infer that the artist believed Shambhala to be located somewhere northwest of Tibet, perhaps in the general area of Khotan. This is consistent with the Bon tradition that their teachings came from the west and included both Iranian and central Asian Shaman elements which have more recently been overlaid by adaptations of tantric Buddhist teachings.

Other Tibetan sources, principally Buddhist, tend to place Shambhala in the mountains of northern Tibet, though there are some sources that suggest an eastern or southern border location, but always in the mountains. The one I feel rings truest, because it accords with the Bon tradition in linking Shambhala with both the cosmic mountain and the spiritual center or community, is described by Stein as being in Yarlung, in eastern Tibet at the mountain Shampo, where the first king of Tibet, Nyathi, descended from above on a kind of mystical beanstalk or rope called a *Mu-tak*—a term which also appears in Chinese literature. *Mu*—even in Japanese today—means emptiness and is the equivalent of the Sanskrit *Shunyata*, the void. After seven generations of kings had been able to maintain contact with their spiritual sources and go up and down the *Mu-tak*, King Digum by accident (inattention) cut his

sacred connection with his sword while fighting his enemies and was prompt-
ly killed. Having no *Mu-tak*, his successors were confined to the Earth. We
already have in capsule form the story of the fall of man—because the king or
shaman lost his ability to fulfil his traditional role of being able to communicate with the heavenly powers and transmit their vision to the people at large.

As described by Stein, the descent of the first Tibetan King Nyathi from
Mount Shampo "took place on a plain called Tsenthang Goshi, or 'King's
Plain with Four Gateways,'" essentially square, therefore, like a fortified camp
or a mandala. Twelve chieftains who had come there to pay religious homage
to the mountain met this being from on high and took him as their king.
They are described as herdsmen, hunters, local inhabitants, twelve petty kings
or twelve Bonpo priests, holy men or chieftains. Their number fits in with the
square lay-out.

The earliest history we have (probably 9th century) says of this spot: "It
was the center of the sky, the middle of the Earth and the heart of the country.
An enclosure of glaciers; the head of all rivers. High mountain, pure Earth, an
excellent country. A place where wise men are, born heroes, where custom is
perfected, where horses grow swift."

This account, taken from Chinese historical sources (the documents of
Touen-houang), gives us several important clues as to how the early Tibetans
thought about Shambhala. Like any place where there was order, it was laid
out as a mandala or rather three mandalas arranged on a central axis, one
above another. Tibetan thought, like that of the Chinese, has always been
moulded by the idea that man was a kind of link or ladder joining the worlds
of heaven and Earth. Here we find Shambhala described as being the "center
of the sky, the middle of the Earth, and the heart of the country," i.e., inside
or under the Earth as the heart is in the body. As we know from other Tibetan writings and paintings, the mandalas of the world above and of the world
below man were similarly constructed as if the lower reflected or mirrored
the higher. The typical Tibetan Buddhist scheme shows the sky as an eight-
spoked wheel and the Earth as an eight-petalled lotus. It was the upper center
that was called Shambhala; the lower one hidden in the heart of the Earth was
called (at least according to Rene Guénon, quoting Saint Yves d'Alveydre)
Agarttha, which in Sanskrit means "ungraspable." As we shall see below, this

scheme of the wheel is the mandala of the *Kalachakra Tantra* which is traditionally believed to have been revealed by the Buddha in Shambhala.

The Kalachakra Tantra is one of the most esoteric Tibetan teachings, associated both with successive Dalai Lamas and with the Panchen Lamas. The version of the Tantra as we have it is usually ascribed to Lobsang Paldan Yeshé (1738–1780), who is called by Europeans the third Panchen Lama and by Tibetans the sixth. He was so fascinated by the search for Shambhala himself that he asked George Bogle, the British envoy who visited him from India on behalf of the British Governor, Warren Hastings, to find out on his return to Bengal what the pandits there think about Shambhala. However the *Kalachakra Tantra* is much older than the 18th century. That remarkable Hungarian scholar, Alexander Csoma de Kőrös, who travelled from Hungary on foot to Tibet early in the 19th century to study the origins of his people, reports that he was told the *Kalachakra Tantra* had been transmitted from Shambhala to Tibet and to India about 965 A.D.

The message of the *Kalachakra Tantra* cannot, however, be dated. It is in essence timeless and the whole teaching is about how to use knowledge of the wheel of time (*Chakra* means "wheel" and *Kala* "time") to get out of time, and thus free of decay and death, which are the inevitable lot of all creatures caught in time. The way out lies through the center, in the timeless hub which is totally empty and still, and around which everything in manifestation and time moves. It moves more and more violently as we leave the center and are thrown to the circumference of the wheel of life. Just as the wheel of the cart moves, the axle alone remaining still. All beings and all life can be placed somewhere on the wheel. All traditions are its converging spokes. At the center there are no more labels, no more words, only stillness and silence; but this is not emptiness as those on the rim imagine the void to be. At the center (and only there) is the plenitude of Being and Joy we can call Life.

Shambhala then can be seen from the *Kalachakra Tantra* teaching as the abode of those who have found their way to the center. It is quite literally a timeless place and, since space-time is a continuum, must therefore also be a placeless place. It stands above history because it stands out of time. We have already seen that it is associated with the beginnings of Tibetan history so we should not be surprised to find that it also has a role at the end of history—alpha and omega. For at the end of this cycle of time the great Tibetan warrior-hero King Gesar (Kaiser, Caesar) of Ling is due to ride forth again with all his troops from Kalápa, the capital of Shambhala, to re-establish, in all its original purity and force, the reign of *Dharma*, that is, of the Buddha's primal teaching, which through the course of history has become tarnished and distorted.

The capital city of the country called Shambhala is here given as Kalápa. This is an interesting Sanskrit term meaning "that which holds single parts together," like a "bundle or quiver of arrows," or "the bells strung around a woman's waist." Yes, indeed; that is what it means to have a center, a point of reference to which everything is related, the glue without which all the little fragments of understanding we have gathered remain fragmentary, not a whole, not holy. Therein lies the difference between information and knowledge, between a string of facts and the understanding to hold them together.

I have long thought that if we could understand the meaning of the word Shambhala it would help to clarify both the origin and the significance of the idea. Unfortunately, I have been unable to find any serious study of the etymology of the word and so, although I do not have the qualifications myself, I am forced to offer a few suggestions to those better able to evaluate and pursue them to a satisfactory conclusion. I am, however, in complete agreement with my friend Professor Elémire Zolla, the great Italian metaphysician, that "metaphysics is concealed in words like pith in stalks, marrow in bones." I am indebted to him for the derivation of the Indo-European root *bha* as meaning "vision" or "light" with the secondary meanings of "sound" or "magic utterance."

As for *sham*, it could either be connected (for reasons given below) with the Indian God Shiva, if the term is ascribed an Indian origin, or with the word *Shamash* of Sumerian origin, meaning "sun," which comes into modern Arabic as *shams*. Thus, apart from the Sumerian sun god, *Shamash*, whose temple was near Babylon, there are known to have been other famous temples dedicated to the sun called *shams* or *shambha* (a) in Balkh, the ancient capital of the Bactrian kingdom in northern Afghanistan; and (b) in Multan which according to Alberuni used to be called "*Shambha-pura* (City of the Vision of the Sun) in the pre-Islamic period." In Multan, the great annual festival of the year was celebrated in honour of the sun, and there are descriptions of the golden idol representing the sun to support this identification. Though the temple was destroyed after Alberuni saw it, the sun god Surya in Multan (as in many other Indian temples) is described as wearing "northern" (central Asian) nomadic dress, including in this case red leather boots, though leather is anathema in Hindu temples. Trade routes to Tibet ran through both Multan and Balkh, so the name *shams* or *shambha* could as easily have been carried to Tibet as the dress from north of the Himalayas to Multan.

If then we see a Middle Eastern derivation in the name Shambhala, *Sham-bha* would mean "light of the sun" or "vision of the sun." Alternatively, if we spell the word Shambala (as it was spelled in most of the early European references to it), this would mean "the sun above" (from the Persian *bala*, "above;" as in Bala Hissar, the fort above Kabul, and many other similar names). Shambala would then mean the "supernal sun," not merely the ordinary visible sun but the principle of Light itself, as coming from the transcendent Sun, the source of all Light.

In Sanskrit literature there are remarkably few references to Shambhala. The *Kalachakra Tantra* and its traditional origin in Shambhala is referred to in Indian tantric literature, where Shambhala tends to be located in the Himalayas and usually in the Swat-Kashmir region according to D.C. Sircar. As Monier-Williams' Sanskrit dictionary gives the meaning of *shamkara* as "relating to or belonging to Shiva" and as *bala* in Sanskrit means "child," Shambala would mean "child of Shiva." However, Danielou gives three attributes of Shiva as translations of the word *shambhu*; Shiva as the "changeless state," as "the giver of peace," and (with Kali) as "the abode of joy."

The only part of the word which seems to be of Tibetan origin is the suffix—*la*, which means a high mountain pass or high place among the peaks, and is used as an honourific term of respect.

When we are dealing with sacred places or sacred symbols, we are not under the obligation (as we would be in the every-day world) to choose one meaning and reject the others. In Shambhala, we are at the center of the world of creative imagination where all divergent thoughts can blend in peace, retaining elements of meaning that might have come from Sanskrit, Middle Eastern or shamanistic sources. Here nothing that speaks truly of the primordial tradition need be rejected. We can keep in our spectrum of meaning the sun, the light, the vision, transcendent amid the mountains; for the Buddhists, the epitome of voidness; for the Hindus, the mountain retreat of the supreme Shiva.

We have already written of one mountain, Shampo, in Yarlung in eastern Tibet where the first kings descended, but there are other references in Tibetan literature. For example, in the *Hundred Thousand Songs of Milarepa* (11th century A.D.), Jetsun (Milarepa) sends Rechungpa, his disciple, to the Shambo snow mountain in the southern Tibetan region beyond Doh for his meditation retreat. The passes in the vicinity of either of these (Mount Shambo or Shampo) could have been called in Tibetan *Shambo-la*. But we need not bewilder ourselves with multiple references to place names when in all probability the particular mountain, whether in the north, south, east or west of Tibet, was called after the traditional prototype mentioned as the origin of the *Kalachakra Tantra* and as the home of the sages, secure beyond place and time. For as Ch'uangtzu says: "The Principle cannot be attained by the eye nor the ear ... The Principle cannot be heard, what is heard is not It. The Principle cannot be seen; what is seen is not It. The Principle cannot be stated; what is stated is not It ... The Principle, being unimaginable, cannot be described either."

Perhaps the neatest expression of this idea comes from Persian literature, from the Sufi writings of the great Persian mystic Suhrawardi. As he puts it, the doors of heaven at the top of Mount Qaf (the cosmic mountain) open on to *Nâ-Kojâ-âbâd*, which literally means "no where place"—a place beyond all places, a place that is nowhere because it cannot be pinned down to a spatial limitation. It belongs to what the Persian Sufis would have called the *Malakut*—or their Zoroastrian forebears would have called *Hurqalya*—the world of pure angelic Intelligences. So is this the world that Trungpa Rimpoche's consciousness penetrated when he looked into his mirror in deep meditation and told us he saw Shambhala? Is this the land of which Milarepa sang, and which Tibetan artists, who are able to see in a way we do not, have painted?

Having begun with the search for Shambhala in concrete terms and having raised the possibility of there being such a place on our planet in the past, and perhaps still today, I cannot simply dispose of Shambhala by saying that it is only an idea that has haunted the imagination of central Asia and of Indian tantrics. One of the surest signs of how far we have deviated from a true understanding of the creative imagination in our own day is that we automatically suppose that if something belongs to the world of *myth* it has no *reality*—it is just (as we say) "imaginary," by which we mean fantastic. It is time we grew out of this simpleminded dualistic way of looking at everything, as either "body" or "mind" when the best doctors are convinced that such a distinction is almost impossible to sustain scientifically. So too with the distinction between myth and history. Today we should be able to see that some myths may be nothing more than folklore or distant echoes of historical events, but others are an expression of metaphysical truths in popular concrete form. Only today's myths are totally false because they contain neither literal nor symbolic truth.

So if we are serious, let us search for Shambhala, not only "from the top," so to speak, but also more modestly and practically from where we are in our mundane three-dimensional world. Maybe it will not be given to us to find Shambhala but if we feel drawn by the idea of it there is nothing to stop us from looking for people or places that might have a connection. So many today are looking for teachers and teachings which have an Eastern or traditional origin. From the point of view which I am exploring, I would say that any authentic teacher or teaching must have, directly or indirectly, a "Shambhala connection." Whether this is admitted or kept secret, it is a remarkable fact that many of the teachings that can be considered esoteric seem to have come from the East and often to have been connected with the high places of the Himalayas or of the central Asian mountains beyond. This area has been so remote and inaccessible for so many centuries that it has served as a kind of deep-freeze in which beliefs and practices have been preserved intact over long periods of time. Since Chairman Mao made China's claim to sovereignty over Tibet effective, from about 1959, Tibetan lamas have as refugees suddenly become more accessible to the rest of the world and interest in their teachings has spread. Their loss has been the world's gain, for it has brought Shambhala closer to us.

Long before the last twenty years, however, there were those in the West who had been touched by the Shambhala idea. So far as I know, Swedenborg in the 18th century was the first specifically to refer to Shambhala in European literature, if earlier references to Prester John's Kingdom are disregarded as being too vague to be linked to Shambhala. In the next century Madame Helena Blavatsky wrote of her Masters from Shambhala, and then the Theosophists took it up. In the early years of this century Roerich's translation into German of the third Panchen Lama's book was published under the title of *The Way to Shambala*. This was followed by what I can only call the Western escapist literature in which people like James Hilton and Lowell Thomas popularized the Shambhala idea as "Shangri-la," the happy kingdom hidden somewhere in the most remote Himalayas where people remain eternally young.

Meanwhile, around the turn of the century more serious and more practical research was going on in central Asia, including Afghanistan and Tibet, by a group of Europeans who called themselves "the seekers of truth." Their quest has been most interestingly described in the writings of G.I. Gurdjieff, especially in his more or less autobiographical book, *Meetings with Remarkable Men*. Now that his work, twenty-seven years after his death, is becoming well known in the West (at least among those interested in seeking for ways other than drugs to expand and transform consciousness), there is inevitably a lively interest in his presumed sources in the East. No doubt anticipating the fruitlessness of trying to retrace his steps through central Asia seventy or eighty years too late, Gurdjieff had been careful to throw dust in the eyes of anybody tempted to engage in this kind of exercise, but the few hints he has given suggest that the brotherhoods, communities, monasteries and great teachers whom he describes may have been located in this part of the world. He mentions specifically the Pamirs, Kafiristan, the Afridis and the Hindu Kush, as well as Tibet and the Gobi Desert. He never mentions the word "Shambhala" but some of his pointers indicate contacts with Tibetan and Sufi masters and with monasteries or brotherhoods in Central Asia combining people chosen from all traditions. Wherever they may have been, the places he describes were exceedingly remote and difficult of access, cut off from the world in high mountain valleys which (from the few clues he has scattered in his writings) could well have been those of this part of the world, stretching through the mountain ranges of Afghanistan, Pakistan, India, Nepal, Bhutan and Tibet. It is suggestive, moreover, that he comes back time and again in the first series of his writings, *All and Everything*, to the solar language of Shambhala in referring to the Supreme as residing on "the Most Holy Sun Absolute."

Carol and I reached this part of the world in 1960, just too late to have attempted to penetrate Tibet itself, but our postings in Sri Lanka (1960–64), India (1967–72), and since then in Iran, have given us many opportunities to spend our holidays driving our Land Rover, or simply trekking on foot, through many of the mountain regions south of Tibet and the U.S.S.R. from Afghanistan to Assam, including specifically Balkh, Bamiyan, Nuristan (Kafiristan), Chitral, Swat, Kashmir, Ladakh, Kulu, the Kali-Gandaki Valley (as far as the District of Mustang) in Nepal, the Solo-Kumbu region near Mount Everest, Sikkim, Bhutan and Assam. Our travels took us to many valleys and high places in the mountains, places of exceptional beauty and power, where there are still today individual teachers and even a few communities—Hindu, Buddhist and Muslim—but there is nothing which I have seen or heard about that would suggest a real Shambhala existing in any of these areas, based on our very incomplete survey. We had of course no illusions that we were in any of these travels "on the way to Shambhala." We were just exploring some of the most beautiful areas of our planet which have always been regarded as a source of inspiration and refreshment by those who have lived in this part of the world. But being especially interested in the traditions which have made these mountains holy, and also in retracing if possible some of the steps of G.I. Gurdjieff, we kept our eyes and ears open for any traces of teachings or teachers that might still be found. Teachers we were lucky enough to find over the years we have lived in the East, but I cannot say that we discovered any trace of existing monasteries or communities that could be considered modelled on Shambhala, or that made any claim to be connected with it.

At the same time, the fact remains that according to every metaphysical tradition, whether Chinese or Tibetan, Buddhist, Christian or Hindu, or Islamic Sufi, something exists in the innermost recesses of our being that is free of the limitations of time and place because it is "here and now." On that central axis the world turns, microcosmically in man and macrocosmically too. In this sense the axis of Shambhala runs through every heart.

Which is not to deny that there may be a Shambhala "out there," too. The absence of specific "proof" proves nothing but that those who might have found such a center would not speak or write about it. Sacred is secret. But if a Mafia of crime can hide itself underground in our big cities, it would be surprising if a spiritually liberated few could not hide themselves even today somewhere in those same cities or in the mountains of Central Asia. "Schools" on various levels have always existed, and we can think of Shambhala as the "School of Schools." We may not have been looking for it in Chitral and the Himalayas in the proper way, but the fact we did not find it does not mean we were wasting our time. The search goes on. Already it has brought us some of our most beautiful and alive moments, especially when we had no prefabricated ideas about what we *might* find standing between us and our direct impressions. The ultimate goal of man's existence here (in the sense in which we have been describing the search for Truth) is perhaps never attained; but something does sometimes happen to pilgrims on the way. They may change. They may become more centerd.

If Shambhala exists on our planet, I am convinced we cannot simply go and find it—it will have to find us. Only by that act of grace, capping our own wish and our own efforts, can we be brought to such a Center.

In the climax of Attar's *Conference of the Birds*, when the last weary and tattered thirty birds (all that are left of the hundreds who started on the great search) finally arrive and find themselves in the divine presence of the Simourg (which means 'Thirty Birds' in Farsi), there is a moment almost of anti-climax. The birds had expected to see God: they find themselves in front of a mirror—they see ... themselves. The shock throws them to the center. They understand at last. But without the whole pilgrimage they would only have seen thirty birds in a mirror.

On the day on which I finished writing this article, a friend in the Iranian Ministry of Foreign Affairs told me the following story of the famous Mullah Nasser Eddin. Once the Mullah was visiting a village in Anatolia where there lived a rival teacher who wanted to show up the Mullah by asking him a question that could not be answered. Accordingly he approached the Mullah when there were many people around him and suddenly asked him, "Tell me, learned Master, where is the center of the world?" To which the

Mullah replied without a moment's hesitation, pointing at the spot on which he stood, "The center of the world is exactly here where I now am." The rival protested that there was no proof and the Mullah answered, "If you think you know better, go and measure the world yourself and find the center."

Tehran
January 13, 1976.

CHAPTER 8

CHRISTMAS IN BHUTAN, 1963

This was written in January of 1964 after a visit to Bhutan while I was High Commmissioner to Ceylon (now Sri Lanka). This "Secret" report has been declassified and was published in "Bout de Papier" in 2004.

So far as I know, I was the first non-Indian diplomat to enter Bhutan. What is more important, however, is not mentioned in this report. My hostess and Colombo Plan colleague, Tashi Dorji, was also Minister of Education in 1963, and she confided during our visit that she was hoping to modernize higher education in Bhutan but needed help from outside to get such a radical departure from their traditions established. I asked her if she was afraid of Jesuits and she replied that the Jesuits had come to Bhutan two centuries earlier and soon given up; Bhutan was firm in its Tibetan Buddhism and not afraid of Jesuits. So I then suggested a Canadian Jesuit, Father Mackay, who I had come to respect as head of Northpoint School in Darjeeling. He was duly invited and spent the rest of his life setting up a complete transformation of Bhutan's education system, becoming in the process a heroic figure still revered in Bhutan.

Office of the High Commissioner for Canada, Colombo, Ceylon, to Under Secretary of State for External Affairs, Ottawa, Canada, No. 42, Secret, January 29, 1964.

Reference: Our letter No. 19 of January 16, 1964.

Subject: Bhutan—A Tourist's Report on the Survival and Development of Shangri-La.

1. In my letter under reference I explained how we came to spend Christmas in Bhutan as guests of the Government of Bhutan. Although I must disclaim in advance any authority or competence for reporting on this remote corner of the Indian sub-continent, I am doing so because my

hosts were remarkably frank with me, and also because (so far as I know) I was the first Canadian official to visit this country. I am, however, taking the precaution of sending my report through our High Commissioner in Delhi [Chester A. Ronning], who will, I am sure, correct my mistakes or add his own comments.

2. Bhutan's policy and Bhutan's problems can be put in two words: survival and development. Since survival must obviously have priority for any Country, I am going to discuss this question first. For many centuries survival for Bhutan has meant survival from India or the British, or whoever were to the south of them. Today of course it means survival from China. But I think we have to bear in mind, as the Bhutanese certainly do, that for most of their history they have looked north, not south. In the 7th Century, Guru Padma Sambhava brought them Tibetan Buddhism, and their life is still moulded in the Mahayana tradition.

3. It was the Chinese takeover of Tibet [political takeover in 1951; invasion in 1959] that not only shocked Bhutan to the core but posed, for the first time in an acute form, the question of national survival. Until then it had been enough for the country to isolate itself, refusing to build roads and closing its frontiers to outsiders even more strictly than Tibet itself. To get into the country at all, the very few permitted visitors, mostly Indians, had to travel for a week to ten days by mule, either from Assam in the south or from Sikkim in the west. The shortest route was from Sikkim through a corner of Tibet to Paro, but this mule route was of course denied to Bhutan as soon as the Chinese occupied Tibet. Therefore, even before Mr [Jawaharial] Nehru [Prime Minister of India] rode into Paro on mule in 1959, it had become pretty obvious to the leaders of Bhutan that their inclination would have to be sacrificed in the interests of survival. They therefore agreed with Mr. Nehru that roads linking at least the main centers of Bhutan with India would have to be constructed as a matter of national urgency. In Lhassa the Chinese had for several years been talking ominously about "Tibet's five fingers"—Ladakh, Bhutan, Nepal, Sikkim and the N[orth]E[ast]F[rontier]A[gency]. Already, about

1955, the Chinese had occupied the former Bhutanese enclave of Kailash after a combination of Chinese threats and intimidation so terrified the Tibetan wife of the Bhutanese representative in Kailash that they had both fled. A few months later the father of the Bhutanese representative in Kailash, who was the Bhutanese representative in Lhassa, was recalled, largely because the Indians were rather afraid that he might be the channel for a deal between the Chinese and the Bhutanese. Since that time, about 1956, there have been no direct talks between Bhutan and China, though unproductive negotiations have been carried on from time to time through the Indians. Not unnaturally the Chinese intimated to the Bhutanese that if they wished to discuss the Kailash enclave or any other question it would be more profitable to do so directly, rather than through Indian intermediaries, but because of Indian pressure based on mistrust, there have been no further official contacts between the government of Bhutan and the Chinese.

Strategic Roads

4. Since India was worried about a power vacuum in this area, it did not take Delhi long to agree in 1960 to construct three strategic roads from India to the central valleys of Bhutan in the west, middle and east of the country. The understanding was, of course, that no corresponding roads would be constructed from the north, as has been done by the Chinese in Nepal. A fifty or sixty mile strip south of the Bhutan—Tibetan border has therefore been left without any kind of road—only mule tracks.

5. Today the road to Paro from Phuntsholing in Assam—that is, the western of the three roads—has been completed so that it is jeepable and can be used in comparative safety by one-ton trucks. In Eastern Bhutan the road to Tashigang has not got quite as far as the road to Paro, but is substantially complete, while the road into the center of the country is about a year behind the other two. Twelve mobile wireless stations already link the northern and central valleys of Bhutan with India and a telephone line to Paro and Thimphu has been three-quarters completed.

Arms and the Men

6. However, on Bhutan's border with Tibet there is still very little besides the difficult Himalayan country—the natural barrier to geography—to stop the Chinese. Bhutan's militia has been expanded from about 3,500 in 1959 to nearly 10,000 today, and about 15 Indian military advisers are training the militia at Wangdi Phodrang in the Sankosh also known as Puna Tsang Chhul Valley. Altogether, more than one half of the annual budget of Bhutan is now spent on defence and there is conscription for military service. But until India can supply arms for the new militia, their training and preparation will not mean very much. Since the Chinese attack in October 1962, Bhutan has naturally been trying desperately to get arms from India (or from anyone else, but the Americans have taken the line that this is India's problem and India has simply not had enough to go around, so that Bhutan has actually received during the past eighteen months only 5,000 rifles from India, each with the princely allotment of five rounds of ammunition per rifle. So, although the tough Bhutanese soldiery are very skilful as archers and would no doubt be quite a problem for the Chinese in the Himalayan valleys as guerrilla fighters, the position today is that the Bhutanese militia could very soon be bypassed or overrun, and it would be up to the Indian Army to rush in troops in the event of any further attack along Bhutan's border.

Chinese Attack Expected Further West

7. Here it must be said that the Bhutanese do not expect that there will be a direct Chinese attack on them. They think it will come, but further to the west, either through eastern Nepal or through the main road south from Lhassa through Sikkim, that is, the road conning out at Gangtok [Sikkim] and Kalimpong [West Bengal]. Once the Chinese had managed to get through these fairly low passes, there would be no natural barriers to slow their descent onto the plains of West Bengal, going straight down to Calcutta. Indeed such a movement would rapidly cut off the great concentration of Indian forces in NEFA, Assam, and North Bengal. We travelled by jeep through the Inner Line (that is, the security zone along

the corridor of north Assam between Bhutan and East Pakistan [now Bangladesh]), and we saw for ourselves the enormous camps and great concentrations of motor transport which make both sides of that road look like one continuous camp for about 40 or 50 miles between Phuntsholing and Siliguri. I don't know what the Bhutanese have said directly to the Indians, but they told me that they were very worried that the Indian Army might be preparing for an attack in the wrong place; that the defeat they had suffered last year in NEFA might cause them to concentrate too much of their strength in that area, whereas in the opinion of the Bhutanese the real threat was the direct route through Sikkim (the Tista Valley) or eastern Nepal (the Kosi Valley).

Chinese Invasion Plans?

8. The Bhutanese seem to think that the attack of October 1962 was mounted by the Chinese initially to correct several deep penetrations which had been made in previous years by the Indian Army north of the McMahon Line [the boundary between Tibet and Assam in British India after the Simla Conference of 1913–14, named for Sir Henry McMahon, Britain's principal negotiator] in the NEFA (as I shall be explaining presently), and was continued as a means of throwing Indian economic development off balance and making India lose face—all the explanations that others have given too—but that it could never have been contemplated as a serious military invasion of India itself. Any further Chinese advance in November 1962 would have had to cope with several crossings of the Brahmaputra River in going further into Assam. The Bhutanese point out that there is no such natural obstacle facing the Chinese once they have come out on the West Bengal plain, where they would only have to advance about 20 miles in order to cut India's supply corridor to NEFA. Therefore the Bhutanese have the rather strong suspicion that the Chinese made their initial attack on NEFA last year knowing, or planning, that this would lead the Indian Army to an injudicious concentration of their forces in NEFA and Assam, which would make it all the easier for the Chinese to cut them off without much of a fight by simply coming

through the Sikkim passes and going down as far as the border of East Pakistan. We ourselves observed how vulnerable that narrow corridor through north Assam is, with only one rail line, one highway and many river crossings (with bridges that could be put out of action); and once the road and the railway had been cut, it would be almost impossible to supply an Army in Assam or NEFA. In that situation the Indian forces would perhaps have to fight their way back across the spur of East Pakistan in order to rejoin the main body of Indian forces in North Bengal. However, these are speculations. The main point to be made in this report is that the Bhutanese I spoke to do expect a further attack by China, though they do not expect it to be directed against NEFA, Assam, or Bhutan, but to come, as I have said, through East Nepal or Sikkim and to be aimed at the lower Ganges Valley. They think such an attack might come fairly soon, perhaps this spring, especially if Mr. Nehru is unable to carry on, and there is confusion in India over the succession.

9. Relations between Bhutan and both India and the United States are not as good as one would expect in this political perspective, nor are Bhutan's relations with China quite as bad as I had supposed they would be. I was given some interesting explanations for this state of affairs.

Relations with India

10. Relations with India are difficult for a variety of reasons, but I think mainly because the Indians are already in Bhutan, and therefore there are opportunities for daily friction that do not occur with the Chinese, who have kept their distance in spite of earlier threats about the "five fingers of Tibet" that I have mentioned, and have not in fact disturbed Bhutanese territorial integrity at any time. The stories given out in Delhi about the Chinese armies having cut through Northern Bhutan on their way into NEFA are flatly denied by the Bhutanese, who regard them as fabrications of the Indians probably intended to cover up part of the ignominy of their defeat.

11. The Bhutanese know of course that they depend on India's help and protection. They know very well that not only their military but their development plans would come to a halt the day that India stopped paying for them; and yet it is perhaps partly this dependence that produces some of the sense of irritation that I encountered in Bhutan with India.

12. The focal point of a good deal of this irritation was the senior Indian adviser, Mr. N[ari]. K. Rustomji [later author of *Enchanted Frontiers: Sikkim. Bhutan and India's North Eastern Borderland* (1971) and *Bhutan: The Dragon Kingdom in Crisis* (1978)]. Mr. Rustomji enjoys the Prime Ministers confidence, but perhaps for this very reason a good many leading Bhutanese, including members of the Prime Ministers family, regard him with suspicion. Although he is serving at the request of the government of Bhutan, and although his role is supposed to be entirely advisory and not executive, he operates as if he was the Chief Minister and not the government's adviser. That is to say, in his planning commission functions he is placing orders and writing plans and specifications, and so on, without always getting the authority of the government. When this leads to difficulties, the Prime Minister has, so far, backed him up and told him to go ahead. But this again makes others feel upset. Miss Tashi [Ashi Kesang?] Dorji, the Prime Minister's sister, for example, told me that she and her younger brother, Mr. Lhandup Dorji, who is Secretary-General of the Planning Commission, although they admire Mr. Rustomji's energy and devotion, feel that he has been behaving in Bhutan as if he were the Dawan or Chief Minister, of the country. In fact, this is a not unnatural attitude for Mr. Rustomji to take, since only a few years ago he was the Indian Dawan for Sikkim. More recently he was the India agent in NEFA responsible for the Indian Army's adventures north of the McMahon Line that I shall describe now, since they are very much a part of the Government of Bhutan's attitude towards India at present.

Indian Incursions North of the McMahon Line

13. I was told in confidence that the Bhutanese government has absolutely reliable information from their own scouts who accompanied the Indian Army, and helped to guide them into the Tibetan regions (which the Bhutanese know so much better than the Indians), that in 1958–59–60 the Indian Army made many penetrations into Tibet, into areas that had always been rather loosely administered from Lhassa, but which were definitely north of the McMahon Line. I was told, for example, of one particular operation (under the direction of Mr. Rustomji, as far as the civil authority was concerned) in which the Indian Army went a distance which was described as "ten days' trek by mule"—in other words, perhaps a zig-zag hundred miles—north of the McMahon Line in the NEFA region, and conducted operations against tribals who have been harassing Indian pilgrims in that area for many years. The object of the operation was apparently to capture or destroy Chinese agents and administrators who the Indians thought, from intelligence sources, were in control of the area. They therefore came in with several hundred men of the Indian army, and when the tribals hid in the hills the Indians cut off all their food supplies for a couple of weeks. They then dropped salt and rations by parachute into the area, and when the tribals came out to get the food they were indiscriminately machine-gunned by the Indian Army, with the result that about four hundred of the tribals perished. Their leader, however, escaped to Lhassa and he was not surprisingly among the scouts who guided the Chinese forces into the NEFA in October 1962.

14. These stories of Indian Army atrocities against the Tibetans carry a lot of weight in Bhutan because the people are cousins of the Tibetans, they write Tibetan, and they speak a dialect of Tibetan. So they really share the sense of outrage that the Tibetans themselves feel when they hear stories such as I have just recounted. Of course there are much worse atrocity stories of what the Chinese have perpetrated against the Tibetans, especially amongst the monasteries, and this is all the more shocking because the Bhutanese are a deeply religious people. But they expect more of the

Indians than they do of the Chinese, and therefore the effect of these stories contributes to the surprisingly widespread feeling which I encountered that the Indians are necessary for them but are not all that welcome.

Indian Aid on Paper

15. No doubt there are economic reasons for this feeling also. The Indian merchants have begun to send in cheap cloth in competition with Bhutanese handlooms. The shops that are beginning to come up (in a country that had no shops until the roads went through) are mostly run by Indians and Nepalese. Then at the government level, as I shall explain in greater detail when discussing their economic development problems, there is a certain feeling that, although the Indians have promised a great deal of aid for economic development, all they have really done so far is to build the roads and write a lot of economic development plans which require a hundred or so Indian experts in the country. And that, too, is a sort of minor irritant in their relations. Expectations have been raised that are not being fulfilled as quickly as the Bhutanese had hoped, and these hopes are therefore turning a little sour.

Relations with the United States

16. Nor can I report that relations between Bhutan and the United States are really much better. This seems to be mainly because the Americans, in their official dealings with Bhutan through the Embassy in New Delhi, have been almost too careful to avoid anything that the Indian government might not favour. This was understandable enough at the time the Bhutanese Prime Minister, Mr. Jigme [Palden] Dorji, was trying to get arms from the Americans in New Delhi when India was being attacked by China, but it is less understandable and excusable to the Bhutanese today. When Mr. Dorji called on Mr. [John Kenneth] Galbraith [Ambassador of the United States to India, March 1961 to July 1963] in New Delhi in October 1962, he explained the defence requirements of Bhutan: how they wanted arms desperately to give them a chance to give a good account of themselves if they were attacked; and how they had even

spontaneously offered India free access to their country with whatever forces the Indian Army wished to send in, in spite of the risks involved in the circumstances to the territorial integrity of Bhutan. All that Mr. Galbraith was able to tell Mr. Dorji at that time was that he thought it was better for India to continue to supply Bhutan with whatever arms could be spared; Bhutan should retain a neutral posture as far as possible, and if the Chinese did come in, Mr. Galbraith concluded, "The Bhutanese would have the sympathy of the whole world." Mr. Dorji was furious—furious because he wanted a chance to fight the Chinese on at least possible terms if they did come, and he was being told to be neutral and expect the sympathy of the world for their corpse. This line was all the more galling to the Prime Minister because of the background, which perhaps Mr. Galbraith himself did not know. [There is an account of this and a later encounter with Dorji in Galbraith's *Ambassador's Journal: A Personal Account of the Kennedy Years* (1969)].

CIA Deal Falls Through

17. While the American Embassy in Delhi was discreetly fending off contacts with the Bhutanese, for the sake of their more important relations with India, the CIA in Calcutta had, in the years 1959–1962, been in secret contact with the trade representatives of Bhutan in Calcutta, with Miss Tashi Dorji and with the Prime Minister himself. Through these channels the CIA said to Bhutan, in effect, that they wanted (without upsetting the Indians) to have closer relations with Bhutan. They hoped Bhutan would maintain its anti-Communist stand and would have nothing to do with the Chinese, and if they fulfilled these expectations of the Americans they could expect from the CIA secret funds for the furtherance of their economic development plans. It was even suggested to Mr. Dorji that he should make arrangements for an economic survey through a Swedish firm that was indicated, and that the CIA would pick up the bill.

18. Mr. Dorji in fact went to Sweden and hired these expensive economic consultants, who came and made a survey, recommending that Bhutan

should develop its potential pulp and paper industry. Then the Swedish firm submitted their bill for the equivalent of Rs.[Rupees] 200,000. Instead of settling the account, as they had undertaken to do, the new head of CIA in Calcutta told the Prime Minister that, unless he could undertake that his government would be more obviously anti-Communist than it had been in the recent past, the CIA saw no reason to subsidise them in the way which had been discussed. Mr. Dorji, in reply, said that he thought it would be an unwise policy for Bhutan to be more openly and even provocatively anti-Communist than they already were, and that if Bhutan's present policy was not good enough for the CIA, they could lump it. The Swedish bill has still not been paid, although Miss Dorji told me that the government have undertaken to pay it off in instalments in rupees, which is of course unsatisfactory to the Swedish consultants.

19. I suppose there is, in addition, a great deal in the American way of life which quite unconsciously offends the traditional attitudes and susceptibilities of a people who have been sheltered for so many centuries as the Bhutanese; and this, together with the background I have given, may account for the otherwise remarkable statement made to me by the Quartermaster—General of Paro, who had been the Bhutanese representative in Lhassa. He said to me that if Bhutan was slated to be run by outsiders in the future, it would be "better to have the Chinese than the Americans." I suppose his attitude was that at least the Chinese were Asians and might not disrupt the Bhutanese way of life as violently as the Americans could. Of course this is an illusion, yet I report it as a pointer to the way these border people feel about their neighbours to the north, and their friends to the south, as well as the friends of their friends—the Americans.

Bhutan's Degree of Independence

20. In discussing Bhutan's survival and its relations with the Chinese, Indians and Americans have clearly been making the assumption that Bhutan is an independent state. This is, as the Indians would be quick to point out,

overstating the present facts. Bhutan is really in a "grey zone" between full independence and the dependence of an Indian state. As reported in my letter under reference, the Indian High Commissioner here, Mr. Kapur, who ten years ago was the Indian political officer in Sikkim and Bhutan, was of the opinion personally that it would be a mistake for Bhutan to have any official relations with outside countries, except India. He conceded that India itself has sponsored Bhutan's application for membership in the Colombo Plan in 1962, but he clearly did not think that this should lead to Bhutan receiving aid directly from other countries. His conception was that any aid given to Bhutan should go through the Indian government. Although his attitude may be out of date, and he told me that he was speaking quite personally, I expect that this is at the back of the minds of most Indians who are dealing with Bhutanese affairs, and helps to account for the reaction they get in Bhutan.

21. The Treaty of [Friendship of]1949, signed in Darjeeling between India and Bhutan, clearly states—"The government of India, undertake to exercise no interference in the internal administration of Bhutan; on its part the government of Bhutan agrees to be guided by the advice of the government of India in regard to its external relations." Then follow clauses providing for an annual subsidy for Bhutan of half a million rupees; and statements that there shall be perpetual peace and friendship between the two governments, and free trade and commerce between the two territories, except that India will be the sole supplier of arms, ammunition, machinery, warlike material or stores for the strength and welfare of Bhutan; and this whole Treaty, it is said, shall last indefinitely and be terminated or modified only by mutual consent. The terms of the Treaty are based on the earlier Treaty of [Punakha of] 1910 between the United Kingdom and Bhutan.

22. Although the terms of the Treaty state that Bhutan agrees to be guided by the advice of India on foreign affairs, in fact this is now disputed in Bhutan. They concede only that India has the right to advise them, in spite of the much more specific language of the Treaty I have just quoted.

But whatever they may think about the legalities of the situation, the Indians have the good sense not to press Bhutan too hard on the strict interpretation of the Treaty, and to give them a good deal of rope in foreign affairs. The prime example is India's support for Bhutan as a member of the Colombo Plan. The contacts that have followed, including the visits to Bhutan of Colombo Plan officials and of the Australian High Commissioner and the Japanese Ambassador in New Delhi, have for the most part been arranged through Miss Tashi Dorji, but I think I am the first member of the Colombo Plan Council whom she has invited to Bhutan.

23. Her understanding of the real meaning of Bhutan's independence is of course much broader than the interpretation that would be accepted in Delhi. She tells me that the Prime Minister and the government have no doubt at all that they have every right to talk to representatives of other countries without giving an account of themselves to India, either before or afterwards. As a matter of courtesy they tell India what they are doing in general terms, but not necessarily in detail, and they hope for economic aid directly from other countries who are members of the Colombo Plan.

24. In fact, Miss Dorji told me that her government are seriously thinking of making some approach to the Commonwealth countries with a view to seeking membership in the Commonwealth. She admitted that this is partly because they could not, in any case, cope with the expenses and complications of membership in the United Nations [Bhutan became a member of the United Nations in 1971, after 3 years as an observer], yet they feel that they would like to have more direct contacts with other countries than are at present feasible. Therefore they would like to start these broadening contacts with the limited circle of friends in the Commonwealth. One of their people had been in touch with the Secretariat, I believe, at the last Commonwealth Prime Ministers' Conference, and they would like to develop this possible expansion of their contacts with other countries during the coming year. She even asked me how to go about such an objective, and I told her, of course quite personally, that

I thought there should perhaps be contacts first with the Indian government about the general proposition, and subsequently a letter should be sent by her government to all governments of the Commonwealth advising them of Bhutan's intention to seek membership.

25. When I asked her what the Indians would think of such a move, she conceded that they might not like it very much, but she thought they were now broad-minded enough not to object. At one time, before the 1949 Treaty had been signed, she told me that there was a strong body of opinion in Delhi that thought Bhutan should accede to the Indian Union, and they wanted to get the Maharajah (now called the King) of Bhutan to accede to India. When this proved out of the question, India had sensibly recognized the situation and even permitted Bhutan to proceed with such acts of national sovereignty as the creation of their own passports (which India has tacitly accepted by putting Visas on them) and with a partial system of coinage (although Indian rupees are still the main notes in circulation with small change in Bhutanese coins), and with new Bhutanese postage stamps, which have just been issued (an application for their acceptance has been made to the International Postal Union).

26. All these attributes of sovereignty distinguish Bhutan from Sikkim, which does not possess any of them. The Treaty governing relations between India and Sikkim is quite specific in reserving not only external affairs but also defence for India, and in practice the Chief Minister of Sikkim is the Indian Dawan. Nothing of the sort would be tolerated in Bhutan. Although at present they may accept even quite large numbers of Indian advisers (for the roads and economic planning), the Bhutanese certainly run their own administration internally.

27. As far as their external status is concerned, while the Bhutanese have in practice been guided by Indian advice in such matters as not having further contacts with China in recent years, and not opening diplomatic relations with (I believe) two Western countries who had been approached by the Bhutanese, still the King of Bhutan was quite specific

on his visit to Delhi about two years ago, saying emphatically that "Bhutan is a sovereign, independent state." In line with this thinking, which is certainly supported by public opinion in Bhutan, as expressed in the National Assembly, or Tshogdu, the Prime Minister, Mr. Jigme Dorji, had also a few years ago wished to be associated with Mr. Nehru when he was negotiating on the Himalayan border with Mr. Chou En-Lai [Prime Minister and Minister of Foreign Affairs of the People's Republic of China]. However, Mr. Nehru turned down the Bhutanese request and has subsequently managed to keep the Bhutanese from having any official talks with the Chinese on their own.

28. Here again the guiding thread of Bhutan's policy is survival. If they need India's friendship and help, as they obviously do in order to have a fair chance of surviving, then they must as a practical matter accept India's advice and hope that over the years the Indians will allow them gradually more and more rope, as in fact seems to be the case. Although the Treaty with India of 1949 does not specifically pledge India to defend Bhutan if attacked, Mr. Nehru has done so in no uncertain terms in 1959 and 1960, and that pledge is regarded by the government of Bhutan as sufficient for their present purposes.

29. Apart from the question of survival and the relations of Bhutan with its neighbours and with other countries, the great question for the government of Bhutan is of course economic development. However, as the defence and political sections of this report have already made it longer than I had intended, I shall send you a separate letter on Bhutan's economic development.

FIGURE 2: *Monastery of Grand Lazva, Mount Athos*

CHAPTER 9

MOUNT ATHOS—
THE HOLY MOUNTAIN

While serving at our new Canadian Embassy in Athens for three years, 1945–48, I tried to visit Mount Athos but because of the civil war no visits were allowed. By 1958, I was in Paris as Deputy Representative on the NATO Council and by then Yugoslavia's Marshal Tito had given up on his attempt at promoting regime change in Greece, the civil war had ended, and visits to Mount Athos were again possible. Mine took place during my summer holidays in that year.

Man's first soundings into space have confirmed the theory that around our planet there exists a field of force similar in form and characteristics to that surrounding a bar magnet. Its lines of force not only extend into space but pass through the Earth itself; presumably, like the iron filings around a magnet, they converge at certain points, Even over the surface of our own bodies it is possible to measure electrically the energies of some of the main centers of activity of our nerve systems. That energy is not equally distributed—there are focal points.

In my own wanderings over the Earth's surface, taking my own crude and highly subjective "readings," I have occasionally come to places I can only describe as alive. Mostly they have been Holy Places, often long before our own era. I cannot, of course, explain why this is so, nor why some ancient places of pilgrimage seem to have dried up and died. But after discounting elements of romanticism, sentiment, and imagination, it is a remarkable fact that certain places have, over many centuries, awakened a vital response in a great many of the Earth's human passengers.

One of these special places is unquestionably Mount Athos. Forget its history, forget the teaching there kept alive in a continuous tradition from the first centuries of our era, forget the witness of dozens of large and small monasteries erected against nature on its rocky ledges over the sea, forget the thousands of monks and their enduring labours to sustain one life and create another. Only look, and open your senses to this lonely spike of rock jutting 35 km into the sea from which we must make our approach. Joined to the rest of the world by an insignificant little isthmus, the whole peninsula looks the other way, outwards, upwards, rising from ridge to ridge until that sudden magnificent cone of rock holds its affirmation against the clouds, the seas and the winds. Austere, barely tolerating the few hard-won olive groves which soften its base, it justifies the Greek legend of its origin, of struggle on a heroic scale. Here Prometheus (he who gave fire to man) struggled with Poseidon, ruler of the sea; and in one mighty effort—no less splendid for its failure—hurled this huge mountain of rock at the sea god. And there it is today—a great pyramid of temple building marble, almost as high as Mount Olympus.

Today the struggle continues, though the scale is now human. There, almost invisible at the summit, an insignificant white outline evoking man's impossibly audacious aspiration towards transformation. It is a little chapel called in Greek "The Chapel of Metamorphosis." "Metemorphosis" is the same word used to describe the change from cocoon to butterfly, a change of being to something with a quite different range of possibilities.

But remember to look down, as well as up. Remember the double-headed Byzantine eagle, looking both ways at once, below the Chapel of Metamorphosis, below the monasteries, below the cliffs, is the sea. Do not suppose that the golden sunset scene is always so peaceful. He who has not felt Athos' storms on his skin has not known the Holy Mountain. Poseidon still lashes back at the challenge to his authority, and below these cliffs lie the ribs of many ships and men. Remember Xerxes and his proud flotilla, the mightiest ever assembled on the sea, all wrecked and drowned at this stormy passage. You cannot see this wreckage from here. But from that difficult path up the rocks, used almost exclusively by the hermits, you can look down in good weather and see with unusual clarity what lies below you. If there is a *memento vivere* at the pinnacle of the Holy Mountain, there is a *memento mori* at the base on every side.

My own first contact with the men of Athos, the monks, was in the bus bringing over thirty passengers rather laboriously over the hills and the bumps from Salonika to Ierrosos, at the neck of land where the domain of the monks begins. At one of our first village stops along the way, two monks got on. One was old and one young. They found places near me. Later there was a stop for coffee and everyone got out. When the bus filled up again, two people who had just got aboard unwittingly took the places the monks had had, and they were left standing in a painful crouched position under the low roof. Several of us tried to get at least the old monk to take our place. He refused and accepted the situation with such genuine good humour and simplicity that I could not but be struck by the comparison with some priests I had seen elsewhere, who would have been very offended if they had not immediately been given their due place. But the equilibrium of these Athos monks was undisturbed by these "little bumps" of a journey in the world.

These first impressions were strongly confirmed in the course of my visit to the Holy Mountain. Among the monks of all degrees, I rarely observed that special form of artificiality which so often afflicts those who minister to the spiritual needs of others in the world, with a "holier-than-thou" attitude. In Athos, one feels that such pretences are recognized as inapplicable. After all, they are all monks. There are no "others," apart from visitors and pilgrims who come mostly during the summer. Some monks may be further on the road to liberation; but rank and status have not the same outer importance they have in the world, either for those below or for those above.

The monks I met on the bus were my first guides, telling me where to go and whom to see, for what I wanted. They were Greeks from Xenophontos and St. Anne's; and what little they permitted themselves to say made me want to visit those they told me could really speak to me.

At Karyes, the "capital," I met the Cabinet that governs Athos—four monks of the highest degree of "Father," chosen from the Council of twenty elected to represent the twenty principal monasteries on the Mountain. Each of the four has a veto, since the official seal that must be affixed to every legal decision is in four parts and each of the four has custody of one of these quadrants. When I said to them that it would be a more peaceful world if organized on the same principle of unanimity, they laughed uproariously. As if it were possible to apply in the world what was done in these special conditions on the Holy Mountain! A splendid joke! Here ended my second lesson.

My third was soon to follow. It had the same quality of simplicity and surprise. Near Karyes I visited a Russian monastery, St. Andrew's, part of which had been destroyed by fire a few weeks earlier, when a monk-farmer had tried to burn some dry grass off a nearby field when the wind was blowing the wrong way. Three old Russian monks—the sole inheritors of a monastery that had once held hundreds and been very wealthy—were cleaning up the ruins. The time came for vespers and one of them went up to the balcony leading to their chapel to hammer rhythmically on a "simandron," or six-foot plank held in the middle. It is the same sound one sometimes hears in the theatre before the curtain goes up, and serves the same warning purpose, as a call to mass. Before the monk went in to pray after hammering out his monastery's special rhythm on his wooden gong, I caught his eye and (gesturing at the burnt chapel across the courtyard) said, "What a pity!" "Why?" he said instantly, adding as a perfectly matter-of-fact explanation, "It was from God." Then he disappeared into the chapel they could still use for worship. Across the court stood the black ruins down whose walls molten gold and silver had flowed from priceless Russian icons and chalices, while the entire iconostasis of 15th and 16th century masterpieces has fed the flames.

It was not fatalism I felt in this monk's attitude. It was something, put explicitly by another monk, who said, "What happens is of no importance: it is how you take it that matters."

The following morning, at Iviron, I had my first real talk with one of the monks. It did not last long; after we got started, it was mostly a monologue; but it has impressed upon me the memory of Father Athanasios, the namesake of the famous founder of monasticism on Mount Athos—or rather he who first gave it institutional form almost exactly a thousand years ago, with the foundation of the Monastery of the Great Lavra near the seaward end of the peninsula, beside Mount Athos itself.

My Athanasios (also a Greek) is not "the first" (*Protos*) or head man of the monastery of Iviron, but according to the other monks I spoke to at the monastery, he is "the best." He is not easy of access. I had to ask three times before I finally managed to see him. He told me later that he finds the tourists "terribly fatiguing" though he is always interested in pilgrims who have real questions and some material. In his speech, as in the way he moves, he has authority—no airs, but presence.

In the great library of Iviron, he brought out for my inspection, after I had told him I had read it in translation, several volumes of the *Philokalia*, on prayer of the heart. He assured me that the *Philokalia* was still widely used as a manual by the monks of many of the monasteries and especially by the monks living in solitude or in houses for two or three around Karoulia and St. Anne's at the tip of the peninsula. I had already heard from one of my companions on the bus that the *Philokalia* was well known at his own monastery at Xenophontos, and in general among the Greeks. My impression is that among manuals of instruction and collections of the early Fathers, the *Philokalia* remains a primary text (though by no means the only one in this category) and is a constant source of instruction for those who go beyond the preliminary grades of their calling.

Clearly, for Father Athanasios, as for the others I spoke to later, the main channel of grace for an Orthodox monk is the liturgy. For this reason the quickest passport to their confidence is the cross around the neck of those baptized in the Orthodox faith. But they are remarkably open to the non-Orthodox as well; and (after the preliminaries) I felt little constraint in their replies because I was not Orthodox. However, they did not conceal from me their belief that the difficulties outside the Church (and deprived of the liturgy and the sacraments) were so great that salvation was almost inconceivable. Indeed, they seemed pretty dubious about the chances for any one not actually working as a monk on the Holy Mountain! It was hard enough for them!

Father Athanasios put it this way: "Life is a market place. Men pass through it, buying and selling. Most accumulate much trash only to find, at the end, that they cannot take it with them. But a few men of discrimination make their transactions in the market solely so that they will be able to buy, before they must leave, the one thing they can take with them. You remember the Gospel? Monasticism is the giving up of everything else for the purchase of that one pearl. It is based on Christ's own injunction to the rich young man (who lacked one thing) to go and sell all that he had, and to come and follow Christ. Only here can we follow Him without distraction."

"But can nothing be done in the world? In life?" I asked.

"After a life of preparation, a monk can be a monk also in the world," he replied. "Outside visits are only discouraged for beginners because it is very difficult and takes much time and practice in prayer. If it were not so, Christ would not have told the young man to sell all that he had."

"Here," Father Athanasios continued after a deep in-breath, "there remains alive what has truly been called a sublime philosophy. By its means, men can become angels. Yes," he added quizzically, "there are angel-men; but there are also men-angels!"

My next instructor was not a monk but a painting. In the big refectory of Lavra—now largely unused—there are a dozen large tables in the hall. All the walls of the refectory are covered with frescoes of perhaps the 14th century, though some have been redone much more recently. On the left as you come in, about 25 square feet of wall are devoted to a remarkable scene. A great fish, with teeth bared and gleaming eye (like the devouring dragon of Tibetan scrolls), is swallowing an ocean of life in which one can distinguish not only sinners but a holy man as well. In the middle of those about to be eaten is a dog in the process of eating a man with each of his two heads at either end of his body. On the dog's back rides a horned black devil, while behind is an angel, using a sort of spear to push someone towards the fish's mouth. The whole lot are being borne along on the waters into the jaws of the great fish, whose head alone fills the bottom of the painting. But of all the figures in the swirling waters, only the saint faces the fish's mouth; only he sees that he is about to be swallowed; and only he accepts what he sees.

"You are always alone. Terribly alone. You never get used to it." Father Nikon was very old, perhaps dying, when he spoke to me of his forty years as a solitary hermit. Yet what he found most difficult to bear was the interruption of his solitude. He knew his life was ebbing; but his one concern was to get back to his cave as soon as his broken arm had sufficiently mended. For two weeks it had been dangling painfully by his side, not even strapped. (I arranged later for the doctor monk to set the arm.)

For the moment Father Nikon accepted his need for the care of the old Russian monk in whose shack he was living when I visited him. It smelt sickly sweet, from the over-ripe fruit of the "prickly-pear" cactus growing thick all around the house. For me, by association, it smelt of death—the sweet smell that hung in the air of London on the morning after the night of May 10, 1941. There too I had been made to feel how alone we really are—in those rare moments when we are not more or less comfortably asleep.

Yet here was Father Nikon, at certain moments very much alive. Forty-one years ago his world had crumpled into dust, like a London building in the blitz; and he—an urbane guards officer who had until then pursued an agreeable life of the senses in the service of his Czar—he turned for help to those who might know how to build something less easily destroyed.

Father Nikon spoke to me with a directness and confidence I had never expected. I had not met him before and had had no reply to my letter asking if I might visit him. So I was not surprised when he was at first more disposed to listen than speak. Finally the moment came when he put a hurdle in front of me. "What do you think," he asked me, "is the essential difference between the Eastern and the Western Churches at the present time?" I replied that I did not know about the Eastern Churches, but that felt I felt in the West that the Western Churches no longer recognized real differences in level, nor understood what that meant. "Parfaitment," he replied with satisfaction. I had passed my test. From then on, he spoke freely.

"The devil," said Father Nikon on another occasion "is fantastically clever. Nobody knows how clever he is. Everywhere he is at work, even here. Already he has distorted and destroyed so much. But people do not recognize him; so his work is easier."

To the ever-present devil, deforming and distorting and dispersing, the monastic answer, he told me, is discipline. First, one must accept a little; then more and more, step by step. To develop this capacity for more discipline (I shall not use the word "attention," as he did not), he gave me an exercise, similar to others recorded in *The Way of a Pilgrim*. But as he indicated that he was acting far beyond his authority in doing so, I shall not repeat it.

For Father Nikon, prayer, silence and discipline were all aspects of one and the same effort—constantly broken, as constantly renewed. He did not put it into words, but he gave me one hint as to the direction of his inner life. "It is necessary," he said, "to be in harmony." Everything pulling the other way was of the devil.

Neither for the world nor for the good government of the Orthodox Church itself was he reassuring. "There is coming a period of frightful decadence" he said very positively. "The decadence of today is only the beginning." A few days earlier he told a friend of mine that contacts between men and beings of other planets would take place shortly; and it would be a terrible test for man. So concerned was he by what he saw ahead for the human race that he read avidly all the science fiction he could lay his hands on and asked me to send him more.

Before dismissing these apocalyptic visions as the evidence of a deranged old age, rather than as evidence of a reality to which our abnormal life makes us blind, we must take into account the frescoes of the Monastery of St. Dionysios, painted several hundred years ago, depicting great black birds (looking not unlike modern aircraft) flying away from menacing mushroom clouds....

Although he did not say so in so many words, he clearly regarded the Holy Mountain as a kind of Ark in which man might, by God's grace, weather the storms to come. In the world, the devil would gain still greater victories, but in the high places of Mount Athos, something was destined to be preserved and passed on. For those outside this benign current of Orthodox teaching, there was no hope of going against the flood. Their advice and direction, he said without mincing his words, was worth no more in matters spiritual than that of "a tailor or a pastry cook."

I accepted Father Nikons final blessing as the benediction of a holy man whom I would not see again. I shall not easily forget the white halo of his hair and beard surrounding (like the silver on an ikon) the finely chiselled aristocratic face. Even in his feebleness, what he gave off at that moment spoke to me more directly than his words. He was full to the brim of gentleness and love.

Father Nikon passed me on, explicitly, to his nearby pupil-monk, Elias, who lives in a little house (or "skete") with an elderly "doctor" monk, Artemis. Elias, who Father Nikon told me, is his favourite pupil. How they communicate is a mystery, since Nikon speaks little Greek, and Elias less Russian.

To prepare himself to take the place of Father Nikon, Elias must also learn to speak with those who come from outside. He is learning English, laboriously from books by himself, in half-hours stolen from his few hours of sleep each night. For when Father Nikon goes Elias will, so far as I know, be the only monk on Mount Athos able to speak a little English; and (apart from Father Athanasios) there are only one or two others speaking French or German.

I stayed three days and nights with Elias and Artemis—two more than I had intended. As I left before sunrise after my first night, Elias said gently that he did not think that little boat would go in such weather. It was raining hard, and a gale was growing from the northwest. But down a thousand feet I slithered with my pack on my back and sandals on my feet, getting wetter and colder by the minute, as my nylon waterproof demonstrated that it was only showerproof. After four hours vainly waiting about the pier, I staggered back to Elias with a headache and fever. The boat and I left 48 hours later, when both the storm and the fever had gone down.

Whether or not I was meant to stay longer on Mount Athos than I had intended, I could not have been either ill or storm-bound in a better place. I was reminded of the time I had broken a bone on one of my first visits to Mendham. In both cases, I got more than just well—I got better.

It was while thumbing through our Greek and English dictionaries with Elias that I suddenly saw the neighbourliness between the Greek words for "prayer" and "attention": *prosefhi* and *proschomen*. The latter means "attention" rather in the French sense and is used also as a warning. The former suggests philologically that prayer is a movement towards well-being, or, more literally, in the direction of wellness flowing up (in oneself). How right that prayer and attention should have the same family tree! What rich psychological meanings lay buried in our languages, waiting to surprise us in a moment of understanding—and then reproach us for having passed them by so often, unaware!

With Elias, I spoke more in detail than had been possible with Father Nikon about inner silence and prayer of the heart. It was when talking to him about the relation of such prayer to breathing—a moment of absorbing interest for me—that he brought me back with a kindly thud: "But that is a detail—just technique. First the mind and heart must yearn to be with God, to open to Him." In different terms, I might have been back in the study bed at Menham. "Just technique...."

To worship God from love, to be in Him without words, and to live this in the liturgy is the monk's way. "*Kyrie Eleison!*" Twenty-one times repeated during the pre-dawn service of matins—again repeated at vespers before sunset—it seemed to me that this was the center of gravity of the monk's effort on Athos. Their life—and also their time—revolves around these special hours of prayer.

For on the Holy Mountain, they do not keep the world's time. Their clocks (and hence their prayers) in all their separate monasteries are synchronized every day, without benefit of radio time signals. When the sun sets below the horizon it is twelve o'clock, and the hands of the clock are adjusted accordingly. So has time been calculated since the days of the Byzantine Empire. (One monastery is the exception: in Vatopedi twelve o'clock is the moment of sunrise. From the eastern side of the peninsula, the monks cannot observe the moment when the sun sets, but sunrise across the sea is plainly visible.)

Elias did not speak much about the liturgy. He read with approval the little Orthodox mass I had in English from before the war, when I had first met the Archimandrite Cassian (from Athos) in Amsterdam. Mine was an abridged but accurate rendering of the mass normally used on Athos, introduced in Russia (in the 10th century?) by St. Basil and St. Chrysostom. I said I supposed it went back further than that. "Yes," Elias replied. "The two-hour mass we use is really the short version edited by St. Basil and St. Chrysostom from the original mass written by the Apostle James for the first monks of the first Church. That mass was used by the Desert Fathers. It has been preserved here. You can read an early copy of it in the library of the monastery of St. Paul where it is sung at a special service once a year on the Feast of St. James. It is not done more often as it takes the whole day—eight hours at a stretch—to go through it all. But that is where our masses come from."

Ten days later, at Meteora, I found myself once more in an Orthodox monastery, once again at a dawn service, this time with my whole family. We had slept all together on the floor of a small room in the picturesque monastery of Varlaam, where Sophie Loren filmed a scene for *Boy on a Dolphin*. But though the site is the most extraordinary location for monasteries I have ever seen (perched on thousand-foot pillars of eroded rock, clustered above the Thessalian plains), the service was a sad disappointment. After the vigour and sincerity of the liturgy in Athos, here was decadence indeed. Three pathetic old men, getting through the flowing sentences anyhow, intoning a whole paragraph in one slur of words, of which only the last was said distinctly—as if to reinforce the contrasting impressions I had had on Athos itself, of weight and content. Here on Meteora, it was but the husks waiting for the next good wind to blow them off their perch, and leave the peaks in undisputed possession of the tourists who already swarm over them, since the Greek government built the good road to the top.

Good monks, bad monks—the liturgy is their yardstick and their measure, as it is their means.

While I was with Elias, I confirmed that Athos is not open to anyone who knocks on the door of their monastic life. Though younger recruits are non-existent for the Russian monasteries and only just enough among the Greeks to maintain their numbers (less than 1500), they do not accept those clearly unfitted, by health or disposition, for the life of a monk.

One evening I told Elias that I had met earlier in the day a Greek at the nearby monastery of St. Anne's. I had taken him for a tourist, but he had told me that he had come to seek admittance to one of the monasteries. Why? Because his father and mother were now dead, he replied, there was no work on his island, his health had not been good, and at least here on the Holy Mountain he would have food and shelter. From his whole bearing, the man seemed more cut out to be a tramp than a monk; but I asked Elias what would become of him. "He will *never* be a monk." he replied with some heat. "I have spoken to him too." "Then what will happen to him?" "He will be tried out as a worker monk; but if, as I expect, he is incapable of working, he will have to be sent back where he came from. We cannot feed useless people here."

"No work, no bread" is an Athos saying. The contemplative life still requires many hours of hard work—usually manual. Elias not only assisted Artemis in tending the monks who fell ill in monasteries within a five hours' walk or climb from his house. He was a carpenter and turned out wooden objects (of no great artistic merit) for sale in the small tourist shops of Daphni and Karyes. A worker-monk helped him, turning for hours at a time the great wheel which powered his lathe. They worked when they needed money for the food they had to buy-beans, canned milk, coffee, bread, eggs. When they had enough, they stopped working in the workshop and used their time in the library or in the chapel. It seemed to be a principle never to accumulate ... "sufficient unto the day" was enough. They had not come to the Holy Mountain for a comfortable life.

Only among the artist monks did I find a different attitude. Their community of half-a-dozen ikon painters does not stop work when they have earned enough for the day's bread. They are specialists, and work in a kind of school, serving up new-style and old-style Byzantine paintings to order, not so much for the monasteries of the Mountain (which have already the finest examples of Greek and Russian ikons in the world) but for Orthodox Churches wherever the name of Mount Athos is enough to double the price of bad copy-painting. The head of this latter- day "school" of artists was suffering from gout: I left him my aspirin supply and headed out for the rocks, with a better understanding of why the hermits leave the monasteries. "The world" dies hard, even on the Holy Mountain.

And the best monks know it. Indeed they seem to make use of this fact as an integral part of their way, One of the famous ikons of Athos shows a monk on the cross, suffering. His nails and wounds are called his "passions" and individually labelled. From the catalogue of "passions" it is clear they have little to do with St. Anthony's temptations of the flesh; but a great deal to do with the suffering of being aware of the sins of pride, self-love and all the negative emotions still dirtying his soul, in spite of years of monastic laundering.

That many monks attain little perceptible to the outside observer is, I think, undeniable. That some carry in themselves a bigness, a cleanness and a vigour of being is equally incontestable. These have no need of the special type of "father's" or "preacher's" hat to distinguish them from the general run of priests. They stand out from the others at once; and they alone do not permit themselves to be photographed.

Could they have attained that clear-eyed quality if they had not found the oral tradition still authentic and alive on Athos? Could they have come that near to perfection by that way if they had not "forsaken all" and left the world? For the world that they and their ancestors have known for many hundreds of years is a hard land. Most monks seem to have come from the poorer families; and a Balkan peasant has no time to cultivate more than his external garden. We had seen how hard was that peasant life of Eastern Europe, for our trip through Yugoslavia and Macedonia had brought us many times into contact with a pattern of life unchanged by either communism or the centuries of occupation: Ottoman, Austrian and German. But the mould of that peasant life is inexorable. Could anything short of complete separation from it give a man a chance of being reborn differently? At least modern life, for all its waste and failure of potential, gives men more time (and in this sense more chance) than the life from which Orthodox monasticism has for so long offered a possible escape to liberation. To meet new conditions, methods can change. The end remains constantly the same.

It is said that one cannot leave Athos. Pilgrims keep coming back. Perhaps I shall be no exception—if I am lucky. But I must leave this little memoir; and to let it stand as notes on a week spent "out of this world," and as a monument to all that I have not yet been able to understand. For we can grasp from such an experience only what, in a sense, we already know. Our understanding can be leavened and strengthened, our search given new life; but we are served, by law, with the measure of our spoons. It takes more than a week to get a bigger one.

CHAPTER 10

UNDERSTANDING OUR RELATIONSHIP TO THE ENERGIES OF THE COSMOS: AN INTERVIEW WITH A SHINTO PRIEST

In Asking for the Earth I have told the story of the original Threshold Foundation based in London, which I started after my retirement with the financial support of Prince Chahram Pahlevi. To give it a thoughtful beginning, he invited a remarkable group of people to a "think-tank" at his island in the Seychelles, between Africa and India, early in 1978. Here we had, among others, Costa de Beauregard and George Sudarshan, the eminent French and Indian physicists; Dean James Morton of New York's Cathedral of St. John the Divine; Father Thomas Berry of Fordham University; Buckminster Fuller; Dr. Michel de Salzmann, the French psychiatrist; Lyall Watson, the South African biologist; Swami Saraswati from India; and Yukitaka Yamamoto, the spiritual head of one of the oldest pre-Buddhist Shinto sects in Japan. What follows is a record of my interview with Yamamoto, who embodied traditional Eastern wisdom.

Yamamoto: For us the primary force is energy which in India is called *prajna*—in China *chi*, and in Japan *ki*. Since its main point of contact with our planet is in the north, we traditionally face south to receive the force in our spine and manifest it out into the world of action through our rituals.

James George: When actually going into meditation, whether facing south or however I may be oriented, I begin to suspect (but I don't know) that one is instinctively tuning in on the frequencies of the Earth's magnetic field, so that the pulse becomes the same, inside the body and inside the Earth. Is this how you understand it?

Y: That is correct. As we see today, the Earth is not just hanging in space all by itself. Earth's energy is completely in harmony with that of the other planets, of the sun—of the whole solar system. So Earth has its own balanced vibration in relation to the whole cosmos. Therefore to be able to tune in to the same vibration or frequency as that of the planet Earth means getting directly in tune with the pulse of the pulse, though they are two aspects of the manifestation of the Cosmos itself. That, in our terms, is to become one with God's vibration. It is to be one with the Cosmos' vibration or energy flow. To get in tune with this cosmic rhythm, which you called "pulse", there are two ways. One is through long and rigorous practice. But there is another channel to become one with the cosmic rhythm. It is through the human psyche and feeling; and perhaps we human beings are given feeling to be able to serve this very great purpose.

JG: That is, through love?

Y: Yes, through love. And at the heart of the matter, before we could manifest what we call love, on the human level, there must be a cosmic rhythm emitting a Force of which our "love" is the merest pale reflection in human terms; and yet it can be the channel through which we are allowed to receive this cosmic pulse, sometimes.

JG: I suppose that is why the tradition you represent takes the Mother as the incarnation of that force?

Y: You are absolutely right.

JG: Even in Islam, which is so male in its conceptions, the Muslim repeats five times a day: "Bismillah al Rahman al Rahim" and the Rahim means the womb of the Mother—therefore compassionate, merciful. It is the female aspect of God that is invoked. Now, since we are on this point, how do you understand the duality of male/female in relation to the One that is All?

Y: If we call the life energy of the cosmos, *chi* or *ki*, it is pulsing, it is rhythm, there is a wave motion, up-down. That already means that it must have two aspects. One can be called the essence of love, the other the essence of intellect. These two essences, intellect and love, come through as the cosmic pulse. Though they are two aspects of the manifestation of the same original force, the essences of intellect and love are seen in our human world as male and female (yang and yin). They are like two eggs in one sphere. In one, love is dominant and intellect secondary. In the other, intellect is dominant and love secondary.

JG: But, both have both.

Y: Precisely. If you apply this concept to the planet Earth, the north is considered as predominantly intellect, and the South is just the opposite, love. But this is in principle, and refers to the combination of what we call spiritual *chi*. When it actually manifests through humans, it is not always the case that intellect is dominant in men and love secondary, or vice versa in women. In practice it may be the reverse.

JG: You are speaking not in absolute terms but of a center of gravity? A relative balance weighted now this way, now that?

Y: Yes, but the marvellous thing about human beings is their variety, and the proportional difference may not necessarily be reflected in their sex or gender. Mostly it seems to follow, but there are many exceptions. And these exceptions are not the accident of nature but because of will; what I would tentatively call "angel's will." This is very interesting, so let me try to be clear. The human being is seen through its cosmic manifestation, through this body of a human being—that's the first point. And when the spirit is sent to be born through a human body, this period of ten (lunar) months and ten days in the womb is the time that is given by the will of (let's say) the spirit world. At that time, or during that period, we begin life as human beings. This is the spirit entering the human body. At the moment of birth we are, in a way, the purest untainted spirit of the higher dimension. Not only on the intellectual level but in instinct, you maintain the original combination with which you were born, whether the intellect dominates or love dominates, regardless of your sex. These traces will be seen in your subconscious, and this many people experience—a brand new place, which you have never seen in your physical form, yet you know this place. Somebody you meet for the first time and yet you have a very special feeling for him or her. These are the proofs of the subconscious world, or your experience before you took human form, as seen in the sea of the subconscious. So no matter how we look at it, in this very body, now, we are related to the higher world, the spirit world, through this very special thing that we have called feeling or emotion or love. I am sorry if this is not altogether clear or relevant to your question.

JG: No, I think it is wonderful. It is absolutely central to our theme. Now in this incarnation of *ki*, energy, is there a parallelism in structure and operation between our bodies and the Earth body?

Y: The life forms that manifest on the surface of our planet must precisely mirror, in structure and function, the energy patterns of the whole of which they are parts. So everything that manifests as life on the surface of this planet carries the energy signature of this planet and conforms to the laws which govern the planet Earth itself, depending somewhat on local variations. In other words, the climate, the chemical or geographical composition of the Earth, all these things influence the way this energy is manifested and within these limitations our human rhythm is also affected. It does not function on all parts of the Earth in exactly the same way—the rhythm does change depending upon the climate, the surrounding vegetation, the soil, how close you are from the center of the energy flow of the Earth itself. And this energy flow is, as I said earlier, captured in China as a science of geography, based on statistical analysis, in *feng shui,* or geomancy.

JG: To serve a sacred purpose is one thing; but it seems very degenerate to use it just to make money burying people! So what is there left today that is authentic and belonging to the real sacred tradition of geomancy?

Y: Remembering all we have said as the foundation, the human function is to serve, in harmony with the energies of wherever you are. Unfortunately, in modern Japan (and perhaps elsewhere) it seems to be very difficult to find that understanding and that service being put in correct order and applied. So because of that lack, even the highest flows of cosmic or Earth energy can now only add to contemporary misery and unhappiness. Although we have what we are pleased to call "development" and high scientific and industrial achievement, people try to work not with but against the higher forces to change or use them for their own purposes. But in the long run it will not work. If it goes too far, the Earth energy will manifest destructively, and there will be a disaster affecting our nation, race or even contemporary civilization as a whole. This will not be the result of going against God's will in a moral sense, but simply the result of our blind mutiny against the natural flow of energy, whose tasks we are obstructing, instead of serving as channels.

JG: It's a matter of law, then?

Y: That's right—the cosmic law.

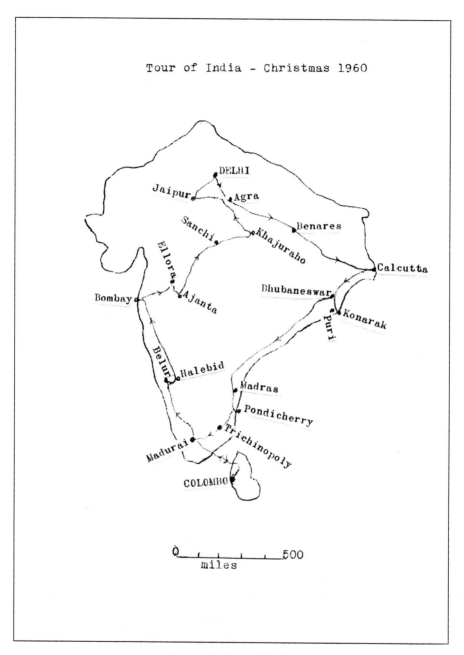

FIGURE 3: *Tour of India*

CHAPTER 11

TOUR OF INDIA, CHRISTMAS, 1960

This chapter is a hasty letter to my father describing some of the highlights of a family exploration of India during our Christmas holidays.

In South India 9.1.61

Dearest Dad,

It hardly seems possible that three weeks have gone by since I wrote to you just before I left on our great trip to India. You will have had the telegram I sent to reassure you that we did not all disappear into the Ganges leaving a dark green ripple but have survived the trip. Now, on the train and ferry from India to Ceylon, I shall begin to catch up on a period when letter writing was out of the question, our time and strength being sufficient unto each day but with not a bit to spare. For we have already completed 3,000 miles, not of North American but of Indian roads, and Carol and the children have been on the go for more than a month.

Nothing has gone as planned, nothing has been easy or comfortable or clean, but all this mass of new impressions has been opening up for us a new world, the very ancient world from which so much of our Aryan World (including Greece and Rome) has so obviously come that the discovery of India is almost as much a rediscovery of connections not previously suspected as it is a totally new field of exploration. In spite of this, we remain foreigners in India, with only the vaguest idea of the inner life of the thousands of Indians we have passed each day—and it is at only one or two points of pilgrimage that we have felt a real common understanding on both sides.

Maybe later I shall try to put certain overall impressions on paper. Now, it is better that I simply say what we have done.

Carol and the children left Colombo by car on December 10 with an office driver to help them get to Bombay via Mysore, Belur and Halebid. I joined them as planned on the 16th, flying over to Bombay after work. It was a great relief to find them all at the airport to meet me.

We sent the driver back by train and went on together to Aurangabad on the 17th. The next day to Ellora and Ajanta, the most extraordinary cave sculptures and fresco paintings in all India. Ellora was the place of worship, Ajanta the school of learning, of a community of Buddhists and Hindus in the Middle Ages. They must have wished to be undisturbed by those who did not share their aims for they built their temples and university in such inaccessible hills that they were only rediscovered early in the last century by some tiger hunters.

In contrast, Sanchi (the next day) was an open center of Buddhism in the time of Asoka. It has a classical simplicity now, with more of the typical Hindu clutter. But no doubt one of the reasons for the contrast is that the Sanchi temples are no longer active, while the Hindu temples we were to see later on are. I wonder if the Greek temples were not very different when they were painted and in use than they are today; different and much "less classical!" Perhaps only in India is mythology alive now.

Khajuraho was our first real introduction to Hinduism—almost too overpowering. Many of the finest sculptured temples in a center that has been open to visitors only for three or four years. God as Love, very graphically on the lower parts of the temple. And no doubt most of those who used these temples understood the idea as literally as most Western tourists.

Here I must recommend to you a book I shall have sent to you from London called *Time of the Mango Flowers* by R. Cameron. It is the sort of historical travel book Carol might have written if Cameron had not done it already, and my highest praise is that it is almost as good as her letters.

I shall not be able now to write of the Taj Mahal, Jaipur and Benares. The Taj will need a letter to itself. It is the most perfect and moving building I have ever seen.

Christmas with the Ronnings [Chester Ronning was the Canadian High Commissioner at that time] for dinner. But we didn't get your letters until we were driving out of Delhi on the morning of the 27th since the office was closed on the 26th. No time to stop for a Delhi postcard, but I shall get one later for Félicité's game. It was wonderful to have news of you there and your cheque too for the trip to Kathmandu, but there was no room on the plane when we could have gone. Instead we went to Calcutta (not on our original plan) to visit a teacher or guru we had heard about in Paris from someone who had visited her ashram in Benares.

Anandamayi Ma is now in her sixties. We had a morning with her, half of it alone with her. I shall not describe it here, it is too important a story to rush under present conditions in the train. But we were much impressed with her, unlike Arthur Koestler in his new book on Indian Ashrams. But then Koestler has not had our preparation in New York and Paris without which we would have understood very little. Instead with Anandamayi Ma, and later at the Sri Aurobindo Ashram in Pondicherry, we found ourselves on the same wavelength as if we had worked in India for years. Methods differ; principles are the same. It is a very good experience to realize it once more, as in Morocco and Mount Athos.

Sorry the train is rough. So was the trip. Often camping in bedless dak bungalows. Boiling all our water, plus using your chlorine outfit. Days of no cooked food except our own soup and tea, biscuits and cheese. But so we stayed healthy on 250–300 miles a day plus sight-seeing. We can sleep when we get home.

Much love,
Jim

CHAPTER 12

ACHAEMENID ORIENTATIONS: DISCOVERING THAT PERSEPOLIS IS SOLSTITIAL

While I was serving in Iran, my wife Carol and I often visited Persepolis and began to wonder whether it might turn out to be a solstitial structure as the central temple of a Zoroastrian Empire. As the sun rose on the summer solstice of 1975, Carol took the photos that established our suspicions. Our findings were presented to an astonished congress of archaeologists a few months later. This report was then published in Volume 15 of A.U. Pope's Survey of Persian Art.

The orientation of Persepolis is solstitial, related both to sunrise and to sunset on the longest day of the year. The sun rises June 21 at exactly 90 degrees to the longitudinal axis of the complex of buildings, viewed from the central stone in the middle of the Tripylon or Tachara, the central building on the site. From this same zero point, on the same day, the sun sets in line with the columns forming the diagonal of the Apadana and cutting its northwest corner. On the winter solstice, December 21, the sun rises (from the same vantage point) over the southeast corner of Darius's Treasury, the first building to be erected at Persepolis. The central axis of this building points to the rising sun of the summer solstice. These orientations are consistent with the metaphysical world view expressed in the Avesta, the Mazdean and Zoroastrian scriptures. That Darius thought in these terms is suggested by his own description of his Empire, with Persepolis at its center, as recorded in the tablets found in foundation boxes beneath the corners of the Apadana at Persepolis.

Much work remains to be done to determine which of the other major Achaemenid and Sasanian buildings are oriented by the sun. In publishing this provisional report on my findings at Persepolis, my hope is that others will join in the observations that should now be undertaken on the solstices and equinoxes.

Since 1972, when I was posted from Delhi to the Canadian Embassy in Tehran, I have been taking an amateur interest in the roots of Persian philosophy, both Islam and pre-Islamic, and in the archaeology of ancient Persia, especially of the Achaemenid period. With the help of friends who know these two rather specialized fields, I began to realize that there might be new insights to be gained by attempting to correlate or bridge research that has been taking place as if in two separate watertight compartments, almost totally isolated from one another. In other words, I began to wonder if the metaphysical doctrines of the Zoroastrians could not shed light on some of the archaeological puzzles such as the orientation of the major Achaemenid palaces and monuments, many of which point not north but 15 to 30 degrees west of north for no reason that has as yet been understood in modern times. At Persepolis, for example, the entirely regular plan of the palaces had been frequently noted with admiration, but their orientation (18 degrees west of north) has usually been attributed to the geographical requirements of the site so as to make use of a small "acropolis" running parallel to a long mountain ridge behind it which, it has been assumed, forced the builders of Persepolis to choose its peculiar orientation.

In Canada, as in the West generally, we are scarcely ever aware of orienting either our cities or our houses in a particular direction, but then it must be admitted that construction in modern times has been particularly "eccentric" in the precise meaning of that word, i.e., off-centered or not having a center. As we fly over any old village or town in Iran and look down into the central courtyards of the larger houses we realize how, in any traditional society, great importance was given to every structure having a center. The nomad Qashgai, Shahsavan and Bakhtiari tents built up with poles held at the center top by a wooden hub, and the similar round reed huts of the Baluchis, are other examples. Moreover, the most important structures had traditionally to be related to the center of centers, and therefore oriented in relation to the Earth's axis or to the polestar, to the sun or the moon or a particular constellation. At this point it is not necessary to go into the history of the Pyramids, Stonehenge or even of the great Gothic cathedrals to make that point, as it is already well established.

Before coming to Iran, we had lived for five years in India, where we had investigated the orientation of great temples such as the one dedicated to the sun at Konarak. According to the earliest sacred writings about architecture in India, the first step in the construction of a temple was to choose an auspicious day, clear and purify the ground, and drive a pole into the central place at what would be, so to speak, "ground zero" for the building of the temple. The pole was supposed to pin the head of the demon serpent underground so that it would not cause Earthquakes later, but no doubt it also served another purpose which was to cast a shadow and facilitate the orientation of the temple in relation to the rising or setting sun. This must certainly have been the case for a temple like Konarak, dedicated to the sun god, Surya. Might it not also have been true, I wondered, in Iran, the other center of the Aryan tradition

During several visits to Persepolis I began to suspect that the orientation of the most famous Achaemenid palace must have had something to do with the sun. The religion and culture of the Achaemenids was, after all, Mazdean (some would say Zoroastrian) and the fire of the sun was a most important religious symbol of that Light which was for them the first principle of all being, representing the deity, Ahura Mazda or Ohrmuzd, who is opposed in the cosmic struggle of light and darkness by his "twin," Angra Mainyu or Ahriman. From the point of view of Mazdean metaphysics, the most sacred day of the year was that on which there was the most light and the least darkness, when Ahriman's shadow was the least present—that is to say the longest day, usually June 21 in our calendar and the 31st of Khordad in the present Persian system of time-reckoning.

My wife and I therefore decided to visit Persepolis at the time of the summer solstice of June, 1975. We were delighted, but not greatly surprised, to find that the sun rose at exactly 90 degrees to the longitudinal axis of the palace. The photograph accompanying was taken at 6:14 A.M. as the sun became visible. The point of observation was from the middle of the Tripylon or Council Hall which stands almost at the center of the terrace halfway down the eastern side of the main acropolis hill overlooking the Hall of a Hundred Columns whose southern wall is shown in our photo to the left of the eastern gate of the Tripylon. At the center of the Tripylon there is a square stone on the center of which a small circle is incised. The block was found by Herzfeld who called it a "measuring stone." Shapur Shahbazi, Director of the Institute of Achaemenid Research at Persepolis, pointed it out to us as possibly the central point of reference for the whole of Persepolis. Our observations support his hypothesis. This zero stone was the place from which our photo was taken. It shows the first rays of the rising sun in the center of the portal. A post placed where we stood to photograph the sunrise would have cast a shadow directly across the site of Persepolis at 90 degrees to the longitudinal axis. The alignment was so precise that the shadow of one column fell at sunrise within one centimeter of the edge of the next column five meters to the west. I am assured by astronomers that although the declination of the sun on the summer solstice in the 6th century B.C. was nineteen feet higher than now, virtually the same results would have been obtained at sunrise on the longest day at least 2,490 years ago when Darius selected the site and the construction of Persepolis began. The second photo was taken from the hill to the east about twenty minutes after sunrise, but the shadows of the columns still fall almost at 90 degrees across the site.

At sunset on June 21, 1975, we again took observations by compass, bearing from the Darius Palace on the western side of the Terrace, and recorded that the sun set 44 degrees to the west of the alignment of the Persepolis buildings. It was only later, when applying this reading to the plan of the site, that we realized that from our zero stone in the middle of the Tripylon the sun had set in line with the columns that once formed the diagonal of the Apadana, the most imposing of all the structures at Persepolis. In other words, Persepolis is not only solstitial in that its basic orientation is determined by sunrise on the longest day, but the north western corner of the most important building at Persepolis points at the sunset of the same day. This elegant "double" orientation may, I suggest, have been a factor in the choice of the site of Persepolis. This is not to deny that there may have been other reasons, including defence, for the move from Pasargadae to Persepolis. It was possible to build better fortifications at Persepolis, and this was important for a building described by Darius as a "fortress" containing his main Treasury.

The next step was to see what happened at the winter solstice, December 21. We had expected that the sun would rise on the shortest day 180 degrees opposite to where it set on the longest, and would set on the shortest day opposite the point where it rose on the longest. In fact there is a distortion created by the thousand foot mountain ridge to the east of Persepolis, the Kuh-i Rahmat, which delays the June sunrise about an hour and a quarter, during which the sun rises 16 degrees above the horizon and swings 9.5 degrees toward the south. Despite this "irregularity," the lines of the summer and winter solstice sunrises and sunsets form on the site plan an approximate St. Andrews' Cross: two diagonals crossing at what, on a flat plain at 30 degrees north, would be 55 degrees but is actually 45 degrees because of the hill to the east. The angles, according to our observations, are shown in the figure. From our zero stone, the sun on December 21 rises over the southeast corner of Darius's Treasury and sets over the southwest portico of Darius's Palace.

Our observations of the solstitial character of Persepolis, to which we had come through metaphysics, had been anticipated five years earlier by a scholar and an astronomer from Germany, Wolfgang Lentz and Wolfhard Schlosser respectively, approaching the problem from the side of astronomy. We had not known of their work on the problem when we made our June observations but acknowledge not only their prior discovery but also their very kind cooperation and great assistance in our subsequent research. Though their calculations about the sunrise on June 21 were correct, they were based on observations made at the site on June 24 and not completed by the winter solstice readings. Our photographic confirmation is, I believe, the first direct evidence to be published based on observations made on the day of the summer solstice. We are also the first (so far as I know) to note the significance of the sunset orientation on that day from the zero stone, and that the winter solstice sunrise, as seen from the zero stone, cuts the southeast corner of the complex.

While I agree with Lentz and Schlosser on their basic thesis, I am not able to follow them (possibly because of translation difficulties, since their articles are in highly technical German) in all the applications of their idea: namely, that Persepolis was a sort of year-round instrument for continuous astronomical observation of sun, moon and stars. Since the buildings of Persepolis were roofed, it would have been more difficult to follow the movement of heavenly bodies than it is in the ruins today. I agree, however, that the solstitial character of Persepolis gave the Achaemenids a ready means of knowing when they had come to the longest day of the year and therefore afforded a check useful for revising their complicated calendar, which was in need of regulation and correction every few years. As Lentz and Schlosser pointed out to me, it would have been much easier for the Achaemenids to check their calendar at the solstices when the sun plainly stops its northern (or in winter, southern) march and turns back than it would have been at the equinoxes when the sun is moving "up" (or in autumn "down") each day with no simple or obvious means of determining when the equinox has actually come. This is one reason al-Biruni thought June 21 was a more important date in the solar year than March 21 (*Now-Ruz* in Farsi) for the Achaemenids.

Taking the solstitial orientation of Persepolis as now clearly established, the question arises as to why the Persians adopted this technique for such a major monument. What was its significance and meaning for them? To unravel this mystery we must examine both the evidence of Zoroastrian metaphysics and the explicit "cornerstone" inscriptions of Darius found under the Apadana.

Let us take first the metaphysical evidence of the Avesta as outlined by Henry Corbin. The Mazdean and Zoroastrian priests thought the world we know conformed to an ideal pattern shaped like a wheel with six spokes radiating from an empty central hub. On the plane of the Earth the key directions were taken from the diagonals formed by (*a*) sunrise on the longest day and sunset on the shortest day, and (*b*) sunrise on the shortest day and sunset on the longest day. Along these lines were laid out the spokes defining the eastern and western regions of the kingdom, the two large segments remaining being divided in half on the north-south axis.

We thus get a diagram or mandala showing six major regions or climatic zones of the world (called *keshvars*) surrounding a seventh at the center. Dividing the regions from one another and surrounding the whole scheme is the cosmic ocean of emptiness, *Vurukasha*, while the hub of the kingdom, the central point of the mandala, is called *Eran Vej*, the "cradle of the Aryans." In its application to the historical kingdom of Darius, *Eran Vej* would have represented the central region, not necessarily in the administrative sense but in the much more important spiritual sense of being the hub, the center, of the power and the glory of the Achaemenid Empire.

In Zoroastrian metaphysics as described in the Avesta, an exactly similar mandala (which is really the ideal prototype of the Earthly kingdom) was

conceived existing, so to speak, in heaven (or in principle) where seven archangels or Bounteous Immortals (*Amahraspands*) presided over the respective
seven spheres. Ahura Mazda had the central position with three male archangels to his right and three female archangels to his left. In the words of the
celebrated Yasht XIX of the Avesta, all seven Immortals have the same thought,
the same speech and the same action, so that they are one in thought, word
and deed. Thus it is impossible, strictly speaking, to call Ahura Mazda "him"
since he/she is said to be both father and mother of the Creation. Ahura Mazda is nevertheless a name of masculine gender in Old Persian.

In addition to the metaphysical evidence which we have cited, there are
two inscriptions which, I suggest, throw additional light on how Darius himself felt about Persepolis. In the northwest and northeast corners of the Apadana, beneath the level of the lowest courses of the walls, two stone boxes
were found in 1933 by Friedrich Krefter. Each box contained one square tab-
let of gold and one of silver bearing trilingual inscriptions of Darius defining
the extent of his kingdom. The inscriptions have been translated by Kent as
follows: "Saith Darius the King: This is the kingdom which I hold, from the
Scythians who are beyond Sogdiana, thence unto Ethiopia; from Sind, thence
unto Sardis—which Ahura Mazda the greatest of the gods bestowed upon
me. May Ahura Mazda protect my royal house."

Now, if one looks at the map of the Achaemenid Empire and draws the
lines which correspond to Darius's description of his own kingdom, it will be
evident that they intersect near Persepolis and moreover correspond roughly
to an extension of the two diagonal lines drawn across the site plan, based on
the sunrises and sunsets of the longest and shortest days of the year. Darius
takes as his first point of reference the area where the Scythians live beyond
Sogdiana, which is where the summer sun rises from the perspective of Persepolis; Sardis in northwest Turkey is where it sets. Similarly, in winter the
sun rises from the direction of the mouth of the Indus (India) and sets toward
Ethiopia.

From what we know of the metaphysics of the Avesta, it should come as no
surprise that the position of the rising sun on the most holy day of the year
determined the orientation of Persepolis; or that Darius's own description of
his Empire appears to follow the Avestan mandala and that he applies it to

Persepolis as the spiritual center through which (as through Ahura Mazda, the cosmic axis) everything on this worldly plane was connected to the macrocosmic ideal, without which nothing could be considered holy or sacred.

It is a remarkable fact attesting to the sacred (and therefore secret) character of Persepolis that contemporaries like the Greeks wrote so little about it, though there are many Greek accounts of the other Achaemenid capitals—Babylon, Ecbatana (the modern Hamadan) and Susa (Shush). Thus Ctesias, the Greek physician of Artaxerxes II who lived at the royal court for twenty years, did not mention it in his writings, though he described the other main centers of the Achaemenids. Some have inferred from this silence that Ctesias never saw Persepolis and that foreigners were kept away from it. This thesis would not, however, explain the fact (which we know from the bas reliefs at Persepolis) that Greeks (among twenty-eight subject peoples) brought gifts to the Great King at festivals and helped to carry his royal throne on such occasions. Therefore I prefer to think of Persepolis as indeed a sacred city, a place of ritual, the spiritual hub and center of the Empire, where the foreigners who came may have been sworn to secrecy. That such oaths of secrecy were effective we know from the paucity of information we possess about their practices from those initiated in the various mystery religions associated with Eleusis, Delphi, and Orpheus.

I would not, however, go so far as to maintain that Persepolis was intended exclusively for ritual purposes, though Pope seems to have held this view. The Darius inscription near the original main gate at the south end of Persepolis describes the place as a "fortress" (*dida*) and anyone who has taken the trouble to climb above the site and study the excellent system of fortifications with massive towers eighteen-meters high overlooking the terrace, itself no mean fortification, must agree. If Darius's first structure on the Terrace was his Imperial Treasury, he wanted to protect it well and did.

At the same time it seems to me undeniable that Persepolis was much more a center of ritual than a place of administration. Wherever the Great King went, the administration went with him. But there is so little evidence of wear on the stairs and passages of Persepolis that we must conclude that the court spent far less time there than at other palaces, such as Ecbatana and Susa, reserving Persepolis for special occasions associated, I would suppose (from the evidence of the bas reliefs and other reasons given in this article), with the main stations of the solar year, the solstices and the equinoxes, especially March 21 (the present Iranian New Year) and June 21, the sunrise that determined the orientation of Persepolis and that probably regulated the calendar.

To supplement our account of solstitial orientations for the buildings on the Terrace, it is worth noting that the two huge rock-cut tombs above the Terrace to the east, those of Artaxerxes II and III, have solstitial features. The temples in front of both tombs face approximately the winter solstice sunset, though the tombs themselves do not. So palaces for the living are oriented to the awakening of the longest and holiest day, tombs (or their temples) to the setting of the sun on the longest night.

Sometimes—but not always. The tomb of Darius the Great and two of the other three tombs at Naqsh-i Rustam, about seven kilometers northwest of Persepolis, face south-southeast (152 degrees east of north) where the rising sun in winter reminds us that the winter solstice, like death itself, is not the end of Light but the beginning of a new cycle of the returning sun. And so it is that the departed kings on the bas reliefs cut into the rock above all their tombs at Naqsh-i Rustam and Persepolis face the rising sun and the sacred fire.

To recapitulate then, it seems to me wholly consistent with its function as Darius's spiritual capital that Persepolis should be placed at the physical hub of Empire and laid out as the Earthly mirror of the heavenly prototype mandala of the ideal or eternal city as Darius must have understood his Mazdean tradition from the Avesta. The very name for Persepolis—*Parsa* used by Xerxes, Xenophon, and in the Elamite inscriptions—may well relate to its spiritual functions if *Parsa* can be linked to the modern Persian word *parsa* meaning "holy pure, one who is versed in prayer." It was after all Aeschylus—not the Persians—who called Parsa "Persepolis."

In this perspective, it seems improbable that Alexander the Great set fire to Persepolis merely as a chance whim or because some dancing girl happened to propose it in revenge for the Persians having set fire to the temple of Athene in Athens. Alexander certainly understood power, including the power of sacred knowledge and the magical power invoked on our plane of existence by mirroring what may be known of the divine model of reality. So we may suppose that in destroying Persepolis, Alexander consciously struck at the root of Persian power by cutting it off from its center and source. Persepolis is then seen as the Achaemenid *axis mundi* in the most profound sense, and with their center destroyed the heart went out of Persian resistance. Though it took Alexander another five years to establish and consolidate his hold on Persia, he had already won the crucial battle at Persepolis.

Partial confirmation of this historical view is found in the archaeological fact that so little treasure has been found in the excavations of Persepolis over the years. Alexander's Greeks had systematically cleaned it out and pillaged it carefully before setting fire to the palaces. Had it been a spontaneous act of arson, much more would have been found in the ruins.

It would be beyond the scope of this paper to enter into the whole question of sympathetic magic as applied to ancient buildings in Iran, though both Persepolis and Takhte Suleiman could be taken as examples. Then, as now, there were those who understood such an idea literally, and those who could understand it in psychological or spiritual terms. Though we have no text on which to base our interpretation, I would suggest that the orientation of Persepolis, and the mandala of the Earthly kingdom of which it was the hub, can be understood on several levels at once. For the people, it was a place of magic and of teaching, a visible and tangible model of a divine order of reality "in heaven." For the priests and most of all for the king, it was a threshold to an inner reality, a state of being, charged with power because it was centerd and perfect. Once it was destroyed, it had no more significance because no more efficacy. This is why in all eastern traditions a sacred image with the least defect is immediately discarded, or sold to a Western tourist. For the Achaemenid initiates, Persepolis before its destruction could be understood as an outward reminder and an aid in that process of centering oneself which is simultaneously one's own conscious aspiration and a blessing from above: a *barakat* in current Islamic terminology. To be in a special place at a special time, and with the help of a particular ritual based on real knowledge, could assist the aspirant to pass over a threshold in himself which by himself he could not pass. Was this not part of the religious purpose and aim of Persepolis and one reason that it had to be so precisely placed and orientated?

It is also worth noting that 1,400 years after Darius founded Persepolis and described its central position at the point of intersection of the solstice diagonals forming his kingdom, the great Persian philosopher-scientist Biruni was using the same sort of mandala to describe the central position of Persia as the crossroads of the diagonals linking Byzantium to Hindustan and Turkestan to Abyssinia.

Is it only modern man that has forgotten how to orient his major structures and to relate both them and himself to the center?

There is, for me at least, a beauty and a completeness that carries conviction through all the detailed evidence which I have brought forward in support of my thesis regarding the orientation of Persepolis. That thesis should now be tested in relation to other Acheamenid palaces and temples. From the rough calculations which I have made, however, based on site plans, I think (in some cases at least) my thesis may well explain the hitherto mysterious orientation of these buildings, but since I have not as yet carried out actual observations, I wish to restrict myself at this time to outlining my idea as applied to Persepolis and to invite others to join with us in the fieldwork that now needs to be done at sunrise and sunset on future solstices and equinoxes in Iran.

I recently noticed that Persepolis is on exactly the same latitude as the pyramids of Giza near Cairo. North or South of this latitude, Darius's "X marks the spot" would not have worked.

CHAPTER 13

THE CITY AND THE MOUNTAIN

As a result of the previous article on Persepolis, I was asked by the leading Tehran English newspaper whether I had made any further discoveries. My response for the "Kayhan International" was given front page treatment on July 28, 1977.

A month ago at the summer solstice (21 June or 31 Khordad of the Persian calendar), how many people, I wonder, of the four million in the capital city of Iran noticed that the sun, on that once sacred day, came up over Mount Damavand? And of those few who noticed, how many asked themselves whether there might be a reason for this—or was it just coincidence?

Before we embark on possible theories, let us have the facts. If you were in the central hub of Tehran, in the City Park (Park-i Shahr), at dawn on the solstice, you would have seen the first rays of the sun break over the horizon at the summit of Damavand, on a compass bearing of 61.5 degrees East of North. This line passes through Tehran, crossing Damavand Avenue (in the east end of the city), which runs not exactly towards the mountain but 10 degrees to the south of it. The mountain itself lies 71 km. from the center of Tehran as the crow flies, if crows really do fly straight.

Seeing is believing. I took a photograph of Damavand at dawn on June 19 (two days before the solstice) from the southern part of Tehran Now (an eastern suburb of the city) from the top of a building under construction—to the astonishment of the workmen who were just walking up as I brought my 400 mm. telephoto lens into action. The photo shows the fully risen sun just to the right (south) of the peak. Since the sun does not rise vertically even on the longest day of the year, the first rays broke closer to the summit. Two days later, and from a little further north, the first rays break above the summit itself, along a path through the heart of Tehran.

Now let us see whether that fact may be significant. To do so we must go back some 2,000 years to the first city that was then established a dozen kilometres south of Tehran, at what we now call Rey.

At that time Rey was called Rhages or Rhaghae/or Rayy. It was then (as now) a holy city, and is mentioned in the Avesta as the "cradle of Zoroaster," though there is no agreement among scholars as to which Rey is meant—there was another in Khorassan in eastern Iran, and Dr. I. Gershevitch thinks the Avesta reference is to that one.

In any case the Rey south of the present Tehran is mentioned by Darius the Great (about 520 BC) and was then a town of growing religious importance. It was there that the Median pretender to the throne of Persia took refuge from Darius. During the Sassanian period (3rd to 7th centuries A.D.), Rey became the "Vatican" of the Zoroastrian world, since it was then the residence of the principal Mobet (or Chief Priest), the *Mas Moghan*, as he was called in ancient times, or more recently *Mobadan Mobet*. And Rey's fierce resistance to the Arab conquest has also been historically recorded.

As we also know from ancient records and traditions, including many references in Ferdowsi's great epic, the *Shahnameh*, Damavand was the sacred mountain of the Zoroastrians—a tradition maintained in the Islamic period when it (as well as Mount Ararat) came to be called Mount Qaf. For both religions it was the cosmic mountain and world axis—the very center of the world. Even for the Parsees and Zoroastrians today, there is a living tradition that the great sages of their faith are still secretly working and teaching the pure remnant of the faithful on Damavand in a hidden retreat called a *Var*. And on our maps of Damavand there are two "vars" to the west of the peak.

As for the Islamic tradition of Damavand (Qaf), it will suffice to recall that it was there that the Great Simorgh revealed his divinity to the "thirty birds," in Attar's *Conference of the Birds* (12th century A.D.): "The sun of my majesty is a mirror. He who sees himself therein ... is as a shadow lost in the sun. That is all."

It would of course be surprising if Damavand were not sacred. At 5,722 metres, it is the highest mountain between the Atlantic and the Hindu Kush. It is, moreover, a perfect snow clad volcanic cone, with as much reason to be venerated as Mount Ararat in Azerbaijan or its twin in Japan, Mount Fuji.

Among all the sun-conscious peoples from the Pacific rim of Eurasia to the Atlantic, the Persians have always occupied a central position, so that at noon in eastern Iran (*Sistan*) for long called *Nim Ruz* (noon day), the sun was half-way from Japan ("land of the rising sun") to Morocco ("land of the setting sun," or *Maghreb.*)

Coming back to Damavand, its peak casts an extraordinary shadow at sunrise on the atmosphere even on a cloudless day, and, at the solstice, its perfect pyramid shadow points to Tehran and Rey, as the night breaks into the blessing of this special day.

Why "blessing?" Because for the Zoroastrians the longest day of the year was the holiest—the day when there was the least contamination of darkness, when *Ahriman* (literally "evil mind" or bad thought) was the least present. The summer solstice was the day of light, of good thoughts, when Ahura Mazda reigns in glory. Hence the importance of this day for the orientation of sacred buildings in Iran, as in many other parts of the ancient world. Persepolis is an outstanding example, as described in my article for *Kayhan International* published on June 22, 1975.

The Avesta itself speaks of the cardinal points of space as the four solstitial sunrises and sunsets, plus north and south. And, apart from Zoroastrian teachings, for all peoples the easiest times to check on the calendar in order to correct it is the day the sun is seen to reach its maximum ascent to the north and begin its descent towards winter, or, conversely, stop its fall descent and begin its rise towards summer. For Egyptians, Druids, Celts, Iranians, Indians and Chinese, the tradition was the same.

I know of no historical or documentary evidence—most of it was destroyed in the 7th and ensuing centuries—but I suggest as a possibility that it was because of its proximity to the apex of the shadow cast by Damavand at sunrise on the summer solstice that Rey became such an important Zoroastrian center in Sassanian times. The sacred cosmic mountain on the holiest day of the year is a powerfully auspicious combination.

That such a tradition may once have existed and not been altogether forgotten is perhaps indicated by a modern fact. Part of the Zulfiqar Order, the highest military decoration in Iran, of which the highest degree is worn only by His Imperial Majesty, the Shahanshah himself, shows the sun rising over Damavand, as it would be seen from Tehran at the summer solstice. This order is not ancient, having been instituted by H.I.M. Reza Shah, nor is it anything but Islamic, commemorating as it does the famous sword of Hazrat

Ali; but this need not deprive modern Iran of feeling respect and affection for still more ancient Persian memories evoked by Damavand and the sun. Being where it is, Tehran may be more blessed than it knows. It is in the right place. Just as Ali has inherited in Iranian folklore many of the attributes and stories originally associated with Rustam and Mithra, so Tehran can be seen, in the long sweep of history, as the inheritor of Rey.

CHAPTER 14

TEILHARD DE CHARDIN AND THE FUTURE OF MAN

This was my contribution to the Geneva Conference on "Education and the Future of Man" in Geneva on April 16, 1981, to honour Teilhard de Chardin.

The first and most obvious question that has preoccupied us all is the one that is almost unaskable because it is unanswerable: Has humanity a future? I don't think any of us would be here if we did not dare to believe, sometimes against the evidence, that the answer to that question is *yes*. At the same time, we would not need to discuss it if the "yes" were automatic, no matter what further stupidities the human race commits against itself and our planet. There is already quite enough evidence that we are not merely capable of blowing up all or most of higher life forms on this our common spaceship, but that we are proceeding to pile up superfluous destructive capacity merely as a continuing reflex to a galloping military and scientific technology that is out of the control of either political or even military forces. British and American top defence science advisors have told us all in clear terms that the scientific establishments—and I suppose the Russians are no different—keep formulating improvements, as research and development advances. Instead of government directing military research, the R&D tail is wagging the dog. Improved nuclear warheads call for improved nuclear missiles, which in turn require better systems to operate and deliver them, with the inevitable clinching argument being that "if we don't do, it the others will."

Seen in this perspective, human survival currently is like a gigantic see-saw in a master game of dominance. If I am up, the other fellow is down; if I am down, the other fellow is up. At its most stable—and it can never be stable for very long—the see-saw holds level in a balance of terror. In these circumstances the people begin to demand the abolition of the see-saw and the changing of the rules of international competition so that they become essentially non-military, and certainly non-nuclear. A start in that direction has at least been proposed by the Canadian Prime Minister three years ago when Mr. Trudeau called for a cut-off in the production of fissionable material (suitable for weapons) on a world-wide basis. One might now add to this prohibition a treaty prohibiting all nuclear weapons testing, another to ensure that nuclear weapons systems would also stand still, and a third to prohibit further production of any existing types of nuclear weapons. Somehow we have to stop the momentum towards war before we can reverse the whole apparatus and get it moving in the opposite direction, of *dis*armament.

Nor is East-West tension the only threat to our survival. Seen on a vertical time stem, human population figures are still exploding in another mushroom cloud that hangs over the planet, weighing down most grievously the poorer developing countries. If this mainly North-South tension due to unequal economic opportunities is not corrected, it may burst into violence even if the East-West balance holds. But what is vital for us to understand today is that no action on anything approaching an adequate scale can possibly be undertaken on North to South technology and resource transfers unless disarmament becomes a reality. The money, through two so-called "Decades of Development," has been going into arms instead of development. On the present rising curve of armaments expenditures, East-West and North-South tensions can only exacerbate each other, and postpone any realistic attempt to create a new global economic order by non-violent means.

If present trends continue and there is no breakthrough on disarmament and none therefore on development—and in today's world this seems all too possible—we shall be a little like the 17th century *Récollets* missionaries from France, who arrived in Canada five years after the Jesuits, travelling by canoe through Canada's Algonquin Indian country, and who had a map showing where the falls were but went over them and died just the same. The special irony in this particular martyrdom was the name of their Order which was dedicated to constant recollection. Here we see all too clearly the metaphor of our times. We have all the information we need in our heads, but we are not acting on it through our bodies and in our feelings, which behave as though they belonged to some separate creature. In other words, we are not integrated people; and for this special sin of non-connectedness and forgetfulness it is possible that we may perish. For I do not think that in the last three centuries we have been learning to live less in our heads and more in what I would call the whole.

This brings us to the perspective that I think is absolutely fundamental to everything we have been talking about during the past week: the relationship between parts and the whole. We have considered from many angles the new climate of opinion, the new age perhaps, which we are now entering. Astrologically we are passing from the celestial sign of the Fish into Aquarius. Psychologically we are passing from a sign of polar opposites (two fish swimming in opposite directions) towards a metaphor of new life and unity, the Water-bearer, as Aquarius is also called. Even if one cannot conceive how our planetary movement out of one zodiacal sign into another can have much bearing on human affairs, one can hardly fail to be aware that during the past thirty years enormous changes have been taking place in the way human beings understand their situation and their society. From my point of view, the key to a clear revisioning that gives meaning to these changes today is, as I have just said, the relationship between the part and the whole.

Let us explore this idea in greater depth from another angle, from the holistic perspective, which I believe to be characteristic of the age into which we are now moving. A great deal of the science of the past 100 years can be seen to be limited by its isolated, flat, linear character. In psychology, behaviourism would be a good example; in physics, the persistence of Newtonian concepts long after Einstein, Bohr, and Heisenberg had shown the limitations of a clockwork universe in which the uniformity of time, space, and causality had been assumed. Examples could be given in almost every other field we can think of to show that a change of paradigm is taking place, amounting, as it ripples outwards, to a cultural revolution, because it is changing the way that we look at our world and what gives it meaning.

The challenge of the new education, therefore, is to transmit the new integrated perspective, in all its freshness and excitement, not as a confrontation with the old but as a more adequate extension of how we used to see things—separately.

For too long education has dealt in separate disciplines with realities artificially reflecting academic divisions. To be able to transmit a more integrated perspective, showing relationships in a whole, we must be able ourselves to see those relationships, and the wholeness. For this we must change ourselves first, to be able to go up to where we can see and be in contact. What does this mean?

The great creative insights, whether in the outer world of science or in the inner world of experience, have always been extremely simple. At the present time, we are witnessing a cultural "polar shift" as upsetting as if the Earth's magnetic pole had suddenly shifted and produced (as the Book of Revelation so clearly expresses it) "a new Heaven and a new Earth." The Earth's pole has shifted five or six times in the past four billion years (and some suspect may fairly soon do so again). In man's much briefer history, there may have been that many major cultural transitions.

But let us understand better what is happening now. To give meaning and purpose and value to the rationalist, reductionist wasteland we have inherited from the metaphysical aberrations of the science of the past 300 years, we have, very simply, to stand it on its head. The most elegant hypothesis is that which explains things most simply. Where a theory has to be stretched to cover the data, it is already suspect, if not out-dated. Can we not now begin to see that all the theories deriving the higher (in the sense of more complex) life forms solely from the lower, without the action of any integrating principles or forces (so to speak) "from above," are about as implausible as expecting all the separate pieces of an electric typewriter to fall into place as an IBM machine on the x-billionth time that they are thrown into the air? Perhaps a simultaneous stroke of lightning will do it! Perhaps not.

Today the most advanced biological researchers, it seems to me, are prepared to admit "mind" and "purpose" into their lexicon, provided such terms are defined as the mind or the purpose of the planet, of "life." Well, that is a step forward towards reality, but we need to go further. General systems theory is telling us about the "Pattern of patterns," the system of inter connections and inter relationships, between parts and wholes on different scales—dare we say "levels?" So what is this *whole* of which this planet (or life as we know it) is a part? What is *its* purpose, into which the purpose of "life" must be fitted in the hierarchy?

Now, as soon as we say the word "hierarchy," the problem in the current cultural evolution becomes clear. The old way of thinking does not want to hear about "higher" and "lower" at all. It wants a world that is strictly horizontal, quantifiable, linear, logical; and it will only admit that there are "worlds within worlds" if all implications of hierarchy are removed. For the old science, there can be differences of scale but not of level, not of consciousness. But "micro" and "macro" traditionally referred to differences of level, not merely of scale on an infinitely horizontal line, as yesterday's science would have it.

The observable world simply does not fit on a horizontal time line of increasing "complexity." There are "quantum leaps." Is the planet not "more" than the rock or the bacteria, and is the animal not "more" than the plant, and is the human not "more" than the animal? And if this *qualitative* difference, this difference (I would say) in the level of being, is recognised, then where does the hierarchy stop? Is the ordinary human consciousness the highest?

Here we have come to a fundamental question. Our response will affect our future. If I have understood correctly the consensus of this Conference, our answer is that the consciousness of the ordinary human being is not the highest, but is capable of linking with it. Apart from theoretical or religious considerations, we each of us have moments of awareness which we recognise as "special"—heightened or intensified awareness, peak experiences, ecstasy, love. At such times we see everything together, related as a whole—not as a logical progression of associations, from A to B to C—the usual "bits" of information with which our mental computers left lobe works. Suddenly we find ourselves in the consciousness of the programmer, not the machine. And the most remarkable thing about this state of being is that I no longer feel it is my consciousness.... For a moment I have awakened into a state in which there is no separation, no you and me, no object and subject, no past and future, no duality, just *Presence*, here and now. In the words of one of Teilhard's most powerful hymns, "The whole Universe is aflame" with the Light of that Presence.

For any person who has been touched by this Presence, there is no longer any question about who is my neighbour. Such a person already knows by direct experience that there are no distinctions of color, creed or culture that can possibly divide the essential communion of humanity.

Is this then the "planetary consciousness" that Teilhard de Chardin said was coming, a new sort of "Christ-consciousness" of which he was an eloquent herald? Big words don't matter, and can even be obstacles for some people. Through awareness, Teilhard wrote simply: "We are becoming a single somebody." What counts now is the *experience*, and exactly how—"scientifically," if you like—to reach it. In that sense we can accept Prime Minister Pandit Nehru's summing up, near the end of his life, when he said in Colombo (when I was part of the audience): "What the world needs today is not politics and religion, but science and spirituality."

But let us make no mistake about it, the change of consciousness that we are talking about as the necessary next step for humanity to aim at, if we are to fulfil our planetary destiny and not just satisfy our insatiable greed for more and more "experience," is not only "a change of mind and heart" but a radical *transformation* of the human being. And although it inevitably must take place through a change in individuals, it is finally not an individual but a collective phenomenon. The breakthrough, for a real "polar shift" in the culture to take place, has to be collective. For this it must affect a certain "critical mass" of the community.

In his recent book *Life Tides*, Dr. Lyall Watson tells a story that he as a scientist finds disconcerting but fascinating. Some years ago, on the Japanese island of Koshima, a group of Macaque monkeys were under close scientific observation for a period of years. When food supplies for the monkeys became short, they were given yams, but the sand and grit picked up by the yams made them rather unpleasant eating for the monkeys, until one day a young female had the brilliant inspiration of washing her yam in the river.

She then taught her mother that yams eaten that way tasted much better, and over a period of many months not only her mother but her immediate family learnt to wash their yams either in the river or (still better) in the sea which added to their flavour. This cultural breakthrough gradually spread among the monkeys until a critical mass—Dr. Watson thinks about 100—were washing their yams. Then quite suddenly and inexplicably, from one day to the next, all the monkeys were washing their yams. And what is even more extraordinary, so were the monkeys on nearby islands and on the adjoining mainland, despite the absence of any direct communication of a kind we could explain to ourselves within the limits of our present understanding.

For the monkeys there was only a change in technology—how to get the dirt off their yams. For us it is also a question of food, but of a quite different order— the higher energy "food" it is possible for us to receive from the air and from impressions. Traditionally, man is an upended tree, with his roots in the air, so to speak. We cannot live five minutes without it. But if our centers are blocked by tension and neglect (forgetfulness), we are like a tree that can no longer receive its nourishment. It is bound to—wither. Man cannot live by bread alone.

My dog may be devoted to me, but he cannot understand me. In the same way we cannot fully understand what is going on above our level of being. The lower cannot "see" the higher, but the higher can see the lower. In accordance with that law, I do not know the planetary or cosmic reasons for humanity growing a new kind of consciousness at this time in history. Our historical and personal experience convinces us that it is possible, and it would not be possible if it were not useful. But how?

If the circulation of energies works in a similar way in the microcosmos (man) as in the macrocosmos, can we suppose (as in Islamic metaphysics) that the Universal Man (*al-Insān al-Kāmil*) is the perfect mirror of the Reality as a Whole? Then only if, in each generation, some of humanity reach this perfection can the finer and more highly charged energies circulate in the collective body of human beings on this planet. From this point of view, man is a link in a cosmic chain, or more exactly a rung on a cosmic ladder, linking the highest and the lowest. Without that link, an octave is missing in the music of creation, in the harmony that is life. And without that circulation of energies through the more conscious human, creation has to stop; it cannot go on to the next step. In such cases, we observe on other levels that death usually follows.

If most really new scientific hypotheses are intuitive leaps (like Einstein's $E = mc^2$, which he "proved" afterwards), let us attempt one such leap together. Supposing there is a Universal Consciousness that intends man to play a more responsible role in planetary maintenance and evolution, how would it initiate us into a new level of maturity, awareness and intelligence appropriate for higher responsibilities? So far, looking back, we can see that danger, obstacles and suffering have always activated the need to respond to major survival challenges, at critical moments on our path through self-consciousness to something more. If the present can be called the Ecological Age (post-industrial, post-technological), then, in Thomas Berry's very Teilhardian phrase, "Man is that being in whom the Earth becomes conscious of itself." Not man as he has been, but man as he could be: the New Man. And to make a new Man, we need new conditions, a new science, and a new education.

In this perspective (which I feel is fully consistent with the thought of Teilhard de Chardin, with Gurdjieff's vision, and with most traditional wisdom), the key to the future of humanity is whether enough human material can be "spiritualised" to serve as an effective link for the circulation of energies that go through us every minute, but which, in our present state of being, we cannot assimilate or transmute into thoughts and feelings and sensations of a new quality of awareness.

This is perhaps a new way of looking at the problem; but the human-as-link ideal is an integral part of every tradition, East and West, North and South. The King or the Priest or the Priest/King (or in other cultures, the great Mother) have been archetypes of the Universal Person linking levels for the health and growth of their people and crops. Humanity asleep could be represented by the horizontal play of forces; humanity awake, by the vertical axis: the pole, the cosmic mountain, the linkage between "heaven" and "Earth." A culture that is all horizontal is a desolate Flatland. One that imagines itself all vertical is schizophrenic and unreal. Life lies in the balanced relationship of vertical and horizontal. This cross, free to move anywhere on its center, describes a sphere, a Unity, which can be created on this Earth, in this body.

The vision of this Unity that animated Teilhard's courageous search, we have seen with our own eyes (at least in photographs) as the sphere of our blue cloud-wrapped spaceship, hanging in the void, vulnerable, beautiful. We have been touched by that vision which has become for all of us the hallmark of the ecological age we appear to be entering: an age in which for the first time a more conscious human being, endowed with a better balance of male and female, rational and intuitive faculties, may become a partner of the Earth in the co-evolution symbiosis René Dubos has shown to be opening before us—*provided* we do not blow it!

CHAPTER 15

THE AMERICANIZATION OF WORLD CULTURE?

As both Albert Einstein and Robert Kennedy discovered independently, there is no effective way to change our destructive human behaviour unless we change our current way of thinking that is producing it. From my observations with the help of what I have learned from Gurdjieff, our ordinary way of thinking is dualistic: either/or; you or me; this or that. It happens automatically, as associations flow from one thing to the next. But whenever we are even minimally present, and the attention is not taken by the ordinary mind, another, more conscious, more awake, mind appears from our sub-consciousness. I call this thought or mind awareness. It is not dualistic but integrative. The more of it there is, the more I am able, as if from a higher place in myself, see that it can be both/and; you and me; this and that. For everything is in reality totally interconnected and interdependent, as science keeps reminding us in a much more limited frame of reference. As Max Plank said in his maturity, everything comes from Mind or Consciousness; and there is only One. So it is unitive, not divisive. What a difference! Can humanity, or part of it, learn to live more of their lives under the direction of their awareness, in resonance with its Source? That would change global culture and destructive human behavior more radically and more rapidly than anything else. That is the great purpose we are here to serve.

> "In the next century, we risk the wholesale globalization of culture. By and large, this will mean an Americanized world culture."
>
> JOHN BIRT, Director General (1992–2000) of the BBC

John Birt's judgment is deeply troubling, as it was no doubt meant to be, to almost everyone, many Americans included, and especially to most Canadians, as we are the most exposed to American cultural influences. There is no denying that some globalization of culture is taking place on the wings of the globalization of the technology of cyberspace. But that does not necessarily mean, as I see it, the Americanization of world culture. For there are other ingredients that are going to flavour the soup. And we can still be thankful that there are many soups—not just one. Who in his right mind wants the globalization of anything—except life?

What is the defining difference that distinguishes one culture from another? There will be many answers to this question, of course, but I would like to propose the following:

Cultures can differ both horizontally and vertically. The essential difference is between what I am calling the horizontal cultures and the vertical, not in the sense of egalitarian vs. hierarchical cultures, but in the sense of cultures recognizing one level or many. Historically, and still today, the basic clash is between those cultures for whom there is something higher than ordinary life, and those for whom there is not. For the past three centuries or so, what we now broadly call Western scientific culture has denied that there is a difference of level, or a higher consciousness, creating and maintaining the universe, and also present within us, in the sense that every traditional culture throughout history has affirmed. The sense of the sacred is almost a lost sense in the profane, horizontal culture that now threatens to engulf the world. Faced with this challenge, there must be a coming together (but not a homogenization) of all the cultures—of East and West, North and South—for whom there still is a vertical dimension, if the higher energies that have seeded all human cultures in the past are not to be disconnected from humanity and thus from this planet. That is the issue, and that is the crisis.

In this perspective, let us consider the relationship of power to culture.

In the 20th century, there have been two centers of world power: North America and Europe. In the 18th and 19th centuries, there was only one: Europe. In the 21st century, it seems likely that there will be three centers: Asia, North America, and Europe. This will be a radically new cultural perspective; for, as we have seen throughout history, cultural dominance follows power. And economic power is shifting very fast, as information, technology, and capital move across borders with the speed of e-mail. It took Britain about 60 years to double economic output per capita; it took Japan half that time; and it took China only the last ten years. In 1960, Japan and East Asia accounted for 4% of world GNP, while North America held 37%. Both groupings now have about 24%. In the nineties, more than half the world's economic growth is taking place in Asia, so Asia will likely outdistance North America within the next decade. Then there will be less likelihood of a globalization of American culture.

When the Europeans (like Mr. Birt) look at the dominance of American culture today, we need to remind them that Asia/Pacific power will soon have a significant impact on what we have known as "American" culture. Indeed, that process has already begun, via California, in the past thirty years with the extraordinary spread of Buddhism in both its Japanese (Zen) and Tibetan forms, inseminating American culture. Twenty years ago, American scholars went to Asia to learn about it; only the hippie fringe went there to learn from it. But that is changing. There may come a time when a fusion of Asian and American cultures produces an Asia/Pacific culture that will be like neither of its original components. If that happens, Europe will, of course, be affected too.

The Greek classical world, and its sequel in Alexander's Empire, the Renaissance in Europe, the Moghul Empire in India (especially under Akbar), the present rise of Japan, and the emergence of Korea, Malaysia, Singapore, Indonesia, and now China, are all examples of the explosive energies of cultural fusions. The "economic miracles" of the Asian countries are being brought about by the Asian graduates of American universities. The fusion of cultures has taken place in their own lives, and it is spreading. When this interchange between Asia and America becomes more of a two-way street, when we in the West begin to learn as much about the inner life from Asian cultures as they are learning from us about the outer life, I believe we could see a cultural transformation that would not be towards a flat homogenized world culture but towards the vertical opening to higher influences. We cannot predict that happy outcome yet, but we can see it as a real possibility, worth working for.

On the way to that goal we can begin now to appreciate cultural diversity the way we are beginning to understand biodiversity. Already the American ideal of a "melting pot" is being superseded by the Canadian vision of a multicultural "mosaic," in which each piece of the mosaic is valued for its own sake and as part of the greater whole.

Perhaps it is precisely for this reason that there is such an unsettling hunger for meaning and values in America. When you find yourself in what Eliot long ago described as a cultural wasteland, un-watered by either a sense of the sacred or an infusion of love of community, you naturally look for what you are missing. Allen Ginsberg finds Buddhism, and Newt Gingrich finds Victorian values. In their different ways, both are groping for something that can stand for the higher and free them from the terror of the "bottom line." If cultures other than our own can help us to find answers to our problems, why not explore them? If our own culture has largely lost touch with the sacred, then can we find that life-giving element in another culture?

Having spent more than half my life in other cultures, I gratefully acknowledge how much I have been helped by that experience. In India, Sri Lanka, Nepal, and Iran I have discovered the inner springs of three of the world's great traditions: the Hindu, Buddhist, and Islamic. As a result, I am no longer the prisoner of the tunnel vision of my own western culture.

For many young Westerners who made the journey to India in the sixties and seventies, when I was there, the culture shock they experienced on their return home was stronger than the one they had felt on arrival in India. For me, too, it was surprising to discover that I am not the same person who had left home some years earlier. I suddenly saw, for example, how I had taken for granted a level of waste and consumption I could no longer tolerate. I now have an inner life of which I had been almost totally unaware. My culture has changed. I am a fusion of East and West. And I feel more whole.

If this can happen to me, it can happen to millions of people for whom multicultural pluralism is not just an idea but an experience that has changed and enriched their lives. I have seen it happening to thousands of others, from both East and West, who are exposed to each other's cultures, and are making their own individual adaptations. It is from these seeds that a fusion of cultures may arise that could, I believe, rescue our own Western culture from its present degeneration, while rescuing much of Asia from its crippling poverty. Those who fear that American consumerism will predominate globally are exaggerating the strength of a culture already in transition, and are underestimating the resilience of a traditional culture that has been around for maybe twenty thousand years longer than this modern aberration. The only real question is whether the fusion of cultures now taking place will lead humanity towards community and participation, or towards the increasing violence of unrestrained individualism, which knows nothing higher than itself.

Increasing prosperity in Asia is shoring up the confidence of people in their own cultures. As one Asian "economic miracle" after another joins the ranks of the relatively comfortable, they see less and less compulsion to imitate American models. Western analysts often make the mistake of thinking that for Asia to progress it must follow in our footsteps by becoming more Western. That no longer seems either desirable or likely to Asians. For now the Asians have seen that they can do well in the world without sacrificing their own cultures in the process. They have seen that the American Emperor has no clothes—that there is much they should actively avoid in the American example, including the highest teenage murder rate in the world. Asian economic success gives them the confidence to take what they find useful but remain true to their own roots, true to themselves. They are learning to honour their differences with America, instead of apologizing for them.

Nor is American culture the monolith it sometimes appears from the outside. I have mentioned the inroads of the "new religions" of Asia, but even science is becoming surprisingly open to dialogue with the great religious traditions. For example, the prestigious Templeton Prize ($1 million) was recently awarded to Dr. Paul Davies, a British physicist teaching in Australia, who sees "the emergence of life and consciousness (as) very significant manifestations of the rather special nature of the laws of physics in a self-creating and self-organizing" universe. The late David Bohm, an American physicist (and a contributor to *Resurgence*) was also a strong influence in building a bridge between science and religion.

Surely the purpose of such a dialogue is the exploration of a cultural meeting ground that can be common to all cultures. Only through such exploration and dialogue can we build a culture which is broad enough to be a global mosaic of cultures, and open enough to let in the light that comes from Above.

CHAPTER 16

REMEMBERING THE GREAT AMERICAN ARCHITECT, LOUIS KAHN

Before Farah Diba met the Shah of Iran and became the Empress Farah, she had been a promising student of architecture. When she had the power to do so, she convened in Iran, in March, 1974, a remarkable gathering of a dozen of the world's leading architects, including my friend Arthur Erickson from Canada and Louis Kahn from the United States. When the Conference in Isfahan was over, I am indebted to Arthur for bringing Mr. Kahn to see me in Tehran, where I was serving as the Canadian Ambassador.

Many years have now passed, but I have never forgotten Mr. Kahn's last words to me that afternoon. I had quickly come to feel a deep rapport and respect for him, and I asked him as he was leaving what he had been searching for through architecture all his life. It would be a pity if I did not record, even now, what may have been his last attempt to express the inexpressible vision at the heart of his craft.

Looking directly at me, he stopped speaking for about half a minute, and then said, very quietly: "Architecture is, after all, our attempt to give form to light; but the life, the energy, the creativity is in the presence of light, as it seeks to manifest in some form. The architect is only the vehicle for this action of the light, if he can get himself out of the way and just see what the light wants to do"

Having said what he came to say, Louis Kahn graciously took his leave and was driven to Mehrabad Airport for his flight to Philadelphia. He never got home. The next day, March 17, he was found dead in the Philadelphia Railway Station men's bathroom.

May he rest in peace and in light!

CHAPTER 17

JERUSALEM—A RELIGIOUS SOLUTION FOR A POLITICAL PROBLEM

Ever since my first visit to Jerusalem, which occurred shortly after I retired from the diplomatic corps, I have felt that there could be no peace between Israelis and Palestinians without some kind of sharing of the city that was holy for both of them, or at least some sharing of the small central core containing the Holy Places. During the years that I was President of the Sadat Peace Foundation (1983–2001), and visiting the area each year, I kept trying to promote interest among the political leaders on both sides in letting Temple Mount and the Holy Places be administered by the Christian, Judaic and Muslim spiritual authorities, giving each a veto on whatever was to be ordained for those few acres, and removing it from the deadlocked political authorities. This was, after all, how Mount Athos has been governed for over a thousand years. The four leading monasteries each hold a quarter of the key to any effective decision, as mentioned in Chapter 9. In the case of Jerusalem and its three faiths, contentious leadership claims might be resolved by agreeing to rotate representation equitably, e.g. alternating Catholic and Orthodox each year. There was some serious interest in this plan among leaders on both sides. I will mention specifically two examples: Zalman Abramov (Likud), the Deputy Speaker of the Knesset; and Ehud Olmert, while Mayor of Jerusalem, before he became Prime Minister. I still think it could prove to be a way around the intractable political stalemate, whenever the political will to find such an escape route again comes to the surface of the conflict.

This article was published in "International Perspectives," Jan/Feb 1978.

If 1978 is to be the Year of Peace in the Middle East, there is going to have to be a great deal more soul-searching, both among governments and among peoples of good will, than seems apparent to a Canadian observing from the wings of the Arab-Israeli stage. Though the wish to find a solution, in this interval of grace when a real solution might just be possible, is undoubtedly present on both sides of the most dangerous confrontation of our times, it is all too easy for those not directly involved to leave the dialogue to the political-leadership of the states most directly concerned; up to a point this is as it should be. Outsiders should not put their noses into what is none of their business. But in regard to the future of Jerusalem there is a much wider community of legitimate concern. Indeed, if this concern does not make itself felt internationally, the key-stone of the arch of concord in the Middle East may elude the negotiating states, whether at a Geneva conference or elsewhere.

I say this because I do not believe there can be lasting peace in the area without a solution for Jerusalem that permits—in practice as well as theory—free access to the Holy Places by Moslems as well as Christians and Jews, and because I do not foresee any likelihood of a political agreement being negotiated on this issue. In the political context, the problem is deadlocked. Can it be lifted from politics and placed in a totally fresh context that is at the same time the one with the deepest roots in history—the religious context?

Political Headway

In political negotiations, with a major effort by all concerned, including the superpowers, I can see headway being made on the question of withdrawal from occupied territories (in accordance with UN General Assembly Resolution 242)—except in the glaringly obvious case of Jerusalem. Even a homeland for the Palestinians may be worked out and guarantees given all round that nobody is going to be pushed into the sea or wiped off the face of the new maps. But will this much progress (so devoutly to be wished) be attainable if Jerusalem remains—as far as the Arabs and the Moslems of the world are concerned—an Israeli occupied territory? Can we imagine the late King Faisal of Saudi Arabia ever fulfilling his life-time desire to pray under these conditions in the silver-domed Mosque of Al-Aqsa, beside the golden Dome of the Rock? Politically, this is a sticking point for both sides.

If there is to be any solution other than a military solution of fact (which is what we have at present) or a military reversal of the present line of control (which is what the Arabs would sooner or later attempt), the only "third force" which could transcend the political-military state of perpetual confrontation and lead to a solution all concerned might be able to live with is the internationalization of Jerusalem as a Holy City under a religious regime composed of Jews, Moslems and Christians. Despite the enormous difficulties of the task, such a regime could (I believe) become a reality if the three religious communities around the world really want it enough. It will never happen if one or other of these communities is bored with the idea. As communities of the "Peoples of the Book" (to use the language of the Koran) we must all want it very much—with the sort of passion that the call of "Jerusalem" generated in the Middle Ages.

Historically, each community has every right to demand such a solution. We each must be more aware of the strength of the claims of all three groups, because none of us have been taught about the basis for the claims of the others. So let us look briefly at the case each community can make for access to (and a share in the control of) the Holy Places that are inextricably inter-linked in the Old City of Jerusalem so that no clever "cutting of the cake" could separate jurisdictions in a manner satisfactory to the three communities. The City must be one and has to be shared.

Special Importance

Take first the Jewish claims, since they come first in time. All three "Peoples of the Book" share the tradition of Abraham but certainly, for the Jews, special importance must be given to their links with the City of David and of Solomon, the City of the two Temples (Solomon's and Zorobabel's), where the Ark of the Covenant of Moses, the two tablets of the Law, were kept in the Tabernacle on the Rock. Traditionally this was the same Rock on the summit of Mount Moriah where Abraham was prepared to sacrifice Isaac, and where Jacob later rested his head to dream that a ladder was set up to heaven, with angels ascending and descending. In other words, the Rock serves as an *axis mundi*, the center of the Jewish psyche, their link as a people between God and man—the door or threshold to a higher world, as interpreted by the Kabbalists. So it is easy to understand why, for thousands of years, Jews have faced Jerusalem to say their prayers. It is their spiritual center.

For the Christians, no less than for the Jews, Jerusalem is the Holy City where Christ was crucified, was buried, rose from the Sepulchre, and ascended to heaven. As Mircea Eliade records the Christian tradition of Golgotha (the "place of the skull"), it "was situated at the center of the world, since it was the summit of the cosmic mountain and at the same time the place where Adam had been created and buried. Thus the blood of the Saviour falls upon Adam's skull, buried precisely at the foot of the Cross, and redeems him."

If Christians orient their churches to the Eastern sunrise (i.e., the East), they are merely following the traditional orientation of the Temple of the Jews in Jerusalem, which probably faced East too.

St Bernard's call "to Jerusalem" ignited the crusading spirit of Christendom to not only capture (or liberate) the Holy Places but also build the City of God on Earth—again a symbol of communication with the "Presence of the Lord," which the Jews had felt in themselves and filling their temple, and which they called the holy *Shekkina,* "The Glory of the Eternal," whereas the Moslems called it *Sakina* in Arabic. The Presence was, and is, the same.

Co-Inheritors

For the Moslems; as co-inheritors of the Abrahamic tradition—the tradition of Jacob and the Prophets (among whom they include Jesus)—Jerusalem has a religious importance second only to Mecca and Medina. The Prophet of Islam describes in moving terms (Surat 17 of the Quran) the Night Journey (*Lailat al-Mi'rāj*), the supreme religious experience of his life—when he rode in a dream on his winged horse one night from Mecca to Jerusalem and ascended from the Rock through the seven heavens to the Presence of God, to the Throne, returning to awaken in Mecca as a new man who had seen God and received a revelation for mankind. As Avicenna's famous Commentary on the "Night Journey" points out, the Rock from which the Prophet rose up to the Throne of God is the same as the Rock on which Abraham prepared his sacrifice, Jacob dreamt of the ladder raised to God, and the Temple of the Jews built here. It is today the site of the octagonal Dome of the Rock, one of the earliest as well as finest monuments of Islam, and (like Mecca) a traditional place of pilgrimage for all Moslems.

If I evoke these three great traditions converging on the Holy City, it is to affirm that all three communities have the right to be in Jerusalem. It is their city to be shared and cherished in common, not placed under the exclusive political sovereignty of any one of them. As long as the present situation lasts, it is my conviction that there will be no secure peace. And I see no way out but for the three religious communities together to internationalize the City; or rather to denationalize it by redrawing the national boundaries around it, leaving it free at the center to run itself, with unlimited access from both sides, east and west, provided only that those who come into the city from outside return the way they entered.

To believe in the possibility of a religious solution for Jerusalem, one must be convinced that it could be made to work: that the three religious communities could actually reach an agreement on who should represent them and how their authority would be administered. The concept of a Holy City is all very well; but the garbage—and the taxes—must still be collected, and law and order be maintained, in what will continue to be an explosive situation. Could it be done without leaning on the military police and administrative resources of either of its neighbours, Israel and Jordan?

For both Christians and Moslems, it would certainly be difficult to resolve the many conflicting interests in deciding who should represent them, since neither community has a recognized central authority. As far as Christianity is concerned, neither the Vatican nor the World Council of Churches makes such a claim; and if they could jointly propose a Christian council for Jerusalem it would be challenged by the Orthodox and Armenian Patriarchs who share with the Vatican traditional responsibility for the Holy Sepulchre.

So, too, for Islam. The King of Saudi Arabia is the custodian of the chief Holy Places, Mecca and Medina; but the Hashemite King of Jordan might be held to have a prior claim to authority in respect of the Moslem shrines of Jerusalem, especially those in the Old City (the Dome of the Rock and the Al-Aqsa mosque). If the Moslems could accept King Hussein's religious custodianship of the Moslem Holy Places of Jerusalem (without implying Jordanian political sovereignty), he would be a logical chairman of the Moslem component of the Holy City.

Once the Jews and the Moslems had been able to nominate their respective representatives to such a Council, the pressures on the various Christian churches to close ranks would become well-nigh irresistible. Christian disunity could not, in the final analysis, be allowed to block a religious solution once such a solution was perceived as attainable. It is only because we Christians can today convince ourselves that it is impractical—or that the squeeze on us is not yet intolerable—that we excuse ourselves from making any effort to overcome the obstacles. So long as the rights of any of the three communities are limited in practice, the light of our Holy City—and our shared tradition—is diminished. Do we not care?

But then, assuming that each of the three communities had been able to nominate its representatives to a Holy City Council, could such a religious Council actually govern the city? I have no competence to draw up a blueprint for such a city government, but I do have one suggestion as to how it might operate. If it is possible for Greeks, Russians, Serbs, and Bulgarians to run Mount Athos as a complex monastic community, it is only one more step to find ways of administering Jerusalem. Perhaps, as at Mount Athos, each of the main communities should hold in its possession a one-third segment of the official seal of government, which must be complete to validate any decision of the proposed High Council. In other words, without the concurrence of each community in Jerusalem, decisions "by majority" would mean nothing. Faced with either stalemate or co-operation, there would have to be co-operation.

Limited Area

Nevertheless, the Holy City proposal should not be too ambitious. If the entire city of Jerusalem were to be brought under a religious regime, it might indeed prove impossible to achieve a workable administration. The Holy City idea would, I think, have a much better chance of success if the map of the portion to be denationalized were drawn in a restrictive way, keeping only to the essential Holy Places on and around Temple Mount (Mount Moriah). The Holy City Council might have a consultative and co-coordinating role in regard to the other holy places scattered around Israel and the West Bank, but by keeping the geographical limits of the Holy City as small as possible it would be not only much simpler to administer but probably easier to negotiate, since it would take only a minimum bite out of the existing sovereignties. Loading too much on the scheme would probably sink the boat.

Another advantage of circumscribing the Holy City, keeping mainly to the Holy Places on Temple Mount, is that under a religious High Council administration Jews might be able to pray on the Mount as well as Moslems, and all Moslems would feel free to go. At present Jews are restricted by the Israeli government administration to worshipping at the Wailing Wall and are not allowed on the top of Temple Mount, while Moslems from most of the Arab world refuse to go there so long as it is under Israeli control. Depoliticize the area and both those religious communities would benefit.

In any case, what is needed at this time is not so much a detailed blueprint for a Holy City administration as the willingness to seek such a solution and to make it work, in the conviction that it is the only real alternative to having no solution at all. Of course Jerusalem can only be solved as part of a general settlement of the Arab-Israel conflict, not in isolation. But what is of greater relevance is that there can be no such settlement without solving the Jerusalem question.

If a religious regime can be created, then, and only then, can Jerusalem once again represent for all three Peoples of the Book their aspiration to create, on this Rock of Ages linking them with God, a city that, in the words of a contemporary Jewish writer (Amos Oz), will truly be the Jerusalem of absolute love. It is a curious twist of history that this ideal solution is now clearly becoming the only one that is practical. Jerusalem can at least become a City of Peace provided it is made, in modern fact, what it has always been in ancient myth—the Holy City.

CHAPTER 18

WHAT DOES GREAT NATURE
REQUIRE OF US?

This is my talk at the All and Everything *Conference in Toronto on April 25, 2009. It was published in the Conference Proceedings, 2009.*

For the past two days we have come together to deepen our understanding of the great teaching Gurdjieff left for contemporary humanity in *All and Everything*. Thank you for deciding to meet in Toronto. Since I live here, that makes it easy for me for the first time to join you, instead of relying, as I have in the past, on reports from others. I am glad to be with you and look forward to getting to know as many of you as possible in so short a time.

The more challenging the conditions we face in life, the more, I find, we need to pay attention to Gurdjieff's seminal teaching and do our best not just to study it intellectually but to practice it together as best we can from moment to moment. After all, we keep saying that this is a "work in life," and in life we all confront the same distractions and temptations, whether or not we are connected with the one of the Gurdjieff Foundations.

In our outer lives, global warming is without doubt the most challenging issue of the 21st century. It may indeed be a survival issue, not only for animals and birds, but also for us. Some of the world's top scientists have begun to question whether humanity can survive this century. Lord Martin Rees, the President of the Royal Society, thinks that the odds are no better than 50/50. Stephen Hawkins seems to have given up on planet Earth and places his hopes on getting human DNA to Mars to start over. What a counsel of despair! Fortunately, most of the scientific experts on climate change still disagree with him, but all agree that the time for effective action is running out.

And what about our inner life? If human behaviour is now accepted as responsible for a very significant part of the problem, how can we change what Gurdjieff calls our "abnormal behaviour?" Can we reread *Beelzebub's Tales* today looking for clues to a deeper understanding of Gurdjieff's call to awaken, so that "the sacred-conscience still surviving in (our) subconsciousness might gradually pass into the functioning of (our) ordinary consciousness?" Ashiata Shiemash showed that it is possible to change human behaviour in this way. "Only he will be called and will become a son of God who acquires in himself Conscience." Now more than ever, we need to hear this call and to adapt our lifestyles and our technologies so that we can serve as stewards of Nature, instead of serving the greedy growth of consumerism and corporation profits that have been steering our economy over the cliff.

Already in the first chapter, "The Arousing of Thought," Gurdjieff refers to human beings, including himself, "as biped destroyers of Nature's good." Only on our peculiar planet, he says, do three-brained beings destroy each other and cause grave problems for Nature. That abnormal behaviour must change. In the distant past, he warns us, Nature has shown that it can take drastic countermeasures when necessary to prevent such abnormalities from impinging on the common cosmic harmony.

> When later … they began to exist … unbecomingly for three-brained beings, and … they had … ceased to emanate the vibrations required by Nature … then Nature … was compelled … to actualize the presences of these three-brained beings according to the principle Itoklanoz, that is to actualize them … the same way … She actualizes one brained and two brained beings in order that the equilibrium of vibrations required according to quality and quantity should be attained.

What a fate for three-brained beings to be reduced to functioning like one-brained or two brained beings!

At the same time, he tells us that unless we begin to live our lives consciously, not automatically, we cannot hope to experience "impulses of self-satisfaction and self-cognizance in correctly and honourably fulfilling (our) duty to Great Nature." But instead of behaving normally, as "beings having in their presences every possibility for becoming particles of a part of

Divinity," we turn ourselves into automatons, "merely into what is called 'living flesh.'" Remember Mullah Nassr Eddin's cautionary injunction: "Better pull-ten-hairs-a-day-out-of-your-mother's-head-than-not-help-Nature."

So what is our duty—both inner and outer—to Great Nature today? What does Great Nature now require of us?

Though it was written many years before climate change became a problem, numerous examples are given throughout *Beelzebub's Tales* of our unconscious human behaviour, which is causing Nature to "huff and puff" in her attempts to redress the damage we humans are causing in our sleepy unawareness. Little do we realize, for example, that in making use of great quantities of electricity for our egoistic satisfactions we are destroying two of the three components of one of the most basic substances in the universe, "the Omnipresent Okidanokh," which some elders in The Work have equated with Consciousness.

It has become indispensable for Nature that humanity stops behaving in ways that, in the next few generations, will, if we do not change, make Earth unfit for most species of animals, including ourselves. If we cannot awaken ourselves from our self-centered dreams, Nature will have to wake us up with shocks of increasing severity—hurricanes, Earthquakes, plagues, forest fires, floods, droughts, and many other signs of the stresses to which unbecoming human behaviour is subjecting planet Earth—or even by eliminating our species, if we fail to understand our duty toward Nature. The awakening of a critical number of human beings thus becomes a human and even a cosmic imperative, for, according to Beelzebub, our aberrant behaviour is affecting the normal evolution of three-centered beings, even on other planets of our solar system, and causing what he refers to as a "cosmic stink."

In my book *Asking for the Earth: Waking Up to the Spiritual/Ecological Crisis* I shared some of my experiences with Mme. de Salzmann in New York and Paris in the Gurdjieff Work and with some of the great teachers of the last century—teachers like J. Krishnamurti, Dr. Javad Nurbakhsh, Thomas Merton, and the Dalai Lama in India and Iran. In that book I was warning, before it was fashionable to be "green," that we were facing a dangerous ecological crisis that could only be remedied by an inner transformation.

The main premise of my latest book, *The Little Green Book of Awakening*, is that Nature is telling us in no uncertain terms that we must wake up.

Gurdjieff said it years ago, and now the situation is critical. In *The Little Green Book* you will see that the latest findings of our best scientists reinforce Gurdjieff's statement, which I quoted earlier. We humans have truly become "biped destroyers of Nature's good." If global warming is not to become catastrophic, Nature clearly requires that we change our energy technologies, our environmental legislation, and much of our wasteful way of living. But above all, I believe, Nature requires that we awaken: we change ourselves consciously and become, as Gandhi put it, the change we wish to see in the world.

To change ourselves, we need a new morality, an objective morality. In one of his lectures at Fontainbleau in 1922, Gurdjieff told his pupils that almost everyone lives with a kind of automatic morality established in him by his culture, his parents, education, and so on. He went on to explain that it is possible to have a quite different kind of morality. By opening up the possibility of a morality that is not automatic and not based on associations, he put this requirement to change ourselves in an even larger context. Let me quote from this little known lecture:

> The objective feeling of morality is connected with certain general, orderly and immutable moral laws, established over the centuries, and in accordance, both chemically and physically, with human circumstances and nature, established objectively for all and *connected with nature, or, as is said, with God.* [My italics.]
>
> The subjective feeling of morality is when a man ... forms a personal conception of morality on the basis of which he then lives. Both the first and the second feelings of morality are not only absent in people but they even have no idea of them.
>
> What we say about morality relates to everything.

As reported by Ouspensky in *In Search of the Miraculous*, Gurdjieff tells us that Nature gives us life and motion—everything. "The flow of impressions from outside is like a driving belt communicating motion to us. The principal motor for us is nature, the surrounding world. Nature transmits to us through

our impressions the energy by which we live and move and have our being."
So how can we imagine that we are here to dominate Nature, not serve her?

Gurdjieff tells us, at the beginning of the First Series, that he is writing *All and Everything* with the aim of solving "three cardinal problems":

> FIRST SERIES: To destroy mercilessly, without any compromises whatsoever, in the mentation and feelings of the reader, the beliefs and views, by centuries rooted in him, about everything existing in the world.

> SECOND SERIES: To acquaint the reader with the material required for a new creation and to prove the soundness and good quality of it.

> THIRD SERIES: To assist the arising, in the mentation and in the feelings of the reader, of a veritable, non-fantastic representation not of the illusory world which he now perceives, but of the world existing in reality.

In other words, his aim is to make a clean sweep of the old certainties in order for the new to penetrate the armour of our inherited and acquired misconceptions and transform us, so that, instead of dreaming, we may become aware "of the world existing in reality," or Nature. What better occasion for such a huge inner shift of consciousness than a time of unprecedented outer changes fast eroding our faith in the old and opening our hearts towards the new, the unknown, both inner and outer? It is a package deal: for there to be a new creation, a new Heaven and a new Earth, there must be a new humanity, or at least a critical mass of humanity, able to serve as a channel for Heaven and Earth to be related, for God's will (or Nature's will) to be done on Earth. Without this vital connection, Mme. de Salzmann warned us many times, "The Earth will fall down"—that is, the Earth will no longer be ecologically sustainable. Two hundred conscious people, Gurdjieff told Ouspensky, could, if they found it necessary, change the world. This is the time for that great evolutionary leap, of which all the traditions have spoken and for which, I believe, Gurdjieff was the herald.

Whenever two or three are gathered together with that intention to change, as we are now, then what we call in the Work "special conditions" may be temporarily created. Special conditions can be said to exist, I suggest, whenever two or three are gathered together to search sincerely for a more direct contact with the energy of presence or life that can animate us, at least at moments, when we are inwardly acknowledging our lack of presence, our need for wholeness, and the insufficiency of our direct experience of "the world existing in Reality." At such moments, a strong wish for being can suddenly surprise us, together with an unflagging awareness of the inevitability of our own death.

So here we are, confronting the fact that our current abnormal human behaviour is creating ecological havoc and that if we do not change, and change quickly, if we do not indeed awaken, then our grandchildren may see the end of the human experiment on this planet. Here we are, realizing that that both the external and the internal changes that are needed are already known and available, so how can we not feel a powerful instinctive awakening response? This catastrophe need not and must not happen. It will not be our inheritance to our children. It would be too stupid for our civilization to be the first to disappear while knowing in advance exactly what we needed to do and to be, and having at hand all the means for making the necessary changes in how we think, and feel and act!

Can we hear again, and in a new way, what Beelzebub says at the end of the *Tales*, when asked a similar question about what can save us by his grandson, Hassein?

> The sole means now for the saving of the beings of the planet Earth would be to implant again into their presences a new organ like Kundabuffer, but this time of such properties that every one of these unfortunates during the process of existence should constantly sense and be cognizant of the inevitability of his own death as well as of the death of everyone upon whom his eyes or attention rests.
>
> Only such a sensation and such a cognizance can now destroy the egoism completely crystallized in them that

has swallowed up the whole of their Essence and also that tendency to hate others which flows from it the tendency, namely, which engenders all those mutual relationships existing there, which serve as the chief cause of all their abnormalities, unbecoming to three-brained beings and maleficent for them themselves and for the whole of the Universe.

CHAPTER 19

THE AWAKENING OF CONSCIOUSNESS NOW

Talk on October 29, 1999, to a Gurdjieff group on the occasion of the 50th anniversary of his death.

When I was growing up in the twenties and thirties, when Gurdjieff was writing *All and Everything*, the spiritual landscape in the West was sadly but aptly described by T.S. Eliot as a "wasteland." For most of us in that culture, God was "dead" even before Nietzsche proclaimed the demise, killed off by a reductionist scientific rationalism that thought all and everything could be explained without God. So the well of the meaning of human life was drying up. Space and time had lost their third dimension. We were spiritually bankrupt, and few noticed or cared. The land was not only waste; it was flat. There was no "higher," and the "eternal" had no root in our experience.

It has taken some of us 50 years to wake up to our common dilemma, and to see that what we most need is to reconnect with that which alone can give meaning to our lives. As E.M. Forester had said: "Only connect!" It is easily said. But how? With what? For that, we needed real teachers and teachings.

And we got real teachers and teachings in abundance. Out of our deep unconscious unease, our incipient sense of need, the teachers appeared to complete the process of conscious awakening. There has never been a time when so many great souls appeared and authentic esoteric practices became so generally available. The brutal diaspora of the Tibetans has been only the most dramatic wave in the dissemination of the seeds of real being. And now the spreading is amplified by the electronic revolution of the Internet, for worse or for better. The spiritualization of the global village has begun. Suddenly, there are "rays to the sun" everywhere. One of these rays—the one that has meant the most to me—is the "Work," or teaching of Gurdjieff, as transmitted to me by Mme. Jeanne de Salzmann.

So, I must bear witness to what I have received from my teachers, even though the fruit of their sowing is far from ripe. I can only tell you how I see it now. (Do not take it as gospel. You have been warned.)

In the 20th century, to reconnect humanity with its Source, Gurdjieff could not use the religious language of earlier times. If "God" is dead, the excessive cult of individuality in the West is still very much alive and could be used to open a channel of returning energy to our unknown Source. If we are not any longer interested in God, then let us begin with what I *am* interested in: myself, I. For I may doubt everything else, but I cannot, in my direct experience, doubt my own existence. I know that I AM. And through that experience let me be brought to recognize the One whom Gurdjieff dared to call "our All-loving Common Father Endlessness." For when I am related with that Light, my little light can be a candle in the world. Only then can I "do."

Yes, there is some risk in this "I AM" approach. I am already too habituated to taking everything egoistically. My wounded vanity does not readily forgive. My pretension to understand knows no limits. I can too easily assume that this "I AM" of Gurdjieff's (or of the Bible) is all about *me* and my personal development. It may take years of inner work to come to the realization that this self-centered attitude of mine is the greatest barrier between me and the impersonal highest in me, which he calls "I." And many more years to see that what I am *when I am* is not different from what you are *when you are.* It is not different from the Highest Presence; it is a drop of the same water as the Ocean. For that cosmic Ocean is indeed omnipresent, as is consciousness. Gurdjieff tells us in his Third Series that the difference between how I am when I am and God is "only one of scale"—and, of course, the scale is inconceivably vast. But the vibration that is the real I in me resonates with the same divine seed of life in you and (if I let it) with the Oceanic Consciousness. When, for a moment, I am truly present, I AM rings true on all levels. Then my physical body is the vehicle for a sensation of love that is not of this world, not of this planet. In *this* moment, I am present, no longer bound to the time of change and successiveness, from past to future. Here and now, I can receive a momentary taste of what always and everywhere IS—the changeless, the eternal I AM.

How ungrateful of me—me again!—to complain that such moments do not last! Perhaps, if humanity is both lucky and diligent, by the beginning of the next millennium human consciousness will have evolved a stage or two towards the state that a few pioneer heralds in our time have shown us is possible, and indeed our birthright. We are here for that evolution. How else could Heaven and Earth be connected? Heaven/man—woman/Earth (as Taoist wisdom has been telling us for millennia) is the linkage. Gurdjieff calls it *Theomertmalogos*, conveying in its etymology the same idea. Without some such permeable membrane, how could life survive entropy and circulate both ways, through involution and evolution, in the cosmos and in us? Hermes Trismegistus put it succinctly: "As above, so below." Today, we can hear that; for though our cultural landscape may still be largely a wasteland, it is certainly no longer flat. We are beginning to "get it." As Dr. David Suzuki recently put it, humanity is now somewhere between naked ape and super-species. We are on the verge of seeing that the threat of ecological doom that we face in this millennium could, if we receive it as a wakeup call, be the threshold of a truly great spiritual renaissance. Because I AM, there is an "above" and a "below" in me. And in that immensity, my ego "I" is ... nothing. Yet "I AM;" and something in me *can*.

D.H. Lawrence felt this, in terms appropriate for the new millennium, when he wrote "The Song of a Man Who Has Come Through":

> Not I, not I, but the wind that blows through me!
> A fine wind is blowing the new direction of Time.
> If only I let it bear me, carry me, if only it carry me!

Fifty years after your death, I thank you, Mr. Gurdjieff, "herald of the coming good," and all your helpers! May your fine wind carry humanity to our intended destination! But we also have our work to do: we must each, with our best attention, trim our own sails.

CHAPTER 20

IMPLEMENTING THE NEW
HEALTH CARE PARADIGM: OUR OPTIONS

*Since Prime Minister Nehru was kind enough to send his Ayurvedic phys-
ician to cure my amoebic dysentery while I was in Sri Lanka, I have had
great respect for traditional therapies, as well as for modern Western medicine. In India I followed Tibetan medicine and later in New York helped to
establish the Chagpori Foundation with Allen Ginsberg, Joan Halifax, Dr.
Philip Weber, and Shakya Dorje to support Dr. Trogawa Rinpoche in his
efforts to spread it in North America. In 2002 I supported Greg and Kate
Sorbara's successful efforts to get Traditional Chinese Medicine regulated
and accepted as part of the Ontario Health Care system. In 1985 I was
asked to speak at a Conference on Health Care at Wilfred Laurier University in Waterloo, Ontario. This is my talk.*

In our culture today, communicating seems to be essentially an electronic
zapping operation. Thus, for both Prime Minister Mulroney and President
Reagan, politics has become the art of the one-liner. Even the day's news has
to be chopped or crushed into crumbs almost as short as the typical 30 second
spot commercial. I am glad that at this Conference in a University setting we
are not bound to trivialize our theme by time constraints that are quite that
rigorous. As I am sure you will all agree, we are faced with choices now that
will vitally affect health care in Canada well into the next century. How we
Canadians decide on our present options will be reflected in the quality of life
of our grandchildren. So it is important to look carefully together before we
leap into the future of our country s health care. It seems to me that we are
at one of those rare thresholds which in retrospect (but seldom at the time)
can be seen to have been the cultural watersheds that can truly be called the
beginning of a whole new way of looking at health and wellness, freed of the
shackles of past conditioning; in short, a new paradigm.

In the largest sense, these rare historical moments occur when "a new Heaven and a new Earth" become perceptible to a small but critical mass of a society. Today we call it a new consciousness. Of those who share in the experience, many can say with Wordsworth "Bliss was it in that dawn to be alive." What I propose we should examine together is whether we can envision a new dawn in health care in Canada arising out of the darkness and confusion and hostility that is all too visible in the health care scene today. One thing is clear: unless we can see what could be, where we would like to go, and the difficulties of getting there, we are not going to reach our new dawn. But if we SEE, and therefore WISH, we CAN. That is my one-liner.

Since I have served Canada more of my professional life in South Asia and West Asia than I have at home, and since my Foundation work in my retirement has kept me mainly in Europe and the United Sates, I must confess that I had at first decided to decline Dr. Maurice Kelly's invitation to speak to you this evening. I do not know nearly enough about what is going on in Canada. But he persuaded me that I could bring an international perspective to your Conference that might be valuable, so that we could look at our options in the light of what is happening in other countries who are also in transition and also face a confusing array of choices. The bottom line, it seems to me, for health care in Canada to have a healthy future, is that we have got to find, through a new paradigm, new roles for a whole range of "healing professions," if high tech medical costs are not to bankrupt our society. The main difficulty today is that we are moving into an increasingly sharp and bitter confrontation between two sides, medical and non-medical, that have no common language to understand each other, and often very little wish to do so. As the success of modern medicine shifts the focus from the control of pathological disease to the problems of keeping people well for daily living in a society of intense stress, it is no longer enough for the doctors, who have no time for all the patients who simply "do not feel well," to dismiss all their alternatives as "quackery," ripping off a public who need protection enforced by legislation. If some degree of cooperation and understanding cannot be worked out between the physicians and the other professionals, we face a raw power struggle in the body politic for control and money. And that struggle could be dangerous for our health, as well as for our economy.

It would, of course, be an oversimplification to present the choices as if it were a matter of following a British/Dutch/Swedish pattern of peaceful cooperation, rather than American pattern of confrontation. There are contradictory trends within each national situation. These are issues being debated today in each country's Medical Association and Ministry of Health. It is not yet sure in any of the countries I have mentioned whether the outcome will be determined in peace or by war. But in the search for peaceful and balanced solutions, I think some countries are ahead of others, and we need not be unduly influenced by what happens in the United States just because they are closer to us and the cultural and political influences are stronger. Let us look around carefully before we opt for what seems today to be the rather heavy-handed and even repressive course our American friends are collectively choosing. We can find a Canadian way that is more like us. Indeed I think the chances of doing so here are quite promising, and it is through Conferences like this one that we may be able to develop the sophistication and awareness in the public that could make a more enlightened solution politically possible.

There is nothing either mysterious or uniquely Canadian about the nature of the problem. Most Western countries in the past thirty years have decided in one way or another to extend the benefits of health care services to their entire population, including those who could not previously afford it. In the process, costs have escalated beyond anyone's expectations without much improvement in the level of wellness of the population as a whole. TB, polio, and smallpox are success stories, but we do not seem to be much further ahead with cancer, and stress related illnesses of mind and body may actually be a good deal worse. Indeed, it may be totally unfair to blame either the doctor or the system for what can, in a broader sense, be seen as a sick culture, producing an astonishing number of premature babies who later come up with nuclear destruction nightmares as children and grow into frightened and alienated adults. To look after them costs about as much as most countries spend on national defence, and may soon cost more, when we have to care for a rapidly aging population, with (especially in the United States) the added cost of an epidemic of malpractice suits. No wonder that in many countries, including France and the United States, hospital and medical insurance schemes are going broke. There *has* to be a better way.

On the horizon, as yet no bigger than a man's hand, I think there is a better way that we can see beginning in all the countries I have mentioned, but especially in the United Kingdom and the Netherlands. Let us look at some examples of what has been happening.

In England, the Threshold Foundation (of which I was the Founder and President) published the first scientific study of the so called alternative therapies. They are not, of course, alternatives in the sense of therapies to use "instead of" medicine, but in the sense of "as well as" medicine. Another term the medical profession objected to in England was "natural therapies"—as if the doctors were practicing unnatural medicine. That is a moot point, but in deference to the doctors, Threshold called its study "A Survey of Complementary Medicine in the United Kingdom." It was carried out by two objective scientists, Stephen Fulder and Robin Munro, who spent two years of research finding out for the first time what was really happening in this field. The results were a surprise to the British Ministry of Health and to the British Medical Association—and to the public at large who suddenly became very interested. Despite the fact that people could get the help of doctors free under National Health, and had to pay for other, complementary therapists, these other therapists were growing in popularity six times faster than the doctors, and so were the numbers of their patients. The growth rate was highest among acupuncturists and homeopaths. Collectively, the alternative therapists were only 14% of the number of doctors, but the gap was obviously closing faster than anyone had realized. Today it is probably about 1:5. And another surprise is that it is the upper end of the social-economic spectrum that goes to the other therapists, the more affluent and better educated. The Queen herself has a homeopathic physician, who happens also to be an acupuncturist. It is the poor who have to forego alternative therapists because they cannot afford such treatment—a complete reversal of the old situation.

As the Threshold survey notes, it is English Common Law that gives the practitioner of complementary medicine his or her freedom to heal without much interference from government. Under the Napoleonic Code legal tradition on the Continent, restrictions are much more often the rule. Yet even there exceptions occur. In the Netherlands, for example, in response to clear surveys of public opinion showing that 75% of the voters wanted freedom to choose, Parliament set up a Commission on Alternative Medicine to foster research, to set standards for the various alternative therapies, to create a data center (like the one in the UK that has sprung from the Threshold Survey), and to consider how payments for alternative therapies could be made under the National Health scheme. I am not sure how far this Commission has gone in the past two years but probably the Netherlands leads in Europe in the registration of complementary therapies and bringing them in to the system in an orderly and regulated way—with the grudging agreement of the medical establishment, and rather loosely under their supervision, but largely self-regulating within each discipline. So in that context, at least, it looks as if a political decision has been taken by the people and all the healing professions are learning to live with it, and with each other. That is an important first.

In the United States, as I am sure you are as aware as I am, the situation is very different. Once the American Medical Association had conceded that the osteopaths should get registration and recognition, it was only a matter of time before the chiropractors achieved the same. They did so by dint of suing the AMA. This confrontational path will probably soon be taken by others who want recognition, with acupuncturists and naturopaths at the top of the list. Despite legal impediments and harassment, complementary medicine is booming in the U.S.A. as in no other country. Threatened by what they see as a rising wave of quackery exploiting the credulous with promises of "natural" cures for everything, the AMA seems to have decided to take the offensive. In New Jersey where I live, there are currently moves to make it illegal to have you baby at home.

With the American Cancer Society and the American Arthritis Foundation, the AMA have got Representative Claude Pepper (Congress' leading senior citizen advocate) to put forward a bill which if implemented may force many alternative practitioners underground. In the latest issue of *Consumer Reports* U.S. Congressman, Pepper says elderly Americans are being "ripped off" to the tune of nearly 10 billion yearly by what he calls "unscrupulous health practitioners and unlicensed charlatans dispensing unapproved medical treatments and outright quackery." We all know horror stories—on both sides. There was the Mongolian masseur, for example, who mesmerized a young lady with obvious breast cancer into not consulting a doctor until it was too late. But then, as the *Utne Reader* points out, no less an authority than the U.S. Congress Office of Technology Assessment reports that surgery for artery disease, chemotherapy for lung cancer, electronic fetal monitoring, and hysterectomy, among others, are far less warranted or effective than the frequency of their use would indicate. So there are problems not only with the cost but with the practice of modern medicine in the United States that have led many people to look to healers who have more time for them and who seem to care the way doctors of my father's generation more commonly did. Here again, I have to say that most doctors in my opinion still care, but the pressures of over work are literally killing. Doctors as a group are among the least healthy professions. Surely, therefore, ways can be found to lighten their load with their cooperation rather than over their dead bodies.

Nor should it be supposed that the battle lines in the U.S.A. are drawn strictly on the basis of professional loyalty. Some of the most outspoken critics of the inhuman mechanistic high tech and high cost of modern medicine are, of course, doctors in every country. Some have joined the holistic medical movement but most have sought to reform medicine from within. Listen to this from the *New England Journal of Medicine* of May 19, 1983:

> A new era is beginning wherein neither the prevention of death from epidemics nor the correction of physiologically measurable abnormalities will be the principal medical challenge. The central objective in the coming era will be the maintenance of improvement of individual patient functioning in the patient's normal environment while he or she performs usual activities. The emphasis on patient functioning is partly founded on probing inquiries that ask whether the high cost of health care is yielding a proportional benefit in health. Public skepticism of the highly technical nature of medical practice and the emotional distance that has grown between the patient and the doctor as the technology has become more powerful may also contribute to a new focus on functional objectives and the concept of the quality of life.

To reform and rehumanize medicine from within is not the whole story, if the paradigm of health remains unchanged, and if medicine is just what doctor's do to you in hospitals, not what better health practices you can learn to heal yourself, it seems to me that we are not going to be able to build a new consensus on an old paradigm—new bottles are needed for new wine. Doctors will undoubtedly have a major part in the putting together of this new paradigm, if they want to do that; but if they resist all attempts to include the health counsellors and Other practitioners to supplement their own services, the revolt of the public wanting choices will explode the system. Before that happens, it would surely be wiser to make the enormous effort needed on both sides to develop dialogue and a common language. When doctors in Canada begin to see how other therapists could help their patients for whom no life threatening disease has been determined, a referral to another kind of practitioner might sit better with the patient than being told he or she would "just have to learn to live with it." Indeed, in the U.K., as the Threshold Survey discovered, almost a third of the patients of non-medical therapists got there by being referred quietly by physicians who did not know what else to do with them. Unless something like that becomes far more common in Canada than it is today, it looks to me as if the financial underpinnings of our health care system are likely to fall apart within a generation.

In my judgment it is already too late in the United States for the AMA to go for total control. The people will resist, perhaps unsuccessfully at first, but in the long run they will get what they want—and they want choices. They want to take a more active role in looking after themselves, not as mere objects in some vast computerized hospital. They want the knowledge and education in nutrition and basic health to be able to do this. They have scant respect for the knowledge most doctors have of what they should eat—and less for most hospital meals. If they have back pain, as many do, they do not accept to be told to take pain relievers or go for surgery. They will not accept for much longer the right of doctors to dispense through pharmacists whatever health food item becomes a hot seller in the health food stores, unless there are proven dangers.

I do not know if this is approximately the situation in Canada at present, but if it is something like that, then I suggest the wisest way to edge ourselves into the new era would be to work towards a consensus in gatherings such as this, and support including physicians and complementary practitioners on the same team because they really need each other, because doctors are going crazy trying to look after those who do not feel well but have no identifiable pathological disease, such as doctors have been expensively trained to treat. For all the current talk about preventive medicine, there are many health problems doctors are less qualified to treat, including (as we have said) diet and nutrition, and cleaning up the environment. Some doctors are already helpfully distinguishing between the very different tasks of attending to pathological diseases, and counselling people on how to tune up better, how to live with less stress, how to meditate or do yoga or run or ski—all functions that may be healing but no one would ascribe to doctors. Yet these are among the ways of keeping people from cluttering up the waiting rooms of overburdened doctors. Instead of trying to get cayenne pepper capsules and herbs out of health food stores and into drug stores that do not want them, the medical doctors might have fewer ulcers if they began seriously to explore (as in the UK) how other healers could work with them in a better disciplined way, each group dealing with its own "quacks," instead of looking to doctors as the policeman of everything that might make you ill.

Why are there today in Canada so few multi-disciplinary clinics in which physicians are working with other therapists as a team, deciding together, in consultation with the patient, which combination of treatments make the most sense in a particular case? The new paradigm seeks larger freedoms, not smaller tighter controls that seem more loaded towards protecting the chemical industry than the public. We do not want to begin talking about the medical-chemical complex, though that sort of alliance seems to be operative in the lobbying in Washington. I hope we are different. Again, we can be if we want to be. We and nobody else can make our own future. When we see this as a real option, we are already implementing the new paradigm.

Finally, let me make one practical proposal that will probably be almost universally resisted. Those who search for a cooperative relationship between all who are genuinely concerned with finding our way through today's crisis in health care management need to find a common language. Otherwise there can be no understanding, no mutual respect and no trust—in short, no relationship. So could the government, or private Foundations with an interest in this question, fund research in this field? Do we really know what is going on in our own country? Do we need a scientific survey, including all points of view but not dominated by any one of them? Do we need funding for research in interdisciplinary communications? Even with funding, it is not going to be easy for the deaf to hear each other in the present emotionally charged atmosphere, but in the process of trying we may find that we open our old understandings in ways that are both personally and culturally liberating. That is what a new paradigm is all about. And I believe Canada has as good a chance as any country in the world to pioneer this major breakthrough towards a sane future, preserving the best of both the old and the new, the traditional and the scientific, in a pragmatic blending of common sense and vision that I like to think is typically Canadian.

CHAPTER 21

SPACE OPTIONS

In the wake of 9/11/01, I became the Chair of an NGO Coalition in Canada called "NO WEAPONS IN SPACE" (NOWIS). We think that we helped to keep Canada out of the Iraq war. Working with Dr. Carol Rosin, president of The Institute for Co-operation in Space (ICIS), a non-profit educational foundation, and Alfred Lambremont Webre, an ICIS international director, we published this plea in the Toronto Star on April 30, 2002.

Canada Could Prevent Weaponization of Space

On June 13, 2002, the Anti-Ballistic Missile (ABM) Treaty will expire following its unilateral termination by the Bush administration, leaving an international legal void that will allow the weaponization of space.

The termination of the ABM Treaty will permit research, development, testing, manufacturing, production and deployment of space-based weapons, and space-based components of the U.S. National Missile Defence System to go forward, instigating a dangerous, costly, and destabilizing arms race in space, impacting all of us.

Russian Minister of Defence Sergei Ivanov has already suggested that if the U.S. proceeds, Russia could deploy its own response to the U.S. space-based weapons system. The stated objectives of the United States Space Command in "Vision For 2020" are to seize the strategic high ground of space to "dominate and control."

There is a rapidly growing worldwide movement to stop this potentially catastrophic arms race in space. This must be stopped before it begins—this year.

As seen from space, Canada lies between Russia and the United States, and, geography aside, no country is in a better position to initiate international action. Since 1982, Canada has led the growing United Nations lobby opposing weapons in space.

Deputy Prime Minister John Manley stated on July 26, 2001: "Canada would be very happy to launch an initiative to see an international convention preventing the weaponization of space." With the strong support of U.N. Secretary-General Kofi Annan, the U.N. General Assembly last Nov. 29 voted 156–0, with the U.S. and Israel abstaining, to prevent an arms race in space.

Almost everyone wants it. On Sept. 28, 2001, Russian Foreign Minister Igor Ivanov had invited "the world community to start working out a comprehensive agreement on the non-deployment of weapons in outer space." At the U.N. Conference on Disarmament in June last year, China had taken a similar position.

But neither Russia nor China will initiate binding action while the United States is unbound. If Canada does not act now, who will? If we do, we will generate far more support and respect than we gathered over our land mines initiative. We could turn the tide that will lift all ships and preserve space as a weapons-free commons.

In the United States, polls confirm that this result is what the great majority of Americans want. When there is almost unanimous international pressure, as well as very strong domestic support, the United States will change course.

In the next few days, every head of government will be receiving, from the Institute for Cooperation in Space, a Space Preservation Treaty, which is the international companion to the legislation introduced as H.R. 3616, the Space Preservation Act of 2002, in the United States House of Representatives on Jan. 23.

The act requires the U.S. to implement an international treaty that will ban all space-based weapons and the use of weapons to destroy or damage objects in space that are in orbit to preserve the co-operative, peaceful uses of space for the benefit of all humankind.

The Space Preservation Treaty is an effective and verifiable world agreement that also will:

- Implement a ban on space-based weapons.

- Implement a ban on the use of weapons to destroy or damage objects in space that are in orbit.

- Immediately order the permanent termination of research and development, testing, manufacturing, production and deployment of all space-based weapons.

The treaty allows for space exploration, research, development, testing, manufacturing, production, and deployment of civil, commercial and defence activities in space that are not related to space-based weapons. Under the terms of the treaty, each nation having signed the treaty shall immediately work toward supporting other non-signatory nations in signing, ratifying and implementing the treaty.

Once three nations sign it and deposit it at the United Nations, Annan is required to report publicly to the U.N. General Assembly every 90 days on the progress of implementing a permanent ban on space-based weapons and on the progress of signing and ratifying the treaty.

Once 20 nations have signed and ratified the Space Preservation Treaty, it will go into force; the outer space peacekeeping agency will be funded and empowered to monitor and enforce the ban on space-based weapons.

Canada's signing of the treaty will encourage Russia to maintain Russia's and China's longstanding commitment to keep space weapons-free and to sign the treaty as well. Together, Canada, Russia, China, and many other nations already on record as supporting such a treaty, can lead the nations of the world in signing the Space Preservation Treaty.

We can and must stop the weaponization of space before it occurs. The signing of the Space Preservation Treaty will put needed pressure on the U.S.U.S. Congress and administration to sign this verifiable and enforceable agreement. This permanent ban on all space-based weapons, worldwide, will transform the war industry into a space industry that will stimulate the creation of clean and safe technologies, products, and services, including new jobs and training programs that can and will be applied directly to solving urgent human and environmental problems.

What can an ordinary citizen do? Contact Prime Minister Jean Chrétien, Deputy Prime Minister John Manley and Foreign Minister Bill Graham immediately. Tell them to lead the way, to be the first to say that they will sign the Space Preservation Treaty. This is the greatest challenge of our generation.

Which Space Vision Do You Want?

Our aims were more fully articulated in a memo that I wrote for NOWIS members in 2004. It has not previously been published. I also shared it with the Secure World Foundation in Boulder, which led to me joining, for five years, their work with Rusty Schweickart and his group of astronauts, cosmonauts, and diplomats who prepared for the United Nations a plan for rapid international action to deflect a meteorite robotically before it could crash catastrophically into the Earth. This report is to come before the UN General Assembly in 2015. For the first time ever, humans have the technology to deflect a meteorite robotically, but some in NASA and the Pentagon would prefer to shatter it into a billion fragments with a nuclear missile.

In the next two years, or about 2004, you and millions of others will have to make a momentous choice, whether you want to, or not. Because, if you think you would prefer to prevent space-based weapons getting into orbit, with the potential that later on some of them will be mini-nukes, then time is running out. One country has already decided it feels free to use them, even pre-emptively, without any international sanction. Other countries are bound to follow suit. Is that the kind of world you want to live in and pass to your children? It is coming down to which vision for the use of space prevails, for that will determine what sort of world we live in: a peaceful world under the rule of law cooperatively verified; or a competitive space weapons race which no nation, even the United States, can win forever and which must therefore end in catastrophe. You still have a choice—a choice between two opposing visions of the future.

"The vision thing," as George Bush Sr. called it, is important. He was right about that. But Margaret Mead was right too, when she said, "Never doubt that a small group of thoughtful, committed citizens can change the world. Indeed, it is the only thing that ever has." The last time the United Nations General Assembly was asked about space-based weapons, in 2003, the international community opposed them overwhelmingly: 159 to 0, with 3 abstentions, including the United States and Israel. Since 1967, there has been an Outer Space Treaty prohibiting weapons of mass destruction from being put into orbit but it has no provision for verification and enforcement. In any case, abrogating international treatie—not signing them—is now the fashion in Washington D.C. The U.S.U.S. Administration has made it clear at the highest level that it is committed to claiming "the high ground" of space to "dominate and control" not only space but the entire world by means of weapons to be placed in space as soon as they can, and Congress has voted the money to do it. How long do we have to stop it? Based on what we already know of the past practices of this Administration in the run up to their Iraq war, we would be naive to take at face value their reassuring statements that space-based weapons are years, perhaps decades, away. That is their way of pacifying the opposition and misleading their opponents until weapons *are* suddenly in orbit (they will say for testing) and it will be too late to do anything about it. The momentum of investment and technology placement will be unstoppable. There is plenty of evidence that they intend to have some weapons in orbit shortly. That "there is plenty of time" is a carefully crafted lie.

If this insanity is to be stopped, the first priority is for the majority of Americans to make the same choice that almost every other nation has made and change their government mandate and the President next November. But that does not mean that the rest of the world need do nothing in the meantime. World public opinion does not carry much weight in American elections but in the long run not even the most powerful country can ignore the world community. Some Americans already realize that China is likely to have a larger economy than the U.S. in another generation. America cannot be sure it can win the arms race in space it is about to start. Over time China, Russia, India, and other countries will feel compelled to join forces in the race.

The only rational course is for a Space Preservation Treaty (yes, there is one ready) to be signed by at least twenty nations, bringing it into force, and in the long run by every space-faring nation, to make this world law effective. This cannot be accomplished in Geneva where the UN Commission on Disarmament has been completely blocked since 1996. The Treaty signing Conference must take place within a year, regardless of the results of the next American election, so that the world community can get the process started and build the political momentum to carry the United States with it into a peaceful future. The establishment of the International Outer Space

Peacekeeping Agency to verify and enforce the ban, as the Treaty states, cannot come into being overnight, even if the Treaty itself can be signed quickly. So the Treaty Conference cannot be delayed beyond the spring or summer of 2005 if space-based weapons are to be prevented. From now on, every day is counted. There is literally no time to waste. Waiting could be disastrous.

But would it not be more disastrous, you may ask, in the mind-set of many Americans today, to entrust our security to the United Nations or an equivalent Space Preservation Peacekeeping Agency, where decision making takes too long in this day of ICBMs, suitcase bombs or vials in a backpack, when we may have to respond in seconds or minutes at most, if we (in DC, NY or SF) are not to be eliminated?

Our response, from our vision of the human community on this planet, is that the mutual trust needed for successful cohabitation is not going to come from unilateralist "go-it-alone" doctrines of pre-emptive action without legal international authority. Security is not going to come from more weapons, even above our heads. We have seen how skewed intelligence got us into more trouble than we bargained for in Iraq. We have pondered what it is in America's behaviour over the years, and especially under the present Administration, that has alienated so many world citizens ... Muslims, for example, in so many countries so profoundly that hundreds of them have blown themselves up in deadly suicides to kill Americans and their Israeli (or other) allies. We have concluded, looking at the patterns of interaction between them, that, in a sense, Bush and Bin Laden feed off each other, action and reaction in fact supporting and justifying (in their respective eyes) their next political or warrior actions in an endless cycle of violence and suppression of liberty and free speech with soldiers on both sides willing to give up their lives. "Homeland Security" will never protect Americans from millions of angry Muslims, and Wahhabi ideology could not incite them to violence if there did not seem to be justification in current American duplicitous behaviour and aggressive policies that are by no means in the great American tradition. That tradition is now being eroded and sullied.

So, if you are an American and you want to live without fear, your best bet is to entrust the international community with your latest space surveillance technologies so that the appropriate international Agencies can be constantly

aware of what is happening everywhere on Earth and can be legally author-
ized to act in seconds to prevent any challenge to the rule of law or any state
acting pre-emptively against whoever they happen to like or dislike. Build
on the existing global consensus that wants space kept free of weapons, since
you have the most to lose if it is not. Sign the binding Treaties and Agreements necessary to prevent all such weapons from ever being deployed and
put all your power and technology behind the verification and enforcement
of a "peacekeeping agency" to make sure that it is effective. Nothing less will
create a viable "new world order." Nothing more is needed to turn this page
in the history of humanity.

Moreover, for people who believe in doing things well and cost-effectively,
there is surely no question that the "internationalist" rule of law solution is not
only politically more astute, easing Muslim (and the world's) anger and resent-
ment, and thus reducing or eliminating suicidal attacks, but it is incomparably
less expensive for Americans—counted in millions, not trillions. Such savings
could better serve human welfare, rather than be devoted to destruction.

Even within the Pentagon and Congress, there are already some signs of
disquiet over the present rush to put weapons into space. Questions are being
raised over why America should take the lead in precipitating a space race.
With the huge technological advantage the United States enjoys at present,
what is the rush? If some other country, such as China or Russia, goes first,
America can amply respond in days or hours, so there is no need to be there
first. That will only prod them into challenging "us" sooner. If we refrain, it is
in their interest to do likewise, perhaps indefinitely. A space weapons race is
not inevitable, unless Americans choose to make it so by going first.

The American military-industrial complex that Eisenhower warned against,
need not fear loss of work or loss of profits. Policing the Earth from the heavens and exploring space, using the most advanced military technologies and
personnel to solve environmental problems, feed the hungry, and educate the
masses in Asia and Africa, while reaching for the stars cooperatively, in peace
with ourselves and with our (as yet unknown) interstellar neighbours—these
are worthy projects for all men and women of good will and good conscience.
Take some transformational projects straight out of the U.S. Air Force Space
Commands budget for fiscal year 2006 and let them serve the common good:

1. Develop and field a space-based radar, surveillance and reconnaissance "to provide worldwide persistent global situational awareness."
2. Develop and field detection capabilities to find chemical, biological, nuclear and high explosives based on a space-based Hyperspectral Imaging System.
3. Develop SATCOM "to form an integrated network-centric system of systems for wideband and protected users with high data rate terminals that will link platforms and satellites and share needed information worldwide."
4. Develop and use on orbit new servicing spacecraft.

In addition, we can develop the use of technology and information services for asteroid and comet hazard mitigation, visit Mars, investigate the moons of Jupiter, and go beyond our imagining into the Universe.

These projects, in the service of a Space Preservation and Peacekeeping Agency, do not foster enmity and terrorism. They do not benefit only a few outrageously, while the others starve and die of new and old plagues. With such beneficial cooperative activities, leaders and world representatives will want to come to the table in peace, and we can all prosper and evolve. Until we learn that lesson from the bitter fruit of current American policies, we shall all share a common fate with a sick planet. When will we wake up and change course?

In this perspective, the timely conclusion of the Space Preservation Treaty and the establishment of its Agency of verification and enforcement, is the sane, cost-effective, morally and politically "right" step, just in time to bring us all a cooperation based security without space-based weapons or weapons that could damage or destroy our satellites—providing real security, for the United States and for the world. Only a Space Preservation Treaty Conference, held within a year, can build an international political momentum sufficiently strong to counter Bush's present momentum within the American heartland, opposing a fraudulent spiritual fundamentalism with a larger and more powerful vision, a conscious vision that carries the power of Truth. By the contagion of Truth, propagated this time by the Internet and its millions of users and NGOs, and pushing every government to pay heed to the demands of the people, we can all come to know that this is the way of conscience, because we can each feel the Truth that is staring us in the face—a vision of peace in space, as on Earth. "As above, so below." That energy, that great force, that Intelligence, is unstoppable, if we can just be open to it, and let it work its magic through us and through our governments, industries, labs, universities, intelligence communities, space agencies, and militaries—all with a common Space Age commitment to this Space Preservation Treaty at the one moment in human history when it can be accomplished. If not now, when? In this global moment, the fate of this world is being decided. What is your response?

CHAPTER 22

A FOOTNOTE ON THE BIRTH OF PETRO-CANADA IN 1975

During the 1973 oil crisis, when the OPEC countries began to use their collective power as producers to double the price of crude, I was serving as Ambassador to Iran and to the five oil states of the Gulf, which I visited twice a year from my base in Tehran. After one of these trips to the Gulf, my friend Gulam Muhammed, then head of the Iranian National Oil Company and a former Prime Minister, gave me this personal advice. "Jim," he said, "your government will never have any idea of what is really going on in the murky world of oil unless you become a player in the international game with the big private corporations who try to manipulate everything for their own private advantage and that of their investors. That is what we in Iran discovered when we set up our National Iranian Oil Company twenty years ago. It has been of great benefit to our people. You should do the same in Canada."

A few months after I had reported this conversation to Ottawa, I was told that the Prime Minister, Pierre Trudeau, had read my report with interest. As far as I knew, that was the end of it, until I came to Ottawa in December, 1975, for the visit of the Iranian Prime Minister, Mr. Hoveyda. During the visit I was told that the Prime Minister would like me to see two of his Ministers, Donald McDonald, the Minister of Energy, and Alistair Gillespie, the Minister of International Trade, after which I was to meet with a group of senior officials chaired by Senator Jack Austin. I had no idea what it was all about, having assumed that the idea of setting up a National Canadian Oil Company had died a natural death on infertile soil during the intervening two years.

My conversations with the two Ministers went off amiably but neither confided to me that they were seriously contemplating the launch of Petro-Canada. Nor did anyone at the meeting of officials. So when Senator Austin casually asked me if I was interested in returning to Ottawa, I did not ask "What for?" but replied equally casually that I was happy in Tehran. With that, Austin thanked me for coming, and I left, only to discover later that he had then reported to the Prime Minister that I was not interested in becoming the first head of Petro-Canada and preferred to remain in Tehran.

This story is not worth telling as an example of officials fighting for public office, but for the subtlety of Mr. Trudeau in testing my suitability for this new office. I never checked on this with him later but in retrospect it now seems obvious to me that he had asked his Ministers not to tell me of his plans for starting Petro-Canada. If after two years I was still keen to see a National Canadian Oil Company, I would surely use my opportunity to push it with two key Ministers. If I did, then they could tell me what was happening. If I did not, they might do better to look for a more eager leader of their new venture. It was an ingenious way of giving me an opening to high office, while testing my fitness for the task. Objectively, I failed the test and am not sorry that I did. By nature, I was better as an Ambassador than I would have been as head of an oil company. But at least I can tell my grandchildren that Petro-Canada was my idea.

Pierre Trudeau had been my friend since we were both working in the Privy Council Office (1948–50). As I have written in Chapter 26, we had drawn closer during his official visit to India early in 1971, and after he retired as Prime Minister he asked me to come with him and Arthur Erickson to Tibet and China. However, the Chinese Embassy declined to give me a visa, knowing my Tibetan connections in India. So all I have from that expedition is his postcard from Lhasa. I regret that I never did thank him for thinking of me for Petro-Canada or explain to him my side of this story. Perhaps I felt even then that I should have jumped at the opportunity. In retrospect, I now feel remorse for putting my own interests first, and not having agreed to serve, as he had when he overcame his natural wish for privacy and agreed to offer himself as a candidate to succeed Mr. Pearson as Prime Minister.

CHAPTER 23

OPENING UP TO NOW

Richard Whittaker, founder and publisher of Works and Conversations, interviewed me in San Francisco on December 24, 2004.

Richard Whittaker: Let's start with the here and now. You're preparing to get married in a few days. So I wondered if you wanted to reflect on that and what's right ahead of you.

James George: It is rather extraordinary at eighty-six to be looking ahead rather than behind. And that is entirely due to the fact that I've fallen in love. I've really found my partner, which is a miraculous thing at any age, but exceptional at my age! Or even at Barbara's [Barbara Wright] somewhat more tender years. [Laughs] That colors everything, doesn't it? When you're in love with somebody, you're simultaneously in love with everyone and everything, aren't you? I think it's surprising that it happens like that. And yet, I think it's quite real.

RW: That energy transforms one's whole outlook!

JG: Yes. We live in such an obviously—or perhaps not so obviously—interdependent, interconnected world. Quantum mechanics is again discovering this, after it was discovered thousands of years ago in the spiritual traditions. And where do we go with this interconnectedness? Is it just a theory? Or is it, right now, the sense between us that the words are trying to catch up with; the much more subtle reality that were sharing, a reality of feeling and intellect and body all at the same time; an awareness of presence, I suppose one could say.

RW: The part where you said, "Maybe it's not so obvious, this interconnectedness," I mean people don't really feel this very often, do they?

JG: No. I don't think they do, because it becomes intellectual, a theory for them, even if they're the scientists who believe this is the case. I heard Hans Peter Durr, the director of the Max Planck institute—Heisenberg's successor—speaking in San Francisco a few years ago, saying with a sort of missionary zeal, that there is nothing in the world, really, but relationship: energy patterns of relationship. Everything that appears to be solid is in fact almost entirely empty. It's held together by these patterns of relationship, different densities and different levels, vibrations basically on different frequencies. Yet when we put it in those words, it doesn't seem to correspond at all to the world our senses are perceiving, or which we are conditioned to think about when we wonder about the nature of reality and the meaning of it all.

RW: Let's talk about relationship in a less abstract way and go back to your own career as a diplomat. One of the basic things about that, I assume, would be relationship. You would be meeting people and wouldn't that aspect, relationship, be an essential aspect of it?

JG: Yes. I think that is a good way of putting it. A less flattering way, as one of my former colleagues once expressed it, perhaps too graphically, was that a diplomat is one who makes a profession out of picking up the shit around the world.

RW: What did he mean by that?

JG: All the discord and violence and paranoia and fear that go into the relationships between cultures and peoples everywhere, and which surface in wars and disputes and litigation. All that make the world disharmonious, when it could be harmonious, disordered when it could be ordered.

RW: So the diplomats work is to deal with the results of the lack of relationship?

JG: Exactly. The lack of relationship is the problem. The diplomat, ideally, is a harmonizer, someone who can avoid the pitfalls of that sort and move in the direction of creating order and peace. Peace is not just the absence of war, it's something much more positive. It's harmony and order, as we were saying.

RW: What are the striking memories that come back to you in terms of your work as a diplomat?

JG: Now were talking about my distant past, because I retired more than 25 years ago, but let me try and respond. To make relationships with people in other cultures, who represent quite different interests in this geo-political world, we have to cut through all the discordant elements that divide people culturally, spiritually and linguistically. What you're really relating to is what it is to be a human being. It doesn't matter whether your skin is brown or white or any other color. It doesn't matter whether you're a Buddhist or a Hindu, a Christian or a Jew; it only matters that we're human beings living on the same planet and we're trying to make sense of this spaceship at this particularly difficult time.

Underneath the "clash of civilizations" that is being spoken about lately, there is now a tremendous need everywhere to find the common threads of a global village. There is a need to relate to a much deeper level of being, not just to the differences, the economic interests and all that which has traditionally occupied most of the diplomat's time. Certainly I found that I had much better relationships in India and Iran, for example, because I was genuinely interested in their enormously rich spiritual traditions and their artistic traditions, and not just in how they were going to vote at the United Nations on this or that resolution or what they were buying from us.

RW: You quote Laurens van der Post in *Asking for the Earth*: "Remembering what was valid in the past makes it part of the present." And I was thinking about how in Japan they have this program of respecting certain people whom they call "National Treasures," because where do the important moments and experiences of human life dwell if not in people themselves? Anyway, they're most alive in the people who are living. I know you have a tremendous amount of experience that would be valuable to others to hear about. How does that strike you?

JG: As much too flattering, thank you. Certainly in my experience the Dalai Lama would be the outstanding example of someone who has become, not a national treasure so much, as an international treasure for all people. He has positioned himself, first of all in his own spiritual practice, and then in what he says publicly as someone who is teaching us how to be, and how to be happy. His emphasis is on finding something which doesn't divide us. We all share a wish to be happy. So he starts from that. He could have started by talking about the teachings of the Buddha, but then a Christian theologian or a Rabbi might say, "Well, you don't even believe in God!"

RW: A wonderful strategy. When did you first meet the Dalai Lama?

JG: I met him first in 1967 soon after we'd arrived in India. I was fortunate enough to have had quite a lot to do with him, partly because he wanted to get some of his people out of the monsoon heat of India. This wasn't very good for the Tibetans who had been used to 12,000 feet elevations and a no-madic life. I was able to work with him to get about 500 Tibetan families into Canada as refugees. This was a good excuse to have a relationship with him that deepened very quickly. I am so grateful to him for giving me insights into Tibetan Buddhism, one of the great spiritual traditions of the planet previously hidden in an almost inaccessible country and now coming out, perhaps, just at the time it is desperately needed in the rest of the world.

RW: Did you ask the Dalai Lama about specific things in the Buddhist religion?

JG: Probably the most important thing he ever said to me, he didn't say just to me, he said it when he was teaching in Toronto last May. After several days of talking about "emptiness," seeing that people were rather mystified by what he could possibly mean by "emptiness," he said, "Well, you can think of emptiness as consciousness."

This struck me as a great formulation for what so many of the great traditions, East and West, have been saying about the importance of being present in the moment; being aware of the fact of consciousness in the moment, and not just the words about consciousness; being aware of consciousness as an energy, you could say. He's made it one of his great tasks to bring that understanding more widely to his own people and to everybody.

RW: He speaks of happiness and then, of course, what is the path toward happiness? That would be the next question. Getting from happiness to emptiness. There must be some connection there.

JG: How can one not be more happy if one is more conscious? It's obvious when you look at it that way, as if emptiness and consciousness are synonymous. But we are using words to describe something so subtle it doesn't correspond to anything in most people's experience.

What do we mean by being *more alive*? Surely being more conscious would be part of that.

RW: We don't have much of a way of talking about that, do we? The world of experience and the world of language here are so greatly different.

JG: Well, feeling can bridge those worlds. We can use that much abused, misappropriated four letter word "love." Surely in our own Judeo-Christian tradition, love still resonates. How can one get beyond the mental formulations about something as subtle as that? But I know very well, and you know very well, when you *feel* in love. This is an alive feeling!

RW: Yes. But that "mental formulation" is the usual thing. I say the word, and just roll on. For instance, let's talk about the word "being." I can say the word, and there's a tendency to think okay, on to the next thing. But that word references a whole spectrum of life, of living existing, with many levels, very little of which I'm in touch with, usually.

JG: It's a very interesting moment in global culture these days, isn't it? One reason is because so many people seem to have a fundamentalist notion of what they mean by the word "God." It does not correspond to anything I would define as sacred. So probably we're at this point, you and I—in terms of language—preferring to use "Being" rather than using the word "God." Being at least is an open concept.

Every time you hear the word "God," even if you don't attach an image of an old man with a beard, at least it's a male image—almost inevitably. "Being" is a word no one sex can appropriate. But it's so easy to start floundering around with these words and lose track entirely of what is actually happening in one's own being.

Probably the most profound thing that can be said about that is that I am being, I am consciousness. I am love. I am life. What does that mean? If I am, then you are, too. It doesn't just apply to me. In fact, this "me" is probably the main obstacle to feeling myself as the same being that your self feels. Is this too far out?

RW: No, but I wonder how your relationship to what you've just said, has changed? You must not have felt the same way when you were thirty years old, let's say. I imagine there's been some evolution, or maybe there are glimpses of a truth, and what is seen is really the same thing—maybe just seen a little more clearly.

JG: I think both are true. It's beyond words, and one has, at a less mature stage of one's evolution, not understood the profundity of some of the great statements that have been made: "God is love" for instance. One can also feel that no words correspond to what is beyond words. When one is in love, one is speechless. But that doesn't make a very good interview. [Laughs]

RW: That's true. Yes. Now I recall you wrote that you had some books in your bookcase by P. D. Ouspensky. How did they get to be there?

JG: *A New Model of the Universe* was given us as a wedding present when I got married in 1942. We read it on our honeymoon. Both of us were very much interested in it. It led to a lifelong connection with the Gurdjieff teaching. Later, in Greece, when the British Ambassador and his wife came to lunch, they noticed the book and told us they were pupils of Ouspensky and helped us to make a connection with Lord Pentland and the Gurdjieff Work in New York on our return to Canada the following year. It was too late to meet Gurdjieff himself, alas, since he had died. So that tells us something about "the patterns of relationship" that run through our lives like underground rivers.

The Dalai Lama said to me once that as he grew up, he had more or less forgotten what he had been in his previous incarnations. He had had that capacity as a child. He knew it, maybe up to three or four years old. Later he only remembered that he'd had had such an experience, and then had forgotten. So in the first years of life, and towards the end of one's life, one perhaps has the same kind of facility emerging, even if you are not the Dalai Lama.

RW: I take that as a statement of your own experience.

JG: Yes. I would hope that in this new century we would see many people coming to a breakthrough in understanding consciousness. It's a subject that science has been avoiding because the best scientists have realized that they were inadequately equipped to measure or deal with it. But I don't think they're avoiding it so much now.

RW: It seems science has confidently assumed that my ordinary mind, along with a scientific methodology, is perfectly equipped to grasp the reality of what this mysterious world actually is, the tremendous faith in Descartes' "I think therefore I am. "

JG: Wouldn't it be much more true to put it the other way around: "I am, therefore I think?" What do I consider myself to be? Thinking is just a small application of being; being is primary. In the vastness of being, maybe I'm lucky enough to have a few thoughts sometimes that correspond to what is!

Time, space; are those fundamental? Or are being and consciousness fundamental? What could it possibly mean to say that being is omnipresent? That's a mind-stopper, right there.

Max Planck, at the beginning of the last century defined reality in terms of what could be measured. If it can't be measured, it's not real . And in the

12th century, the time of St. Thomas Aquinas in Europe, the pre-eminent Vedantist philosopher in India, Shankar Acharya, was saying just the opposite, "Anything that can be measured is illusion, maya." The root meaning of *maya* is measure. Anything measurable, by definition, is illusion; unreal. So take your pick!

RW: That's a wonderful juxtaposition; the Vedantist view and Max Planck's view. Well, we're talking in quite a big way….

JG: Probably too big.

RW: A wonderful passage written by Lee Hoinacki, an ex-Dominican priest, comes to me. He got the idea to walk the pilgrimage to Santiago de Compostela, and he asked his friend Ivan Illich, "Should I do that?" Illich said, "Yes, but keep a journal." Hoinacki was already in his sixties, and with very little preparation, he left alone on a thousand-kilometer walk. He writes how, at one point walking along reciting the rosary, he suddenly felt himself absolutely present in a way had never experienced before. He was absolutely right there as he took each step, feeling his legs, his feet, his hands, his breathing, smelling the air, feeling the air around him, seeing what was right in front of him and all around him; utterly present. I know you know what I'm talking about.

JG: I think it's absolutely true and well said. When one is in love, one is present in that way. All the senses, very alive. One isn't talking about it to oneself, but it *is* that.

RW: That's another aspect of Hoinacki's experience; the inner talking must have stopped completely.

JG: Exactly. Words or thoughts can distract one from the direct awareness.

RW: I wanted to ask about being with the Hopi elder, you mentioned in the book. You were with him when he was performing the morning prayer as the sun rose. What was your experience with this man?

JG: Grandfather David was then ninety-eight, I think, and very, very alive. He was trying to convey to anybody who could hear it, that the world we inhabit, and what happens to us here, depends on our state of consciousness. These ceremonies were intended to keep him in touch with a consciousness he considered sacred, and to co-operate with that he would say, "If I don't do these ceremonies, the rains won't come. Our people won't be able to eat."

Everything depends on the attention bringing one to a state of presence—as you were just describing—and sustaining that in ordinary life, not just thinking about it; actually living it.

RW: Were you with him just for that morning?

JG: No. I was helping him to prepare a letter he wrote to the United Nations. It was eventually circulated to every delegation at the UN General Assembly in New York, warning all peoples that humanity was about to face what was probably the greatest crisis in our collective human history because we were mindlessly fouling our nests and destroying our air, water, and land, driven by our greed. No species destroys its own habitat, consciously. We were simply asleep, frighteningly asleep.

RW: There are a lot of very frightening things going on in the world right now.

JG: One doesn't have a direct sense yet that there is a purpose to what is happening beyond my minuscule understanding of it, and beyond my ability to control outcomes. But if I begin to feel, not think, but feel, that my body has been very intelligently designed, designed with a need for being, a need for meaning, a need for what we call the sacred, as we consequently become more open to that, there is a sort of two-way presence active some of the time; or at least, there can be.

Take the final scene in Gurdjieff's *Struggle of the Magicians* where the white magician is saying: "Oh Lord God and all of your assistants, help me to be more conscious so that less evil will enter Thy creation." If we have been designed to become conscious, which is after all our only evolutionary option, our consciousness is not finished. Our human consciousness is just beginning perhaps, to flower.

So at the frontier of the force that is manifesting, creating all that is, and the evolutionary response that is coming back to that Source, if these two forces in us are conjoined in our awareness in what the alchemists call the "sacred marriage," that conjunction can produce the transformation of human consciousness. We are not doing it; we are only here for the process, to watch it as a kind of observer. That's what I AM, as St. John would say.

RW: The idea that we are not "doing it" but just "becoming aware" is something so foreign to our whole culture of power, control etc.

JG: Yes. It's an entirely different direction, and I feel that if we don't get it as a species, and fairly soon, our species will not make it. Other species have gone into the dustbin before us, but we have the possibility, I think, of waking up to a very different consciousness than has been generally available so far.

In every spiritual tradition, the pioneers have done it in the past, and right now the challenge is to have that awakening spread to a critical mass within a limited time. Probably this century will see whether it's going to go down or up. The Astronomer Royal in England, Sir Martin Rees, wrote a book two years ago predicting that in the next hundred years humanity would either go extinct or evolve, and he is not willing to bet on the outcome.

RW: Krishnamurti wrote in his notebooks about looking at the new spring leaves, so tender that the sunlight came through them. We need to be like that, he said, to find an openness which would allow these forces to come through us freely, but where can we find a model for such a thing in popular culture?

JG: It's become a sort of new age cliché that we are "co-creating our world," but I think there is a sense in which that's true. We're beginning to have that capability if we can embody the consciousness that is present always and everywhere.

RW: What you brought up with the prayer in *The Struggle of the Musicians*, that evil enters the world through unconsciousness—that's something one doesn't hear talked about much, the problem of the unconscious.

JG: Well, let's call it the sub-conscious as Gurdjieff does. The real consciousness, for him, is in the sub-conscious.

RW: That's a very interesting idea that our real consciousness exists in our sub-conscious. I can't think of anyone else who formulates it that way.

JG: I can't either. These deep insights take a while to work their way into what Jung called the collective unconscious and finally, we hope, to percolate up to the collective consciousness, if we can call it that. In experiments with rats we have seen an inheritance of more rapid learning. The next generation of rats will learn more quickly to swim through a maze and not drown. And maybe humans will learn how to be more conscious, more present, because of the inherited learning that takes place almost by itself. We all stand on the shoulders of those who came before us.

RW: A very hopeful thought. Did you ever meet Carl Jung?

JG: No, but I feel much more in harmony with his way of looking at it, than with Freud's.

You see, Consciousness is permeating human beings to the degree that it can, but we're not receptive. We're not allowing that penetration. Our fixed ideas, our cultural conditioning are shedding consciousness like a raincoat sheds water! We're not getting the shower of blessings that we could, at any moment.

Even in the course of this conversation, there has been a good deal of floundering, but at times something has come through. I don't feel what I've said is just from Jim George. The only decent stuff is coming through Consciousness itself. The same for you, isn't it?

RW: Well, making a leap here, I'm reminded that I've had some unusual experiences. I've had what gets reported as an "after-death experience," of being in this golden light one reads about. It's both love and light at the same time. I know you described in your book something that must have been similar, the experience that came to you while you were sitting alone that one morning in Switzerland.

JG: Yes, in Chandolin. I think these experiences are happening to more and more people, and they are indicative of the possibility that humanity is almost ready for that critical mass shift. Perhaps the pressure cooker is exactly what we need; this pressure of seeing how extraordinarily stupid we're being in collectively damaging our environment; and even the political pressure cooker we have now. Are we being shown one side of our potential, the face of violence and fear and domination, in order to awaken us to a quite different potential of love and light and peace?

[Barbara Wright comes in and joins us]

JG: Well, Richard was talking of his near death experience, which I found very interesting. In order to get there, there has to be a dying. There has to be a submission. Without that submission, you wouldn't have had that experience.

RW: That's true.

JG: And this is what is important. As long as I think I can do it, then I'm blocked. Part of love is to submit. [Turning toward Barbara] I don't mean you submitting to me, but both of us submitting.

Barbara Wright: Yes. There is a submitting, a moment when the usual agenda-forming stops. I have felt that way at various times, and I can say that I learned from those times. Sometimes just by watching, too. Something in the body learns.

JG: I remember Bill Segal saying to me that he learned more about waking up from Gurdjieff by watching his back in the sauna, than by anything he ever said to him.

BW: That really implies that we learn in the body. When the mind is quiet, the learning goes right into the body. Of course, we think that learning in the body is only about how to move in a different way, but there is a more complete learning on that level too. If the body is open in a certain way, the impressions go in and a real learning, which includes the mind and the feelings, takes place.

For me, right now, learning consists not so much in knowing immediately what to do, but in knowing there is a choice, an awareness of choice. In the unconscious part, there seems to be no choice. The next stage for me is knowing that I have a choice between a couple of things, and knowing what they are. Then, perhaps I can choose more intelligently, or not. But the first step is awareness.

RW: Earlier we were talking a little about how in our culture we have models of power and control and no models of openness and awareness. We could say we're conditioned to act from tension, and what we lack is relaxation.

BW: I've actually had people say to me, "Well, obviously you don't care," because I'm not tense. That's strange isn't it? I'm very interested in this. We're all that way....

JG: Until we all change. And, if not now, when?

CHAPTER 24

FOUR BOOK REVIEWS

In the last thirty years I wrote many book reviews for Parabola Magazine, *but these four are the most meaningful for me. The third review, "Awakening Higher Consciousness," was written with Francis Childe, a Canadian who for years served UNESCO as head of its World Heritage sites.*

Indira Gandhi: An Intimate Biography by Pupul Jayakar

The biographies of the great political figures of this century have examined everything from their philosophy of politics to their sex life—everything, that is, except their souls. Pupul Jayakar's biography of Mrs. Gandhi reveals not merely the political astuteness—and failings—of her friend, but allows us to share in the inner struggles of India's first woman Prime Minister.

The struggles have an epic quality, sensitively, and movingly recorded by Jayakar, who was not only the Prime Minister's close friend for thirty years, but was for several years India's unofficial Minister of Culture, presiding over the great Festivals of Indian art in London and New York. In addition, Jayakar was Mrs. Gandhi's link with J. Krishnamurti who helped the Prime Minister come to terms with her demons when she declared a state of emergency and ruled by martial law for a period of twenty-one months in the 1970s, and later in 1984, when Sikh terrorists had taken refuge in the Golden Temple in Amritsar and Mrs Gandhi sent the Indian Army in to get them out.

As Jayakar's careful researched intimate biography brings out, Mrs. Gandhi embodied in her own person the conflicts between East and West, tradition and modernization, service and ambition, humility and pride, idealism and pragmatism that typified the best of the Indian elite of her generation. Born to politics (however reluctantly) as Nehru's daughter and heir, educated in Switzerland and Oxford, she nevertheless retained a deep inner connection with what was most authentic in the culture and spirituality of India. She loved her people and drew energy from their love for her. Yet she was impatient to move them into the 20th Century, sometimes in spite of themselves.

Seeing India's population explosion negate all efforts to raise living standards, she embarked on programs of sterilization that were not always as voluntary as they were supposed to be. The popular reactions were violent, and were violently suppressed, ushering in the Emergency that led to her downfall—for a time. Jayakar's unique ability, as a friend and as a spiritual counsellor, to tell the Prime Minister's story from the inside of her agonizing doubts and final confession of error makes compelling reading for anyone interested in the *human* dilemmas of political power and spiritual development. For this is the drama of politics played on the Indian stage alongside the *Mahabharata*, where integrity and motive are more important to the verdict of history than success and failure.

Was the influence of her son Sanjay mainly responsible for her excesses and the consequent Emergency? Prime Ministers have no such easy way of escape from history. She herself must also have taken the decision to send the army into the Amritsar Golden Temple of the Sikhs, and it was two Sikhs in her personal bodyguard who finally gunned her down.

A few years later, her surviving son, and successor as Prime Minister, Rajiv Gandhi, met a similar fate in South India. Who can say that mythologies are not still being made in India today? All the elements of a Greek tragedy are present, and it takes a Sophocles or a Jayakar to set them down for our inner reflection—"emotion recollected in tranquillity." But the emotions are all the more significant when they are projected in a life of heroic proportions, the life of one who not only plays her external role to the utmost, but is at the same time seeking to save her own soul and her own cultural heritage. Mrs. Gandhi led such a life, and we can be grateful that she has found a biographer capable of portraying her life in its spiritual fullness and depth.

I have only one regret. Jayakar does not mention Mrs. Gandhi's fateful decision to break her international agreements and test a nuclear device—"for peaceful purposes," as she said, in 1974. This could not have been an easy decision for a Prime Minister who, two years earlier, had led the way towards restoring the planet at the first great United Nations Conference on the Environment, in Stockholm.

Hammarskjöld—A Life by Roger Lipsey

As Roger Lipsey's magnificent life of the most remarkable United Nations Secretary General, Dag Hammarskjöld, reveals, it has taken 50 years to begin to understand the inner dimensions of this great diplomat who, more than any other person, embodied the spirit of internationalism and gave voice to the world's crying need for peace in a world of warring nations.

Great men do not appear every day, and when they do it takes time to recognize their true greatness. It seems to me that this is because their greatness lies in their unseen relationship to that which is the Source of all life and of all meaning in our ordinary world, whether or not we dare to call that source God.

Sir Brian Urquhart (one of Hammarskjöld's principal assistants in the United Nations Secretariat) had already written what Lipsey himself describes "as the best biography we shall ever have" of Hammarskjöld before Lipsey set to work. Lipsey, however, had unparalleled access to private correspondence and the best translators from Swedish to help him to understand the subtleties of what Hammarskjöld described as his "negotiations with myself ... and with God" in his private notebook, posthumously published as *Markings*. Even more important, I feel, is the fact that my friend Roger Lipsey has spent his own lifetime of experience and search trying to live an awakened life in today's world. He is fascinated by Hammarskjöld's spiritual journey, which was formed by his selfless devotion to not just the idea of peace but "that something or someone" that Hammarskjöld felt as the Source of all that is. Lipsey admires the lonely courage of a man who had almost no companions on this journey but many who were mainly interested in frustrating his attempts at practical compromises that would advance peace, if even in the most modest steps. Hammarskjöld wrote in *Markings* a month before his death, "In our era, the road to holiness necessarily passes through the world of action," and Lipsey recognizes Hammarskjöld as a man actually aware of living the frictions of daily life as a spiritual discipline. Only a fellow-spirit could have the intuitive understanding that Lipsey brings to the appreciation of Hammarskjöld's greatness. For Hammarskjöld was not only, I would say, the greatest Secretary General but a spiritual exemplar for our "global village" today.

With Endnotes and Bibliography, this is a 752-page study of Hammarskjöld's life that follows a man who was the youngest son of a Swedish Prime Minister and unexpectedly was thrust into what his predecessor described as the world's most impossible job. As Secretary General from 1953 until his plane crashed (or was shot down) in what was then Rhodesia in 1961, Hammarskjöld played a part, sometimes successful, sometimes not, in salvaging peace and justice from violence and hatred, in China, the Middle East, Suez, Tunisia, and the Congo. Lipsey gives us front-row seats at all the great occasions when the world "let Dag do it" and not least in his famous confrontation with the head of the U.S.S.R., Khrushchev, demanding the Secretary General's resignation, which the General Assembly, after listening to Hammarskjöld, declined to give him. Lipsey gives us a vividly intimate look at all these dramatic events.

During the first four years of Hammarskjöld's tenure, I was assisting the Canadian Foreign Minister (later Prime Minister) "Mike" Pearson at the United Nations. We often met with Hammarskjöld, but I had to wait for Lipsey's book to read some of the private notes Hammarskjöld and his staff were exchanging during the night-long debates of the Suez crisis in 1956, while Hammarsjkjold and Pearson were hastily inventing a UN Peacekeeping Force in response.

Of course I had little idea of Hammarskjöld's spiritual nature until *Markings* was published after his tragic death. What I did know at that time, and appreciated, was Hammarskjöld's courage in insisting on creating within the Secretariat building what he called a Quiet Room, which he felt was needed because "we all have within us a centre of stillness surrounded by silence." This was not a priority among his mostly very secular colleagues who would have found very different uses for the space.

For readers of *Parabola*, I think it will be of less interest to compare Urquhart's biography with Lipsey's more nuanced account of Hammarskjöld's outer life than to concentrate here on what Lipsey reveals of the Secretary General's inner struggles to serve his great calling selflessly. *Markings* is a great resource for this, and we can resonate to his cry to

Thou,
Whom I do not know
But whose I am

As all the great teachings affirm, only when I am fully present is it possible
for a human being to be united with the Source of action and be the vehicle
for the action of a higher force in our world. But how? What does it mean?
Here are three passages from *Markings* cited by Lipsey:

> I don't know who or what put the question, I don't know
> when it was put, I don't even remember answering. But at
> some moment I did answer yes to someone or something
> and from that hour I was certain that existence is meaning-
> ful, and that therefore my life, in self-surrender, had a goal.
>
> From that moment I have known what it means not to
> look back and to take no thought for the morrow.

Consciousness emptied of all content,
In restful harmony—
This happiness is here and now,
In the eternal cosmic moment,
A happiness in you—but not yours.

In that faith which is 'God's union with the soul,'
You are one in God,
And God wholly in you,
Just as, for you, He is wholly in all you meet,
With this faith, in prayer you descend into
Yourself to meet the Other.
In the obedience and light of this union,
See that all stand, like myself, alone

Before God,
In that faith … *everything* has meaning.

How did Hammarskjöld develop such deep experiential insights all by himself "alone before God"—without a spiritual guide or community? When *Markings* was first published (1964), Lipsey tells us, "It revealed a person whom scarcely anyone had known as a religious seeker, taking his lead from Albert Schweitzer for ethics and from medieval Christian mystics for the conduct and direction of inner life. He proved to be Pascal-like in his critique of self and society, Montaigne-like in his questioning, Augustine-like in his need and willingness to chronicle his hard journey." On his final flight to Africa, Hammarskjöld was translating Martin Buber's *I and Thou* into Swedish. At the United Nations Headquarters, I was aware that two of my friends, the Permanent Representatives of India (Dayal) and of Pakistan (Bokhari), were having long talks with the Secretary General about spiritual questions. However, I believe that all these various influences on Hammarskjöld were of less importance to him than his familial Christian background. He was always a practicing Christian; and all the other influences he explored only strengthened and deepened his understanding of his faith.

Lipsey has also told us more than anyone else about Hammarskjöld's "monasticism," and the reports circulated by friends of his predecessor suggesting he was homosexual. Hammarskjöld never married, but Lipsey's objective research concludes that the question doesn't matter—he was a monastic. Also, with the help of Susan Williams's latest findings, Lipsey says that the jury is still out on whether Hammarskjöld's last flight crashed or was shot down, but it now looks more likely that those, both black and white, who wanted him dead succeeded, and that their cover-up is at last unravelling.

Thanks in large measure to Hammarskjöld, the United Nations has not failed, and there has been no nuclear World War III. We are still here to contemplate his outer and inner greatness. Even President Kennedy felt it, calling him "the greatest statesman of our century." Hammarskjöld had once told an audience at the Museum of Modern Art, "If we are to prevail,, we must be seers and explorers." Lipsey continues: "Seers are not wholly of this world; they know another…. Explorers belong to this world; they like maps and terrain and challenges. Dag Hammarskjöld was both seer and explorer. Without "noise," as he used to say—that is, without calling attention to it—he brought spirit into public life and learned through public life to care still more for the point of rest at the centre of our being."

Thanks to Lipsey, we now know much more about an important figure and also about his inner life in the midst of the United Nations noise, as Hammarskjöld put it. But how many more human beings, unknown to us, may now be serving as vehicles for the action of spirit in our world? That question gives me, and I trust you, grounds for hope.

Awakening Higher Consciousness: Guidance from Ancient Egypt and Sumer **by Lloyd Dickie and Paul Boudreau.**

When two scientists, Dickie and Boudreau, who specialize in ecology and biology, and who have spent a year together exploring the wisdom hidden in ancient Egyptian temples, decide to share their discoveries about awakening higher consciousness, they face two problems, even when they are friends and come from the same city—in this case, Dartmouth, Nova Scotia. To maintain their academic standing, they must present solid rational evidence that there is any such reality as higher consciousness, and that, at the dawn of civilization, our remote ancestors may have understood a more subtle level of reality better than we have.

The second problem they face is to find a common way of expressing their individual discoveries. Co-authorship is never easy, but these two have nevertheless managed to produce a truly remarkable study.

In their introduction, Lloyd Dickie and Paul Boudreau recall Arnold Toynbee's insight—that in a "time of troubles" like ours, ancient myths can help in the search for a better sense of the meaning of life, of the Self, or of higher consciousness. For, as our authors affirm, "ancient myths contain the oldest expression of who we are":

> We in the West can trace our cultural roots directly to myths written down 4,500 years ago! But the challenges modern societies face lie in understanding what these myths are telling us and determining how we can make use of them in our everyday life to awaken our higher consciousness...
>
> The primary purpose of the myths is to urge us to awaken. The wonder is that they seem to be so difficult to hear. The myths also speak of the need for struggle.... They repeatedly point out that the real evil for us is isolation and the separation of parts. Using symbolism, they also show that under the ordinary circumstances of life the desire for individuality leads to isolation. When one's desire becomes the opposite of what is needed to achieve wholeness, transformation is blocked. Isolation leads to enmity and division, while

integration leads to positive relationships and wholeness. The struggle in life is the work of embracing and reconciling opposites: love—hate, joy—sadness, hope—despair, and so forth.... So ... we hope that our readers will see these myths in a new light that will contribute to their explorations of themselves and the world around them—to help them find and establish a stronger Self within themselves.

From these extracts, it is clear that this book aims at a new interpretation of what Joseph Campbell called "the Hero's Journey," taking advantage of better modern translations of the ancient texts and of the insights of Schwaller de Lubicz and G.I. Gurdjieff, among others. The "Guidance from Ancient Egypt and Sumer" in the subtitle of the book tells us how we can learn from these ancient myth makers to free ourselves from the ordinary analytical mind, discovering the "mind in the heart" that Schwaller de Lubicz speaks of in *The Temple of Man*. The difference, our authors say, may be "between intuition and thinking, or between induction and deduction." The interaction between these two minds "is the essence of myth itself."

This book is not just an academic study about the beginnings of civilization. For Dickie and Boudreau,

These stories of wisdom are not about others, about the dead, or about the past. They are about us, now. The symbolism of Osiris warns that our part in understanding the differences between death and awakening to life can be played only if we maintain an active role in the continuing struggle between preconception and perception. So rapidly are our fleeting moments of clarity destroyed by our habitual, day-to-day preoccupations that we need help to even be more aware of their existence. We need to be fully aware that we are participants in this myth if we are to maintain attentiveness. Only by awakening can we turn towards the possibilities for living as a re-membered being, existing in the everlasting present ...This realization of the need for help to mount the struggle is behind the religious teachings of all ages.

In this connection, we were glad to learn that the more accurate translation of the title of what we all know as *The Egyptian Book of the Dead* is *The Book of the Coming Forth by Day*. Yes indeed; let there be Light! "The Egyptians saw [one's individual purpose] as becoming united with the light and life-bestowing properties of the eternal sun itself." In preparing initiates for life after death, by learning to "die before you die," the priests of Egypt were using esoteric methods that subsequently entered Greek culture through Empedocles and Pythagoras, early Christianity through the Gnostics, and Sufism through Hafez and Rumi.

Although they recognize these linkages, the authors have said little about what is now known about the detailed practices of breathing with awareness that led the Pyramid Texts to speak of mortals feeding on air, feeding "on the gods' food, the food on which they feed." Nor do they connect these practices with the development of higher being bodies that may not die when the physical body dies. Yet there are many cases where the *ankh* of Eternal Life is associated with the *ka* or soul in a ladder of possible transformations. They take *sahu* ("astral body") as meaning just "our biological germ plasm." We think it was much more than that and are including in this review a striking image of Horus, the New Man, "the one born not of flesh but of spirit," initiating a pupil (symbolized by the pharaoh) into the absorption of the higher elements in the air—"the gods' food"—in what Gurdjieff believed were esoteric schools of repetition.

Coming from a scientific background themselves, the authors share their amazement in discovering, through Giorgio de Santillana and Hertha von Dechend's *Hamlet's Mill*, that the earliest Egyptian architects were using the sophisticated mathematical ratios of *pi* and *phi*, and their astronomers were fully aware of the precession of the equinox, long before the Europeans were.

We have concentrated on the Egyptian parts of this great book, but our authors have done a great job in discovering many parallel themes in the traditional stories of Sumer, Akkadia, and Babylon, as well as in the magnificent epic of *Gilgamesh*. So readers of this book have much to look forward to and enjoy, even when some parts may seem heavy going.

PHOTO: F. CHILDE

FIGURE 4: *Horus as teacher*

We suspect, as co-reviewers, that our co-authors have sometimes solved their differences of view by putting both their versions into the book, and this may explain the redundancies. But this is a minor problem, and perhaps in the end we would do well to take note of what no less an authority than Gurdjieff says about the ancient tales and myths. Writing of his own experiences as a boy listening to his father recount the legend of Gilgamesh, he says: "When the beneficent result of the impressions formed in my childhood from the narratives of my father finally became clear to me—a result that crystallized in me a spiritualizing factor enabling me to comprehend that which usually appears incomprehensible—I often regretted having begun too late to give the legends of antiquity the immense significance that I now understand they really have."

JAMES GEORGE & FRANCIS CHILDE

One Mind by Dr. Larry Dossey

In the 20th century, our "poet canaries" were warning us of the Waste Land we were creating by our unnatural separation of ourselves from anything sacred, from any higher Source Intelligence. And now in this century, we see that the consequences of such aberrant human behaviour are already threatening the ecological stability of our planet and the very survival of our civilization. So it is high time for us to reawaken to something closer to the original seed vision of humanity, but rooted, as it must be now, not only in the deepest spirituality but in the most advanced science.

Stepping up to this formidable task is a seasoned internal medicine physician, Larry Dossey, who has served as chief of staff of Medical City Dallas Hospital and has written 12 books including a *New York Times* best seller. I have been reading (and writing) books on this subject for 20 years and *One Mind* is, in my opinion, the best overview of not only the unifying principle but also the unifying fact of life that we call consciousness.

Consciousness. How else is a doctor to understand the fact of distant healing, by prayer or good wishes, which has now been rigorously documented in scientific studies cited by Dossey? What better explanation can physicists find for the fact of entanglement, now that they have found that at the quantum level nothing exists separately, that everything is interconnected in a web of life that is seamless, universal and endless?

When I was getting the Threshold Foundation started in London in 1978–79, I knew a visiting American scientist, Russell Targ. I was fascinated to learn more from Dossey in this book about Targ's subsequent work with remote viewing, and how, in the next two decades, he documented his work at Stanford, which proved to be of such value to the CIA and other intelligence services. As Dossey reports, Targ came to the conclusion that almost anybody can be trained to "see" and draw pictures of what they are seeing thousands of miles away. Remote viewers in California, for example, draw a series of pictures of Soviet submarine installations in the Arctic that are then confirmed by aerial reconnaissance, but in much less detail. How can those who think of consciousness as nothing more than the product of our brains explain that?

And when someone is clinically dead, not just for a few minutes but for an hour or more, and comes back to their body and tells the doctor and nurses exactly what they were doing at the time they assumed their patient was dead? Dossey quotes this sort of experience as told by Harvard professors who have faced ridicule for telling their out-of-body stories while searching for a broader, deeper, truer science than that provided by the reigning paradigm in our universities.

We are just beginning to acknowledge how many scientific discoveries have come through the medium of insights and dreams: from Mendeleyev's Table of the Elements to von Kekule's insight into the structure of the benzene molecule? Is One Mind, one consciousness, one presence, the common thread guiding us towards flashes of insight of the Whole coming from the mind of "the Being of beings," to use Gurdjieff's trenchant phrase? And is this kind of scientific insight really any different from spiritual or religious insights? No less a scientist than Einstein said he was "only interested in God's thoughts—the rest are details."

So is God the One Mind? Dossey continues, "If the One Mind is the source of all information that is known or knowable, then it is omniscient. Omniscience is a characteristic usually assigned to the Divine. And if the One Mind is nonlocal—not localized to specific points in space, such as brains or bodies, and not confined to specific points in time, such as the present—then it is omnipresent and eternal, characteristics usually attributed to God."

Nevertheless, Dossey is careful to hedge his own answer: "No, but..." He leaves the question unanswered. At the same time, the whole book is testimony at least to the convergence of One Mind and God, in the upper reaches of the Great Chain of Being. He quotes the great physicist David Bohm's credo: "Deep down the consciousness of mankind is one." For Nobel physicist Erwin Schrodinger, the One Mind is God, and in that Mind humans are not just like God, they *are* God—as "the mystics of many centuries, independently, yet in perfect harmony with each other ... have described." The central Hindu aphorism, "I am That!" is the same affirmation as Shrodinger's. As Dossey makes clear, he thinks that though the Buddha, al-Hallaj, Meister Eckhart, and Christ used different words, they were pointing to the same Reality.

If great scientists and great sages can agree that human beings have the capacity for an experience of consciousness that is omnipresent, omniscient and eternal, then why are most of us still living in an automatic mode of consciousness that the perennial philosophy calls "sleep?" Why can't we just wake up?

Dossey writes, "I have intended this book to be a way out of hell—the hell of the particular moment in history where we confront threats to our existence that our forebears never imagined, an earth that is being degraded by the sheer fact of our existence and short-sighted choices.... My message is that there is a way of recalibrating our collective response to all of these problems—a move that then permits a cascade of solutions to fall into place. This approach requires rebooting our ethical and moral stance towards the earth and towards one another ... I believe that the concept of the unitary, collective One Mind, a level of intelligence of which the individual minds of all sentient creatures are a part, is a vision that is powerful enough to make a difference in how we approach all the challenges we face ... as something we feel in the deepest way possible."

I love this book. It strengthens our faith and our hope and (best of all) our love of consciousness. It can help us towards being real human beings, able to be aware of our essential oneness and live it, transcending our habitual selfishness, and waking us up, moment by present moment.

CHAPTER 25

THE OMNIPRESENCE OF CONSCIOUSNESS

This interview by David Ulrich, photographer, teacher, and author of The Widening Stream: The Seven Stages of Creativity, *was published in the Winter 2014–15, issue of* Parabola Magazine *under the heading "To Let the Light In."*

James George is a retired Canadian diplomat who served with distinction as High Commissioner to India, and Ambassador to Nepal and Iran. Chögyam Trungpa called him "a wise and benevolent man, an ideal statesman," and the Dalai Lama refers to him as an "old friend." He has known many important spiritual teachers of the 20th century and has a long-standing commitment to environmental issues. A founder of the Threshold Foundation and president of the Sadat Peace Foundation, he led the international mission to Kuwait and the Persian Gulf to assess post-war environmental damage. He is the author of *Asking for the Earth* and *The Little Green Book on Awakening*. He lives with his wife, Barbara Wright, in Toronto.

I had the good fortune to spend a long weekend retreat in May with Jim and Barbara in Boulder, Colorado. In spite of the intensity of the weekend, Jim graciously agreed to a conversation, and we met in his home at the foot of the mountains. At age ninety-six, Jim is lucid and sharp, like a translucent diamond radiating the wisdom and experience of a well-lived life.

DAVID ULRICH

David Ulrich: I am touched by the question you raised in your *Parabola* review of Larry Dossey's book *One Mind*: "Is one mind, one consciousness, the common thread guiding us towards flashes of insight of the whole from the mind of the 'Being of Beings,' to use Gurdjieff's trenchant phrase?" Could you speak more about the relationship of one mind to our search for consciousness?

James George: Well, you're leaping into deep water right away. Let's swim!

What I'm coming to lately is an end-of-life conviction that there is more to consciousness than what is produced in my little head, or yours. Both of us have the capacity, at times, mysteriously, to get beyond whatever this small consciousness is doing and telling us. When we are able, when we are sufficiently still and relaxed—letting it happen, not doing it—we can receive a resonance from a greater consciousness.

Many spiritual masters I've known, and also eminent scientists like Carl Jung, echo this belief. Just before Jung died, the BBC managed to interview him. And he was free enough at that stage of his life to say things without looking over his shoulder and worrying about his scientific reputation. He said: "Man cannot stand a meaningless life. Something in us sees around corners, knows beyond time and space, so may continue in that state after our physical death. Those who fear death as the End, die soon. Those who think they will go on, die old."

Fear is constricting. In fact, so are all those self-concerns for one's reputation, for one's ideas, even for what the next association is telling me. For example, am I just thinking of what I should say to you now? Or am I open to something that could be quite new, that is not really coming so much from me as from this source consciousness that many traditions have called "I"? I'm referring to the consciousness that manages to see what things are, what I am, and to not get caught in the next reaction or judgment or association—because all of these are functions; and consciousness is not a function.

DU: When I experience an echo or a hint of that consciousness, there's a distinct experience that something can move through me. And I even begin to feel impotent without that sense of connection to a greater knowing.

JG: I think our entire culture has been rendered impotent by its disconnection from that consciousness, from anything that we could really call sacred. It's so sad that even such a great mind as Francis Crick [co-discoverer of the structure of DNA] could say: "Well, I'll tell you what consciousness is. The brain produces consciousness the way the kidneys produce urine."

DU: No, no. But then you have someone like Erwin Schrödinger [Nobel physicist] who wrote: "Consciousness is a singular of which the plural is unknown." The search for consciousness occupies a lot of my attention because I recognize that I am not conscious and not whole. I have an idea of this phrase "one mind," that I associate with a mental activity. But for me, ironically what we call "one mind" is carried in part on the wings of feeling.

Chögyam Trungpa used as an entry point to inner work what he called basic sanity, but then later changed it to basic goodness. It seems to me that one mind or consciousness is deeply related to the whole of myself, which includes feeling, not just mind as I know it.

JG: Without being in love with consciousness, we can't reach it, and it can't reach us while we're preoccupied with all that is going on in our ordinary thought, our ordinary bodily habits, sensations, movements, and our ordinary emotional reactions. These are what I am calling functions.

It's as if we have two natures: a functional nature; and what many people have been calling a spiritual nature or a soul. But that language is suspect these days because we have been so careful for the last couple of centuries to separate from the superstitions of the past that we have involuntarily cut ourselves off from the sacred, and even from God.

DU: I think we also have to ask where this is leading us as a culture. Something is going down. And I have grave concern for the earth. It seems to me that we really need to come into a relationship with the sacred, with the search for consciousness, if our world is to continue on a healthy path.

JG: I agree. In the environmental movement that I've been part of for 30 years, I've been saying that the problem is not just in our technology or in our corporate system, but inside ourselves. What has to change more radically is my whole attitude to nature, from one of domination to an attitude of stewardship. It's a hard sell these days, though the need for such a radical change has been laid out in all of the great traditions.

When we talk about the need for a less self-centered attitude or for waking up, it's a change of consciousness, a change of mind from an identified mind that is just presenting its next automatic association—and assuming it can control our entire life that way—to a mind that is still and open and able to receive something from this greater mind that Carl Jung was invoking earlier. Like you, I am searching for who I am, and by now I know that I am not going to find an answer in my functional machinery, ticking away automatically, but in my essential mind, just aware attention, watching.

As the Dalai Lama has been pointing out in recent years, the Tibetan language has two words for these two very different kinds of "mind": The ordinary automatic mind that they call *Sem*; and this other receptive stillness, which has no judgments, no associations, that they call *Rigpa* and translate as "awareness." It's a beautiful statement in a few sentences of what has previously been a very secret Tibetan practice called *Dzogchen*, closely allied to what Gurdjieff and others have taught as the wordless way of being totally present now, in this moment....

We're all designed with this possibility. But what is obstructing the realization of that human potential...

DU: ... is me!

JG: It's me. This narcissistic preoccupation with my story, my difficulty, always has a kind of negative touch to it, because I am complaining about what is wrong with me either physically or mentally. And the quiet, impartial, impersonal mind, consciousness, with which I could be connected, is blocked by that.

It is so important to understand awareness as a connector to something greater than me, to my source, really. My presence is the doorway to that, even at the moment that I acknowledge that I don't know who I am, and I see my lack of presence. But that is the beginning of a real wish for it, a wish to be.

And when I have that wish, then maybe something can reach me that is of an absolutely different quality. I may perceive it as an axis of light running down through my physical body, which has a different origin. Gurdjieff says the physical body comes from this earth, and this other ... my essence ... comes from the stars, from the sun, from higher up, in a sense, closer to the source.

We have such a resistance to even the theoretical idea that we could, right now, you and I, be breathing an air charged with the omnipresence of consciousness, the omniscience of consciousness. We've all had, perhaps rarely, a direct experience of a moment when I knew everything at once, and I was aware not just of what I'm calling this present moment, but of past, present, future, as one eternity. These are just words at this moment. But I remember it wasn't just a word, it was a flash of light, of electricity from the top of my head to my toes. And it changed something in my cellular structure that persists today. I feel that now. And everybody has this possibility for a change. As you say, we have to be aware of our need, in order to be receptive to this source consciousness, to wake up in a larger sense.

DU: You just created a link. We have to be aware of our need, but in order to be aware of our need, we need to really see ourselves as we are.

JG: Yes, see ourselves as we are, not trying to change anything and not trying to develop a soul because I've heard that it could be done, which is a mental idea. How do I include all of me: mind, body, feeling? All the functions have to be integrated. It's not a search to escape from this altogether wonderful system of functioning that is a terrible master but could be a wonderful servant in a whole human being.

For the moment, I stop thinking, start sensing and feeling so as to integrate all the parts. Can I have a complete sensation of the body? Then, is it possible…. [*a few moments of silence, a gradual quieting overtakes the room.*]

You see, each center has its own possibilities, ranging from its ordinary, automatic way of functioning to a more conscious way of being. When the mind becomes aware, there is clarity. When the body becomes aware, there is a sensation of life. And when the feelings are aware, there is the presence of love. These experiences, I find, come and go from the practice of the Work over the years. And when they go, can we at least stay in front of not knowing, without trying to change anything or do anything? Then it's more of an effort to be here until something relaxes enough to let the light in from a crack in my shell.

DU: We need this in the world today. How do you see this question of the search for consciousness amongst us, individually and collectively? People say that this could bring something very fine into the world and even help heal the planet. It has to start with my search, but could this connection to one mind have broader cultural and ecological implications?

JG: All the great traditional records of inner experiences at the highest level of humanity—in different cultures, in different times—are united in saying that this is what we are designed to experience and to serve. The purpose of a human being is to serve as an intermediary so that this one mind can reach the low level of this planet, which desperately needs that infusion of life, of energy, in order to survive. And if a human being is required as a conductor, a bridge between those levels, then whether you or I achieve anything towards our own salvation is secondary to the contribution we are called to make as a service to this transmission of energy, when we are less asleep.

DU: I find myself moving in a direction where I wish to work for myself, I wish to work for others, but more and more I'm finding myself wishing to work for the world.

JG: All the great traditions confirm that we can do all three at the same time, in the same life. But now, only now. Our inability to be here now is the blockage. And what blocks is our identification, our thinking about how to do it, and just being identified with the thought of it.

So, let it go, sense and listen, so that something can act on us when we are sufficiently present to receive it.

DU: That's beautifully stated, and I feel as if I am receiving a teaching right now. And it touches something in me.

I think people instinctively want this. How to help engender this search in ourselves, in others, and in the world so that we can begin to uplift, individually and together?

JG: All the great traditions take it as a given that life and consciousness have a higher source. But the scientific approach, in its reductionist present-day paradigm, keeps insisting that life and consciousness "evolved" from lower forms of matter. Science has now managed to unify energy and matter, $E = mc^2$, but we have no conception scientifically of how life or consciousness might give rise to everything that we call energy and matter, from the top down so to speak. And yet there have been important scientific voices with the courage to express a more traditional view. This is what Max Planck, the founder of quantum mechanics, came to in his maturity:

"All matter originates and exists only by virtue of a force which brings the particle of an atom to vibration and holds this most minute solar system of the atom together. We must assume behind this force the existence of a conscious and intelligent mind."

This is the same man who is much better known for his youthful axiom: "If it is not possible to measure it, it is not real." The Saint Augustine of the Hindu world, Shankaracharya, in the twelfth century, made exactly the opposite point, observing that in Sanskrit the root of the word "measure" is the same root as the word "illusion": Maya. Therefore he was saying if it can be measured, it's not real. The real world is immeasurable.

DU: If the real world is immeasurable, can it be experienced or perceived?

JG: I can't reach it, but it can reach me. On a more ordinary level, when I was setting up the Threshold Foundation in London in 1978, one of my friends was Russell Targ. He was based at Stanford and was training remote viewers for the CIA to work in padded cells where there are no exterior vibrations. They would be given targets and asked to draw what they could see in their minds, what they could visualize. For example, they were asked to see what the Murmansk Soviet submarine facilities looked like. This was such a secret area that no spies could get near it. A U-2 spy plane would fly high over the facility and take photographs, which gave considerably less definite information than what the various remote viewers had drawn. How do you explain that fact? Were each of the remote viewers tuning into the same, omniscient one mind? Targ thinks no other hypothesis is tenable and says that almost anybody can be trained to do it.

Distant healing is also now accepted scientifically as a fact. You don't have to be touching somebody to heal them. If your prayer or power as a healer is real, you can heal somebody a thousand miles away. It doesn't matter—there's no space or time for that reality. It obeys the laws of another unknown world. To contact that world, we must re-tune our awareness and attention. Only the essential particle of life/consciousness in my organism can resonate with its one mind source. I am That.

Trungpa related basic goodness to primordial goodness. It's primordial, and yet it's spacious; and it's now, and yet it's eternal. It's foundational, and it's immediate. These paradoxes are just ways of saying we can't think about it. How to find in ourselves, in this moment, something in us that knows its source? There is an order, a design, a lawfulness that is wonderful. We can rejoice in it and be uplifted by it—not just reject it because we have no way of measuring it rationally. I remember Michel de Salzmann coming up with half-a-dozen adjectives, saying the real world is immeasurable, ineffable, intangible, omniscient, omnipresent. But, he added, it is still, for us, palpable. In this sense, over the years, the Gurdjieff Work has given me a new conception of God. And that is exactly what Gurdjieff said he had come here to do.

It's not a mental conception, but a deeper conviction that could draw everything and everyone together in the love of consciousness, the faith of consciousness, the hope of consciousness.

CHAPTER 26

AFTERTHOUGHTS

Looking back, I see my five years in India as the high-point of my diplomatic life, and my most memorable time in India as the four days in January of 1971 before Prime Minister Pierre Trudeau's official visit to India. During these days Mr. Trudeau and I were on a rather undiplomatic mission. We had known each other as friends when we were both serving in the Privy Council Office, or Cabinet Secretariat, in Ottawa in 1948–9. Before his official visit to India, Pierre had asked me whether I could arrange for us to have a few days together during which I could introduce him to the "real India" of sacred places and saintly teachers that he had glimpsed during his earlier visit to the country as a student. Thanks to the very understanding attitude of the Foreign Ministry in New Delhi, I was able to take him to see not only some of the great places, like Khajuraho, Fatehpur Sikri, Mathura, and of course the Taj Mahal under a full moon, but also introduce him to two of the leading Tibetan Rinpoches, to disciples of Mahatma Gandhi and of Krishnamurti, and to the Canadian Jesuits in Benares. But our most striking encounter, I believe for him as for me, was our morning with Anandamayi Ma at her ashram on the banks of the river Ganges near Benares.

Anandamayi Ma was then a 75-year-old Hindu from Bengal, regarded all over India as a remarkable saint and teacher. In Chapter 11, "Tour of India, Christmas, 1960," I have written about our first visit to her in 1960. This was my third.

From the moment that we sat down on the floor with her and her interpreter, I could see that she understood that this was no courtesy visit and that I had brought her another seeker of truth, struggling, under the impact of her presence, to find some rational explanation for the factual experience of how an illiterate Bengali woman, who could scarcely sign her own name and had never read a book or had a human teacher, could respond with such wisdom and intelligence to his questions about the nature of the human condition. Later, I was able to help him follow, at least mentally, the indications she had been giving him as to how he might, with practice, expand his horizons through a form of meditation that amounted to being fully present at each moment. But this was too much for his Jesuit-trained mind to accept in one short visit. Instinctively, he respected her. He could see that she was reading his thoughts. Her sensitivity and understanding was beyond anything that he had ever encountered. But he could not bring himself to abandon the promptings of his well-furnished mind and all its rational associations. He could not shift his trust from his mind to the unknown One Mind (see Chapters 24 and 25 as the source of our primitive consciousness, even when she was demonstrating for him that this miracle was humanly possible. He was in the same predicament as was Henry Corbin in front of Dr. Javad Nurbakhsh, as I described in Chapter 4: the Westerner trusts his mind; the Sufi, his heart.

In 1972 I was in Ottawa between India and Iran postings, and the Prime Minister invited me to lunch at 24 Sussex. Before lunch Pierre's wife, Margaret, was showing me around their official residence. At the top of the stairs, she pointed to an embroidered banner hanging on the wall, proclaiming *LA RAISON AU-DESSUS DE LA PASSION* ("REASON ABOVE PASSION"). And she said with a laugh "That is what I live with—and he put it next to the bedroom!"

In retrospect, I feel I was being shown, in these lessons, how difficult it has become for any Western intellectual to free his attention from its identification with the ordinary associative thinking that has come to rule our daily lives, isolating us from the life-giving energies of an all-pervasive Consciousness, or One Mind—the "boundless luminosity" of the *Dharmakaya* in Tibetan Buddhist terms—that knows no restrictions of time or of space, but for most of us is beyond our knowing. On his recent visit to the United States, the Karmapa observed that the general lack of confidence in that quality of consciousness was what was putting our civilization in danger. All I can say about it is that it *is* … just as I actually, in this present moment, *am*. But that is incontrovertible.

As I see it now, it was Gurdjieff's mission, once he had found his way to be penetrated by that One Mind, to articulate, in language the Western mind could grasp, the skilful means that, if practiced diligently for years, could make it possible for human beings not just to think and feel and move differently but to be in a different state, to be. In my experience, "I AM" is at the heart of that practice and at the basis of Christ's original message, as I suggested in the Introduction. I hear it in Krishnamurti's call for a "choiceless awareness."

After our meeting with Anandamayi Ma, Trudeau asked me if this was what she had been trying to convey to him. He told me that he had been reading Krishnamurti and understood the human potential of making a shift from ordinary thinking to this direct awareness. Can enough of us follow Anandamayi Ma, the Dalai Lama, Krishnamurti, and Gurdjieff, among others, into such esoteric practices so that human behaviour will change in the only way it can, from the inside out, allowing the higher to penetrate the lower part of our nature? Nothing less fundamental will, I say with trepidation, avert the breakdown of our civilization, as climate change takes hold of our world, and our grandchildren wonder angrily why we did so little to stop it.

Pierre Trudeau was a very private person, so it is not surprising that his interest in India has never been understood as anything more serious than tourism. It is time for me to reveal a little of the spiritual exploration that we shared together so long ago. He had a deep search to understand. It gave him a freedom from conventional thinking and standard reactions that made him, in or out of office, such an interesting man. And on this occasion his reputation for breaking boundaries did him no harm, though it probably irritated Ted Heath, the British Prime Minister, who was officially conferring with Indira Gandhi in New Delhi, while most of the media attention was covering Trudeau's unofficial encounters elsewhere.

Shortly before completing this book, I was greatly encouraged by reading the latest reflections of my friend, Lee Smolin, physicist and founding member of the Perimeter Institute, which is hoping to formulate a scientific "theory of everything." In *The Singular Universe and the Reality of Time*, Lee has (in partnership with his co-author, Roberto Unger, Professor of Philosophy at Harvard and currently a Minister in the Brazilian government), come to the remarkable conclusion that nothing less than a completely new paradigm, a new cosmological theory, will suffice, if the many problems in physics and philosophy are to be resolved. He proposes the reality of time as the basis of their new cosmology: "All that is real is real in a moment, which is one of a succession of moments," and because the laws and states are "properties of the present moment," they can evolve. On this basis, I hope we shall soon see a new paradigm for science that will enable West and East, science and spirituality, head and heart, to come together with mutual respect in a common search for the One Reality. As Gurdjieff has been telling us, life is real only when we are completely aware of the present moment. That existential sense that "I am," he repeated, is our chance, moment by moment, to change ourselves and our world for the good.

As the French say, perfectionism is the enemy of the good. It is time for me to let this "Last Call" go to my publisher as it is, and then, with such being as I can muster, wish sincerely that it will be of some help to you on your journey. So may all of us join together in this prayer from Pope Francis' great Encyclical of June 18, 2015:

> A prayer for our earth
> All-powerful God, you are present in the whole universe
> and in the smallest of your creatures.
> You embrace with your tenderness all that exists.
> Pour out upon us the power of your love,
> that we may protect life and beauty.
> Fill us with peace, that we may live
> as brothers and sisters, harming no one.
> O God of the poor,
> help us to rescue the abandoned and forgotten of this earth,
> so precious in your eyes.
> Bring healing to our lives,
> that we may protect the world and not prey on it,
> that we may sow beauty, not pollution and destruction.
> Touch the hearts of those who look only for gain
> at the expense of the poor and the earth.
> Teach us to discover the worth of each thing,
> to be filled with awe and contemplation,
> to recognize that we are profoundly united
> with every creature

as we journey towards your infinite light.
We thank you for being with us each day.
Encourage us, we pray, in our struggle
for justice, love and peace.

So now it is up to you, and to me, and to everyone, to awaken to consciousness as best we can. On August 22, 1947, at the Harvard Club in Boston, less than three weeks before he died, the great Buddhist art historian, Dr. A. K. Coomaraswamy, put it this way: "May you come into your own, that is, may I know and become what I am, no longer this person So-and so, but the Self that is also the Being of all beings, my Self and your Self."

CHAPTER 27

SOME POEMS

"Whenever I am in love, I am ashamed of everything I have ever written about love." (Rumi)

So am I.

Nevertheless, Rumi shared his poems with others.

So why not?

"As above, so below."

I know a secret lake
Deep in the jungle
On the other side of the world
From where I call "home."

"In the beginning,"
In the centre of Ceylon,
There was a Paradise,
A Garden of Eden.
For priests and kings,
Painters and warriors
And people. Above, the fort,
Piercing the Sun Door to Heaven;
And below the rock, gardens,
And this mirror lake
In the jungle. But for those
Who find the way to its shore,
Here is a magic vision of reality
Not as we see it in daily life
But as the camera sees, inversed,

Everything upside down, trees
Standing on their heads, the rock
Resting on empty sky, so peacefully
I have to ask myself which half
Is real, the upper ordinary
Or that extraordinary in the lake's mirror?
Maybe my mind's conditioning
Has got me used to shadows
On the cave and I need Plato
To upend my view. Is it then
Only the "Hanged Man" in the Tarot pack,
Hanged by his feet, who sees
The right way up? Or we who look
Into this lake? Look again.
There are two levels of reflections.
Below the surface of the mirrored fort
See the sun's logs and drowned trees,
Where a black water snake slides
Into their shadow.

Worlds within worlds-within
One Law, one Order, One
All comprehending, all embracing Love.

                    Sigirya, Sri Lanka. 1963

Vézelay

The midsummer sunset casts its red robe,
Lovingly, around the stone fabric of the Madeleine—
Red for the Scarlet Saint, that other Mary
(Not the Mother, Not the Virgin), Mary Magdalene,
Who "loved much." Let Shakti wear red at sunset; then,
And let us build her temple on the hilltop
Where we can still kneel on the bed rock—
What better bed under the clear blue sky!
And may the sun, the moon and the stars be our witness!

So, facing the stars, His head to the Easter sunrise,
Lies her Church, as the holy body of Christ, He who redeems
Even those who love excessively,
Until there is nothing left but tears
And one last vial of the most costly scent
To wash and perfume our Lord's feet
And dry them with that richly flowing hair
That was the power and the glory
Of the Madeleine.

Christ's body, giving form to her Church, lies prone
Where the pilgrims' routes from the north branch at Vézelay ,
Where those bound for St. Jacques de Compostelle
Parted from those heading for Jerusalem.
Looking down the nave, Mary's statue at His feet,
Christ's head (the choir of the church) is slightly off centre
Tilted (no doubt intentionally) to the left,
To the side of the heart, towards those who love;
Not to the right, the side of the practical Martha,
Doing the sensible thing, as reason might direct.
No, do not seek here the Basilica of the head!

Lift your eyes (and your hearts) to the capitals of the nave
And see how many heads are being severed.
Is this an epic of decapitation?
Is Mary Magdalene as keen as Salome
To have our head on a charger?
Did even John the Baptist think too much?
Did Mary baptize better with her tears
Than John with all his watery words?
Who, then, served the unspeakable Word
That is Love? Is Mary's love
The secret of the reintegration of Man,
As Eve's love is the not-so-secret
Cause of his fall? (Oh, blessed fall—
Without which, no redemption!)

How, then, can we call it "accident" that in such a Church
The vine is everywhere in evidence?
For if He is, as He said, the True Vine,
His Church should be the Tavern
Where our water is transformed into His wine
And the marriage of Heaven and Earth
Celebrated with Joy; yes, with Joy!

No wonder the puritan people of the head did not understand.
No wonder they felt affronted by the richness and beauty.
No wonder they burned the body of your Church, Mary,
And scattered the powerful relics of your love
So that in later ages men would say
That a "Christian tantric" is a contradiction in terms.
Yet for those who know how to read the trace remains.
Certainly you know, Mary, it was Love and Love alone
That raised your brother Lazarus from the dead;
And you know, Mary, without the least sentimentality,
That Man plus Woman makes a Whole, neither are separately.

Your Church, even after the ravages of the destroyers and the restorers,
Still speaks with unmistakable authority
Of that transformation of energy which happens by His grace
When egocentric man is upended, as you see in your Church several times.
But what does it mean to be hung or crucified
Upside down? Surely with this "conversion" the heart
Comes above the head, rules the ego, instead of the "normal" way round.

On the rim of the great wheel of time
Around the sun disc of the zodiacal year
Of which Christ is the *axis mundi*, the wheel's hub,
Turn the months and the seasons on the tympan above the portal,
Starting with bread for January—shades of Demeter—
And ending with the old man of the year,
December, carrying the old woman off stage,
To begin the next cycle
Of human transformation
By love, in love, for Love.

So Mary, lover of God, pray for us!

Basilica of St. Mary Magdalene, Vézelay, France, July 26, 1976

What Is Real? Who Am I?

It takes a while to see that
These are two sides of the same question,
To see that there is only one cosmic field
And the knower of the field,
Who is not different from the field:
The I who is aware of the field's Greatness
And of my own nothingness—
In the zero point of surrender.

If only for a moment, in a long life,
I have been aware of living
In a field of Consciousness, Intelligence,
Unbounded in either time or space,
In the Wholeness of Life
Of which I AM
A unique hologramic particle
Manifested by the Unmanifest
With unconditional Love.

Then I am awakened to the One,
For I am That! That I AM!
Always, everywhere.
But … how quickly I forget!

So, as Rumi says, "There is a field—I'll meet you there."
(That is, if I remember.)
For how could we ever meet anywhere else?

May 28, 2002

From Knowing to Being

When Newton saw the apple fall
He calculated gravity
Would pretty well account for all
The forces of a clockwork world
That God had set in motion, then
Left ticking by itself until
The question would arise in men,
Why the whole world continued, when
The clockwork by itself should stop
When its entropic spring must flop.

From Einstein, Planck and Bohr to Bohm
We seem to be getting close to home
In seeing that the clockwork part,
Out there, in us and everywhere,
Though very strong is not quite all—
That time, space, energy and mass
Need life and light and love to pass
The test of truth and wholeness, for
Without them we would be no more.

After a century of knowing
We have a heavy debt that's growing
To balance what we think we know
With what we are in essence, so
The unknown being that is me,
And you, and you—we might say "we"—
May survive time eternally.

December 12, 2009

Martha and Mary—Doing and Being

When I was young, I could do anything—like that—
But what to do, and how, I did not know.
And now I'm old, the 'what' and 'how' I know
But the ability to do has left me flat.

"The Lord giveth and the Lord taketh away"—
But somehow I'd like both on the same day!

Or maybe, through God's grace, before I die,
I'll see that I already AM both earth and sky—
There is no 'thing' to do, so I can see
That I already AM all I can be.

March, 2007

Icarus and the Angel

Icarus:
Your light, my love, is palpable,
Your body incandescent;
Within your eyes I see myself—
A moment evanescent—
Enfolded in your wings of peace,
Aspiring upward for release.

But when on angel's wings, I rise
Above both time and space
I fear the melting of the wax—
The fall back to my place—
For death is underwriting love
Upon this earth for realms above.

The Angel:

Fear not, for you are made, like me,
Of stardust, the Creator's breath,
And a free field of glory light.
For your real nature there's no death;
Together, no duality
Can touch our immortality.

At the Margin

Cottage musings by the Lake

Out of the corner of my eye
I see a blur of fur flash by—
Where rocks meet lake
Along the shore
At the margin.

And from behind my inner ear
I in the distance dimly hear
A woodpecker hammer at the bark
Of some dead tree
At the margin.

My mind picks up the sensory cue
And thinks how life begins anew
When sperm meets egg
And penetrates
At the margin.

Returning from my make-believe
A beaver surfaces to breathe
While further out a fish
Swallows a fly
At the margin.

The wall of every cell, I think,
Limits what enters at the brink
Permitting what gives food and life
To nourish us
At the margin.

Is that how world began from soul,
Big bang erupting from black hole?
At least I know what I don't know
When now I AM
At the margin!

July 2000, McGregor Lake, Quebec

Prayer

What's real?
The question stops me:
In my body, in my mind
And in my beating heart.

What's real behind these forms
In intergalactic spaces and in me—
What is the beingness that makes the Unity?
Behind our clumsy words, our changing thoughts,
What is the pure awareness that just IS,
Serenely present, totally awake,
Unconditioned and immutable?

I pray for tastes of that Reality,
That Light our darkness cannot comprehend,
That Life for lack of which
Our world may self-destruct.
That is my prayer
Addressed to what I constantly forget
But which, in truth, I AM.

May 7, 2008

Without Love

Without love
Even the song birds are silent,
So should I be surprised
That I cannot remember myself—
That my life is a sleep and a forgetting—
Without love?

And not only for me.
Every society and the earth itself,
Bound by the same laws,
Will fall down
Without love.

To get this far
Towards an awakening of the human
Has taken maybe fifteen billion years
Of conscious loving. So are we
Going to let it all go
Without love?

What use is all our knowing,
Money and power? They only
Hold me captive and alone
Without love.

No need to talk about it,
Even to myself. One touch
Of your hand reminds me
That until now I was
Without love.

So let us wake up, joyful as this spring,
Birds singing in the sun,
Holding each other close,
As if the world depended on our love,
Though in that state we know
That everything that is could never be
Without love!

May 26, 1992

"Poems are made by fools like me
But only God can make a tree!"

Sometimes it seems to me
That I'm a tree
Drawing my substance from the Mother ground,
And circulating it around and around
In circles that give life with every breath
Throughout this trunk that stands against my death.

But then again, maybe,
I see that the real tree
That I could be
Is upside down in me,
Roots in the air,
Like rumpled hair,
Drawing down energies
I scarcely know
By a reverse osmosis
With the same thirst
With which the tree
Draws water from the earth.

And when both trees together
Are, for a moment, working well in me,
I feel a birth
Of a new kind of love—
A field of energy—
An atmosphere—
In which there's no above,
No below either,

A vibrant wholeness
In which all of me
Proclaims ecstatically
"I AM A TREE!"

Earth Day, April 22, 1990

Love Equations of an Unknown Sufi

There is no beloved but the Beloved!

$L-MI = O^2$
"When I am in love,"
As Rumi says so well,
"I am ashamed of all
I have ever written *about* love."

There are no words for the heart's
Leap when I see you, touch
Your lips, contain you in my arms,
Remember you in my being,
Breath of my breath,
Life of these old bones!

Let the data bank upstairs
Store past impressions
And retrieve them in associations.
The mind, the "me," is not your lover;
Even if he talks passionately and acts
The part, he is not your lover;
Love has nothing to do with the past
(Memories are for the mind)
And is oblivious of the future
Which is only a print-out projection
Of the past. Love is NOW.
Or nothing—an imposter.
The heart beats time
But its centre is timeless

Only when I empty myself to myself
Die totally—am reduced to zero—
(And how can this happen more wonderfully
Than in loving?)
Can the cup of this flesh
Contain the joy, the very wine of love.

Is that why I sometimes feel
I love you most fully
When you aren't with me?

1 = X

Who are you?
And why do I love you?

After all
We have met only twice,
And each time
We couldn't talk much.

But what need of talk
With you
Who ARE—
What? Who? How?
HA!

1 × 1 = 1

You know what I felt
Because we participate
In each other's state—
Or did tonight.
If I stop to think
How strange, yes, extraordinary
It all was
For me, the only "Westerner"
(The mind says).
But the heart knows better,
Knows how familiar it was,
How timeless
Is truth
And right gesture
And love.

So one evening
Is a thousand years old
And the first Communion together
Is only the first this time around.

2 - 1 - 1 = 0

I love you:
Take away I
Take away you—
Love IS.
Isn't it?

$1 \times 1 = 1$
But $1 + 1 = 2$

Are you a mirror
For me? Or a veil?
If I plunge into your lake
Shall I find refreshment
Or hit my head on a rock?
Love is so subtle
And those who sense the goddess
Must be careful—
But not too careful
Because Tara opens
And closes her gates swiftly.

If at the moment of opening
I reflect Her truly—
And if you do—
There is beauty and love
And such joy
Beside which
The body's is nothing.

But if you want
Something from me
(Or I from you)
We find each other
As two veils
And whatever we do
Is wrong and flat
For we never get
Beyond twoness.

Since words speak
Only to the mind
I must look into your eyes
To see the third (that is single)
Above the two,
To see whether the heart
Is clouded or pure,
Is veil or mirror.

Do you yourself know?
Do I?

For the New Year, 2006

Maybe it's time, for time to have an end,
Maybe it's time to die before I die,
And by that dying live,
In time no more, in NOW,
Awakened from the dream
That is a lie, pretending to be true;
Awakening to life as presence too;
The Omnipresence that is everywhere
Except where thought excludes, by its too tight embrace,
Awareness of what's felt, a direct taste,
Clear of the past and of the future too,
Free of the trammels born of "me" and "you."

July 2, 2010

Surfing on a wave of love,
I see the Earth from high above
Where "either/or" becomes "both/and,"
Where "you" and "I" go hand in hand
Because we both have come to see
That "I" is One, so "we" are We
And "Amness" is our constancy
Throughout all space, eternally,
Since all that matters is to BE—
So simply *be* That, gratefully.

For Global Oneness Day, celebrating our Oneness with all life.

The Victorian poet, W.E. Henley, facing the darkness at the end of his life, famously affirmed "I am the master of my fate, I am the captain of my soul."

I'm not the master of my fate, nor the captain of my soul,
But it's enough, for me at least, to know, just once, that I am Whole!

October 24, 2015
Bridgepoint Rehabilitation Hospital,
Toronto

FURTHER READING

To read about Gurdjieff's Work, begin with these books, starting with Ouspensky's book.

P.D. Ouspensky

In Search of the Miraculous
Harcourt, San Diego/New York, 2001

G.I. Gurdjieff

All and Everything:

Beelzebub's Tales to His Grandson
Penguin Arkana, New York, 1999

Meetings with Remarkable Men
E.P. Dutton, New York, 1974

Life Is Real Only Then, When "I Am"
E.P. Dutton, New York, 1978

Views from the Real World: Early Talks of G.I. Gurdjieff
Viking Press, New York, 1991

Note: I have not included page references for my citations from *Beelzebub's Tales to His Grandson*. These are now readily available by subject in an invaluable book, *Guide and Index to Beelzebub's Tales*, Toronto: Traditional Studies Press, 2003. Second edition.

ABOUT THE AUTHOR

JAMES GEORGE (September 14, 1918–) was born and educated in Canada's largest city, Toronto, Ontario. He was a 1940 Rhodes Scholar from Ontario but postponed his studies to serve during World War II, first as an ordinary seaman and later as Canadian Naval Historian Overseas. His diplomatic career, which began in 1945, belongs to the Golden Era of Canada's international influence, from Lester Pearson (Foreign Minister and Prime Minister) to Pierre Trudeau (Prime Minister). After serving as deputy head of Canada's United Nations delegation in New York and of its NATO delegation in Paris, and later as Minister at the Canadian Embassy in Paris, George served as Ambassador or High Commissioner to all but two of the countries between Turkey and Burma, always seeking to deepen and broaden relations with cultures other than his own. While High Commissioner in India, he was credited by the Commonwealth Secretary General with having helped to avert a war between India and Pakistan in 1971. During the oil crisis of 1973, while Ambassador in Iran, he recommended following Iran's lead in starting a National Oil Company; his report lead to the creation of Petro-Canada in 1975.

After retiring from the Foreign Service in 1977, he co-founded and directed the Threshold Foundation in London (1977–82), served as President of the Sadat Peace Foundation (1983–2002), and chaired the Canadian coalition "No Weapons in Space" that helped to keep Canada out of the war in Iraq. For five years he was a member of the Panel on Asteroid Threat Mitigation of the Association of Space Explorers, which is working towards getting United Nations agreement to coordinate global cooperation to avert a catastrophic impact from an asteroid.

He is the author of *Asking for the Earth: Waking Up to the Spiritual/Ecological Crisis* (1995), and *The Little Green Book on Awakening* (2008).

He lives in Toronto with his wife Barbara. His email is geojam6@gmail.com.

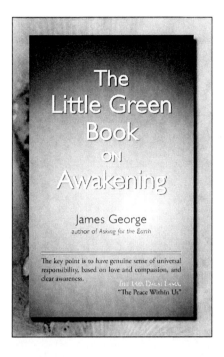

As we confront the challenges of climate change, James George calls us to wake up and stop our careless treatment of our planet before it's too late. At the same time, he shares his own practice towards waking up-the practice of Presence, known to all spiritual paths and simply and eloquently presented in this book. As he writes: "To become aware of the omnipresence of Consciousness may be the next great leap in human evolution and the foundation of the new paradigm in which both science and spirituality can find common ground. For consciousness is the field that connects—not separates—everything with everything."

"This book eloquently cries out to the world for a radical blending of environmental sensibility and spiritual insight."

—JACOB NEEDLEMAN, author of *The American Soul*

$15.95   184 pages, paperback   ISBN: 9781581771121

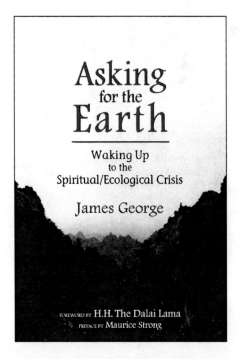